Dictionary of literary

PSEUDONYMS

a selection of popular modern writers in English
second edition

FRANK ATKINSON

CLIVE BINGLEY   &   LINNET BOOKS
LONDON   HAMDEN · CONN

FIRST EDITION PUBLISHED 1975 AS
DICTIONARY OF PSEUDONYMS AND PENNAMES
THIS SECOND ENLARGED EDITION FIRST PUBLISHED 1977
BY CLIVE BINGLEY LTD 16 PEMBRIDGE ROAD LONDON W11 UK
SIMULTANEOUSLY PUBLISHED IN THE USA BY
LINNET BOOKS AN IMPRINT OF THE SHOE STRING PRESS INC
995 SHERMAN AVENUE HAMDEN CONN 06514
SET IN 10 ON 12 POINT PRESS ROMAN BY ALLSET
PRINTED AND BOUND IN THE UK BY
REDWOOD BURN LTD OF TROWBRIDGE AND ESHER
COPYRIGHT © FRANK ATKINSON
ALL RIGHTS RESERVED
BINGLEY ISBN 085157-239-1
LINNET ISBN 0-208-01662-7

In memory of Mahatma Kane Jeeves

Library of Congress Cataloging in Publication Data

Atkinson, Frank, 1922-
    Dictionary of literary pseudonyms.

    First ed. published in 1975 under title: Dictionary
of pseudonyms and pen-names.
    1. Anonyms and pseudonyms. I. Title.
Z1041.A84 1977   423'.1   77-5047
ISBN 0-208-01662-7 (Linnet)

CONTENTS

Introduction to the First Edition iv
Introduction to the Second Edition viii
Real names. 1
Pseudonyms 117

We had a bottle of port for dinner, and drank dear Willie's health. He said, 'Oh, by the by, did I tell you I've cut my first name William, and taken the second name Lupin? In fact, I'm only known at Oldham as Lupin Pooter. If you were to 'Willie' me there, they wouldn't know what you meant.'

The names wished on us by our parents don't always please, and lots of people fiddle about varying the order of the components to suit themselves better; or they manage to get themselves nicknamed. The Grossmiths, in the piece quoted above from *The diary of a nobody*, satirised this harmless foible—but quite gently. And they did allow young W L Pooter, who could not come to terms with life as a Willie, to prosper as Lupin. His champagne flows at the end of the book.

Choosing a pen-name

Authors are great name-fiddlers, and many have performed quite drastic nomenectomies in order to achieve a satisfactory pseudonym. Arthur Elliott Elliott-Cannon lopped off Arthur and the spare Elliott; Reginald David Stanley Courtney-Browne excised his three forenames, and most understandably, Richard Nathaniel Twisleton-Wykeham-Fiennes writes as Richard Fiennes.

Many people would like to adopt an entirely new name, but most of them are inhibited by family and friends, business and other encumbrances. In the separate world of books, however, writers please themselves. They choose the name, it is solemnised on the title-page and perpetuated in lists, catalogues and the less-probing bibliographies.

Generally speaking, there is no deep thought, and little ingenuity, in the devising of pseudonyms. Obvious punning and word association provide one popular method: for example, Cecil John Street became John Rhode; Morris West about-faced to Michael East and Owen Seaman thought up Nauticus. Very basic anagrams or part anagrams, such as Melusa Moolson for Samuel Solomon, John Gannold for John Langdon and Walter De la Mare's Walter Ramal, come a close second.

Producing a more profound pseudonym takes a little longer. *Life* magazine carried a letter from Edward Stratemeyer, author of the Rover Boys stories in the 1920s, explaining how he got his pseudonym of Arthur M Winfield:

One evening when writing, with my mother sitting near sewing, I remarked that I wanted an unusual name—that I wasn't going to use my own name on the manuscript. She thought a moment and suggested Winfield. 'For then', she said, 'you may win in that field.' I thought that good. She then supplied the first name saying, 'You are going to be an author, so why not make it Arthur?'

Stratemeyer added the M himself, reasoning that as M stood for thousand, it might help to sell thousands of books.

Corey Ford, in his *Time of laughter*, quotes this Stratemeyer letter, and also gives a highly dubious version of how he selected a pseudonym for himself. 'Unfortunately', he writes, 'I did not have Mr Stratemeyer's mother to help me out. So I shut my eyes, opened the New York telephone directory at random and put my finger on a name. The name turned out to be Runkelschmelz, so I threw the phone book away and thought up John Riddell.'

Part of a package

It is not always personal preference alone that motivates an author's name change. Often it is done to match a particular type of book, on the grounds that any product sells better under a familiar label. Westerns, for example, should appear to be the work of lean and saddle-sore cowpokes, a six-shooter in either hand—with which, presumably, after bacon and beans round the ole campfire, they whack their typewriter keys.

So, when offering their readers *Rustlers and powder-smoke, Hopalong Cassidy, The big corral*, or similar horsesweat, the respective authors Charles Horace Snow, Louis L'Amour and Archibald Lynn Joscelyn, become Charles Ballew, Tex Burns and Al Cody.

Romantic fiction, on the other hand, is not expected to be penned by the Bucks and Hanks of this world. That *genre* requires authors' names suggestive of crisp, clean blouses and commonsense, yet with a hint of madcap moments; names like Elaine Carr, Phyllis Marlow and Caroline Holmes—all three of which are pseudonyms of one Charles Mason.

Tandem names

When two writers work together and decide to share a pseudonym, they rarely come up with an Ellery Queen. (And even Danny and Lee took some time to drop Barnaby Ross in favour of the peerless Ellery.) Usually, like married couples naming their house Marjalf or Gladern, they make one name from bits of the two. Kelley Roos is made up from two surnames (Audrey Kelley and William Roos), as is Manning Coles (Adelaide Manning and Cyril Coles).

The two first names of Constance and Gwenyth Little, lopped fore and aft, form this couple's pseudonym of Conyth Little; while David Eliades and Robert Forrest Webb decided on David Forrest for their joint works.

Hilary Aidan St George Saunders and John Leslie Palmer, on the other hand, settled firstly for Francis Beeding as a joint pseudonym and later for David Pilgrim, simply because they liked these names.

The game of the name

All this suggests that the pseudonym business is a bit of a lark. For the most part, as far as British and American writers are concerned, it is. Although some of them are compelled (or find it politic) for professional or contractual reasons not to publish under their real names, very few can be in fear of serious prosecution or persecution.

It is often said that some writers adopt pseudonyms in order to deceive the taxman. At best, this could be only playing for time. Death and taxes are still the two certainties of life.

So it really is a game—a mixture of fantasising, crossword puzzling and riddle-me-ree. When the game gets a good grip on a writer he may soon, like John Creasey, Michael Angelo Avallone Jr, or a number of others, clock up a double-figure pseudonym total. Some real fanatics for false names have acquired bumper collections. François Marie Arouet is usually cited as the top man in this field. In addition to the pseudonym Voltaire, he is credited with some 136 others; but most of them he used only for signing letters. Within the scope of this work, however, Lauran Paine leads the field with sixty-five discovered pennames.

What a tangled web

The real name-pseudonym area of research is more full of snags than most. In the first place there is the writers' intention to deceive. This may be an ephemeral and relatively light-hearted intention—as witnessed by the number of authors who freely declare their pen-names in the various biographical reference works. Or it may be a serious and long-standing determination such as that of the former librarian Eric Leyland, of whom Lofts and Adley, in their *Men behind boys' fiction*, say: 'Written nearly 150 books for young people . . . and another 100 books under various pen-names which are strictly private.'

Shifts do occur, from the second group to the first, as circumstances change—usually for business reasons. The commercial success of a writer often leads to her, or his, pseudonyms being blazoned on dust jackets and in advertisements.

Secondly, there are the publishers. With few exceptions, those contacted in the course of compiling this work may be divided into two groups. One group considers authors' pseudonyms to be such close and vital secrets that any enquiry after them is treated, at best, as an impertinence but, more often, as attempted subversion. The other group consists of firms carrying on business in cheerful ignorance of the true identity of many of those whose work they publish. Enquiries there cause amused surprise that anybody should be interested. As to practical help, well that's not possible because no-one really knows and then, you see, royalties are mostly paid to authors' agents and no-one, apparently, cares.

Call me Sappho, call me Chloris
Of the writers who kindly replied to our enquiries, a number were vague about the various names under which they had written. Of those who were certain, two gave spellings of their pseudonyms which differed from those on the title-pages of their books. It is not surprising then, that the great catalogues of the British Museum and the Library of Congress, and the *British national bibliography* and the *Cumulative book index*, are sometimes at odds with one another as to whether a name is real or assumed. For the period 1900-1950, volume eight of Halkett and Laing's *Dictionary of anonymous and pseudonymous English literature* is a further contender except, of course, when it quotes the British Museum catalogue as its authority. Since 1968, the cumulations and indexes of the *British national bibliography* have not distinguished between real names and pseudonyms.

A few threads teased out
This dictionary is limited to writers in English and the selection has been made from those writing in the years 1900 to date. It is hoped that it will help librarians and booksellers to answer some of the many questions which are asked about authors—particularly contemporary authors—who write under more than one name. It may also assist in solving some of the queries about pseudonymous contributors to newspapers and magazines during the early decades of this century.

On a less practical, but equally justifiable level, there is the intention to satisfy people's curiosity. W. P. Courtney called his book on British anonymous and pseudonymous writings, which was published in 1908, *The secrets of our national literature.* In the first paragraph he wrote: 'The pleasure of finding out the secrets of our neighbours appeals to most minds.'

Many readers are even more curious about their favourite authors than they are about their neighbours. This book may give them some small pleasure.

April 1975

F. A.

INTRODUCTION TO THE SECOND EDITION

There are now over 8,000 names and pseudonyms in this dictionary—an increase of more than one-third over the first edition total.

A number of names have been included or varied as a result of comments received from correspondents in many countries, to whom I am very grateful. Most of the additional names are of North American authors, which makes this a more representative selection of modern writers in English.

Once again many authors, and colleagues in libraries and the book trade, have given me information about authors' names and I am grateful to them all.

I am especially grateful to Eric Leyland for giving me a list of his pseudonyms, previously kept strictly private; and to W. Howard Baker for patiently explaining the circumstances under which he and Wilfred McNeilly have used, and continue to use, the pseudonym W. A. Ballinger jointly and separately.

The exigencies of the publishing business have imposed a very tight schedule on the preparation of this edition. I acknowledge, with gratitude, the fact that it would not have been completed on time without the help of kind friends and the invaluable assistance of my wife who shelved her own work during the final weeks.

Broad Oak
Heathfield Sussex
March 1977

Frank Atkinson

Real names

Who gave you this name?
My godfathers and godmothers.
—Church of England Catechism

AARONS, Edward Sidney
  Ayres, Paul
  Ronns, Edward
ABRAHALL, Clare Hoskyns
  Drury, C. M.
  Drury, Clare
ABRAHAM, James Johnston
  Harpole, James
ABRAHAM, Peter L.
  Graham, Peter
ABRAHAMS, Doris Caroline
  Brahms, Caryl
ABRAHAMS, Henry B.
  Henry, B. A.
ABRAHAMSON, Maurice Noel
  Chub, Sergeant
ACWORTH, Marion W.
  Neon
ADAM, C. G. M.
  Stewart, C. R.
ADAM, Robin
  MacTyre, Paul
ADAM, Ronald
  Blake
ADAM SMITH, Janet Buchanan
  Carleton, Janet
ADAMS, Agnes
  Logan, Agnes
ADAMS, Charles William Dunlop
  Montrose

ADAMS, Cleve Franklin
  Charles, Franklin
  Spain, John
ADAMS, Clifton
  Randall, Clay
ADAMS, Franklin Pierce
  F. P. A.
ADAMS, Henry
  Compton, Frances Snow
ADAMS, Herbert
  Gray, Jonathan
ADAMS, Samuel Hopkins
  Fabian, Warner
ADDIS, E. E.
  Drax, Peter
ADDIS, Hazel Iris
  Adair, Hazel
  Heritage, A. J.
  Mao
ADLER, Bill
  David, Jay
ADLER, Irving
  Irving, Robert
AGATE, James
  Prentis, Richard
  Sir Topaz
  Warrington, George
AGELASTO, Charlotte Priestley
  Watson, C. P.
AIKEN, John
  Paget, John
AINSWORTH, Mary Dinsmore
  Salter, Mary D.
  Salter Ainsworth, Mary D.
AITKEN, Andrew
  Arnold, Wilcox

1

AITKEN, E. H.
  E. H. A.
AKERMAN, Anthony Charles
  Anthony, Charles
AKERS, Elizabeth
  Percy, Florence
ALBANESI, Effie Maria
  Rowlands, Effie Adelaide
ALBERT, Harold A.
  Priestly, Mark
ALBERT, Marvin H.
  Quarry, Nick
  Rome, Anthony
  Rome, Tony
ALDRED, Margaret
  Saunders, Anne
ALDRICH, Rhoda Truax
  Truax, Rhoda
ALEXANDER, Colin James
  Jay, Simon
ALEXANDER, Janet
  McNeill, Janet
ALEXANDER, Joan
  Pepper, Joan
ALEXANDER, Robert William
  Butler, Joan
  Temple, Ruth
ALGER, Leclaire Gowans
  Leodhas, Sorche Nic
  Macleodhas, Sorche
ALINGTON, Argentine Francis
  Talbot, Hugh
ALINGTON, Cyril Argentine
  Westerham, S. C.
ALLAN, Frederick William
  Leo, Alan

ALLAN, Mabel Esther
  Estoril, Jean
  Hagon, Priscilla
  Pilgrim, Anne
ALLAN, Philip Bertram Murray
  Cabochon, Francis
  Phillip, Alban M.
ALLBEURY, Theo Edward le
  Bouthillier
  Butler, Richard
ALLDRIDGE, John Stratten
  Stratton, John
ALLEGRO, John Marco
  McGill, Ian
ALLEN, Henry
  Fisher, Clay
  Henry, Will
ALLEN, John E.
  Danforth, Paul M.
ALLEN, Stephen Valentine
  Allen, Steve
  Stevens, William Christopher
ALLEN-BALLARD, Eric
  Allen, Eric
ALLFREE, P. S.
  Blackburn, Martin
ALLISON, William
  Blinkhoalie
ALMOND, Brian
  Vaughan, Julian
ALPERS, Mary Rose
  Campion, Sarah
AMBLER, Eric *and* RODDA,
  Charles
  Reed, Eliot
AMES, Francis
  Watson, Frank
AMES, R. F.
  Black, Jack

2

AMIS, Kingsley
  Markham, Robert
AMY, William Lacey
  Allan, Luke
ANDERS, Edith Mary
  England, Edith M.
ANDERSON, Betty
  Canyon, Claudia
ANDERSON, *Lady* Flavia
  Portobello, Petronella
ANDERSON, Martin
  Cynicus
ANDERSON, Poul
  Craig, A. A.
  Karageorge, Michael
  Sanders, Winston P.
ANDREWS, Claire *and* ANDREWS, Keith
  Claire, Keith
ANDREWS, Naomi Cornelia
  Madgett, Naomi Long
ANSELL, Edward Clarence Trelawney
  Crad, Joseph
ANSLE, Dorothy Phoebe
  Conway, Laura
  Elsna, Hebe
  Lancaster, Vicky
  Snow, Lyndon
ANTHONY, Barbara
  Barber, Antonia
ANTHONY, E.
  Parr, *Dr* John Anthony
ANTHONY, Edward
  Cleo et Anthony
  Gate, A. G.
APPLEBY, Carol McAfee
  Morgan, Carol McAfee

APPLEMAN, John Alan
  Daley, Bill
  Montrose, James St David
APPLIN, Arthur
  Swift, Julian
APPS, Edwin *and* DEVANEY, Pauline
  Wraith, John
ARD, William
  Kerr, Ben
  Wills, Thomas
ARDEN, Adrian
  Ariel
ARMSTRONG, Charlotte
  Valentine, Jo
ARMSTRONG, Douglas
  Douglas, Albert
  Windsor, Rex
ARMSTRONG, Paul
  Right Cross
ARMSTRONG, Richard
  Renton, Cam
ARMSTRONG, T. I. F. *see* FYTTON ARMSTRONG, T. I.
ARSHAVSKY, Abraham Isaac
  Shaw, Artie
ARTER, Wallace E.
  Kay, Wallace
ARTHUR, Chester Alan
  Arthur, Gavin
ARTHUR, Frances Browne
  Cunningham, Ray
ARTHUR, Herbert
  Arthur, Burt
ARTHUR, Ruth M.
  Huggins, Ruth Mabel
ASHBROOK, Harriette Cora
  Shane, Susannah

3

ASHFORD, F. C.
  Charles, Frederick
ASHLEY, Arthur Ernest
  Vivian, Francis
ASHMORE, Basil
  Marlin, Roy
ASHTON, *Lady*
  Garland, Madge
ASHTON, Winifred
  Dane, Clemence
ASHTON-WARNER, Sylvia
  Henderson, Sylvia
  Sylvia
ASIMOV, Isaac
  Dr A.
  French, Paul
ASTON, *Sir* George
  Amphibian
  Southcote, George
ATKINS, Frank A.
  Ash, Fenton
  Aubrey, Frank
ATKINSON, Frank
  Shallow, Robert
ATKINSON, John
  Aye, John
ATTENBOROUGH, Bernard
 George
  Rand, James S.
AUBREY-FLETCHER, *Sir* Henry
 Lancelot
  Wade, Henry
AUCHINCLOSS, Louis
  Lee, Andrew
AUSTIN, Benjamin Fish
  Nitsua, Benjamin

AUSTIN, John *and* AUSTIN,
 Richard
  Gun Buster
AVALLONE, Michael Angelo Jr
  Carter, Nick
  Conway, Troy
  Dalton, Priscilla
  Dane, Mark
  De Pre, Jean-Anne
  Michaels, Steve
  Nile, Dorothea
  Noone, Edwina
  Stanton, Vance
  Stuart, Sidney
AVENELL, Donne
  King, Charles
AVERY, Harold
  Westridge, Harold
AVEY, Ruby D.
  Page, Vicky
AYCKBOURNE, Alan
  Allen, Ronald

BABCOCK, Frederick
  Mark, Matthew
BABCOCK, Maurice P.
  Bea, Empy
BABER, Douglas
  Ritson, John
BACKUS, Jean L.
  Montross, David
BACON, Elizabeth
  Morrow, Betty
BACON, Josephine Dodge
  Lovell, Ingraham
BAILEY, Francis Evans
  Wilson, Ann

BAILEY, Gordon
 Gordon, Keith
BAIN, Kenneth Bruce Findlater
 Findlater, Richard
BAIR, Patrick
 Gurney, David
BAKER, Anne
 Cross, Nancy
BAKER, Betty
 Renier, Elizabeth
BAKER, Laura
 Minier, Nelson
BAKER, Louise Alice
 Alien
BAKER, Marcell Genée
 Miller, Marc
BAKER, Marjorie
 McMaster, Alison
BAKER, Mary Gladys Steel
 Stuart, Sheila
BAKER, Ray Stannard
 Grayson, David
BAKER, William Howard
 Arthur, William
 Ballinger, W. A.
 Reid, Desmond
 Saxon, Peter
BAKER, William Howard *and*
 MCNEILLY, Wilfred
 Ballinger, W. A.
BALCHIN, Nigel
 Spade, Mark
BALDWIN, Dorothy
 Jones, Clara
BALDWIN, Gordon C.
 Gordon, Lew
BALDWIN, Oliver
 Hussingtree, Martin

BALFOUR, Eve *and* HERNDEN,
 Beryl
 Hearnden, Balfour
BALFOUR, William
 Russell, Raymond
BALL, Brian N.
 Kinsey-Jones, Brian
BALL, Doris Bell
 Bell, Josephine
BALLARD, Willis Todhunter
 Ballard, P. D.
 Ballard, Todhunter
 Bonner, Parker
 Bowie, Sam
 Hunt, Harrison
 Hunter, George
 Hunter, John
 MacNeil, Neil
 Shepherd, John
BALLINGER, William Sanborn
 Freyer, Frederic
 Sanborn, B. X.
BALOGH, Penelope
 Fox, Petronella
BAMBERGER, Helen R.
 Berger, Helen
BAMBERGER, Helen R. *and*
 BAMBERGER, Raymond S.
 Aresbys, The
BAMFIELD, Veronica
 Wood, Mary
BANBURY, Olive Lethbridge
 Lethbridge, Olive
BANDY, Eugene Franklin Jr
 Franklin, Eugene

BAR-ZOHAR, Michael
  Barak, Michael
BARACH, Alvan Leroy
  Coignard, John
BARBER, Dulan Friar
  Fletcher, David
BARBER, Margaret Fairless
  Fairless, Michael
BARBER-STARKEY, Roger
  Shropshire Lad
BARCLAY, George
  Kinnoch, R. G. B.
BARCLAY, Oliver Rainsford
  Triton, A. N.
BARCLAY, Vera C.
  Beech, Margaret
BARCZA, Alicja
  Orme, Alexandra
BARFIELD, Arthur Owen
  Burgeon, G. A. L.
BARKER, Albert H.
  King, Reefe
  Macrae, Hawk
BARKER, Clarence Hedley
  Hedley, Frank
  Seafarer
BARKER, Dudley
  Black, Lionel
BARKER, E. M.
  Jordan, Nell
BARKER, Ilse Eva L.
  Talbot, Kathrine
BARKER, Leonard Noel
  Noel, L.
BARKER, Michael
  Barker, Jack
BARKER, Ronald Ernest
  Ronald, E. B.

BARKER, S. Omar
  Canusi, Jose
  Squires, Phil
BARKER, Will
  Demarest, Doug
BARLING, Muriel Vere
  Barling, Charles
  Barrington, P. V.
  Barrington, Pamela
BARLOW, James
  Forden, James
BARLTROP, Mabel
  Octavia
BARNARD, Marjorie Faith *and*
  ELDERSHAW, Flora Sydney
  Eldershaw, M. Barnard
BARNES, Patricia
  Abercrombie, Patricia Barnes
BARNITT, Nedda Lemmon
  Lamont, N. B.
BARNSLEY, Alan G.
  Fielding, Gabriel
BARONAS, Aloyzas
  Aliunas, S.
BARR, Patricia
  Hazard, Laurence
BARR, Robert
  Sharp, Luke
BARRADELL-SMITH, Walter
  Bird, Lilian
  Bird, Richard
BARRAUD, E. M.
  Johns, Hilary
BARRE, Jean
  Lindsay, Lee
BARRETT, Alfred Walter
  Andom, R.

BARRETT, Geoffrey John
    Anders, Rex
    Blaine, Jeff
    Cole, Richard
    Kilbourn, Matt
    Macey, Carn
    Rickard, Cole
    Royal, Dan
    Sanders, Brett
    Summers, D. B.
    Wade, Bill
BARRETT, Hugh Gilchrist
    Bellman, Walter
BARRINGTON, Howard
    Stone, Simon
BARROW, Albert Stewart
    Sabretache
BARROWS, Marjorie
    Alden, Jack
    Dixon, Ruth
BARTLETT, Marie
    Lee, Rowena
    Rift, Valerie
BARTLETT, Stephen
    Slade, Gurney
BARTLETT, Vernon
    Oldfield, Peter
BASCH, Ernst
    Ashton, A. B.
    Ashton, E. B.
    Ashton, E. E.
BASHAM, Daisy
    Aunt Daisy
BASHFORD, *Sir* Henry Howarth
    Carp, Augustus
BASS, Clara May
    Overy, Claire May

BASSETT, Ronald
    Clive, William
BASTIN, John
    Sturgus, J. B.
BATEMAN, Robert Moyes
    Moyes, Robin
BATES, Herbert Ernest
    Flying Officer X
BATT, Malcolm John
    Malcolm, John
BATTYE, Gladys
    Lynn, Margaret
BAUM, Lyman Frank
    Akens, Floyd
    Bartlett, Laura
    Cook, John Estes
    Fitzgerald, *Captain* Hugh
    Metcalf, Suzanne
    Stanton, Schuyler
    Van Dyne, Edith
BAUMANN, Arthur A.
    A. A. B.
BAUMANN, Margaret
    Lees, Marguerite
BAX, *Sir* Arnold
    O'Byrne, Dermot
BAXTER, Elizabeth
    Holland, Elizabeth
BAYBARS, Taner
    Bayliss, Timothy
BAYER, Eleanor *and* BAYER, Leo
    Bayer, Oliver Weld
BAYLISS, John Clifford
    Clifford, John
BAYNES, Dorothy Julia
    Creston, Dormer

BAYS, J. W.
  Roadster
BEADLE, Gwyneth Gordon
  Gordon, Glenda
BEAR, Joan E.
  Mayhew, Elizabeth
BEARDMORE, George
  Stokes, Cedric
  Wolfenden, George
BEAUCHAMP, Kathleen Mansfield
  Mansfield, Katherine
BECHOFFER ROBERTS, C. E.
  Ephesian
BECK, Lily Adams
  Barrington, E.
  Moresby, Louis
BECKER, Peter
  Vul' Indlela
BECKER, Stephen David
  Dodge, Steve
BECKET, Ronald Brymer
  Anthony, John
BEDFORD-JONES, Henry
  Keyes, Gordon
  Wycliffe, John
BEDFORD-JONES, Henry;
 FRIEDE, Donald *and* FEARING,
 Kenneth
  Bedford, Donald F.
BEEBE, Elswyth Thane
  Thane, Elswyth
BEESTON, L. J.
  Camden, Richard
  Davies, Lucian
BEETON, D. R.
  Barratt, Robert
BEHANNA, Gertrude Florence
  Burns, Elizabeth

BEILES, Sinclair
  Wu Wu Meng
BEITH, John Hay
  Hay, Ian
  Junior Sub
BELANEY, Archie
  Grey Owl
BELL, Alexander
  Young, Filson
BELL, Eric Temple
  Taine, John
BELL, Gerard
  Landis, John
BELL, John Keble
  Howard, Keble
  Methuen, John
BELL, Martin
  Oates, Titus
BELLASIS, Margaret Rosa
  Marton, Francesca
BENARY, Margot
  Benary-Isbert, Margot
BENCHLEY, Robert
  Fawkes, Guy
BENDER, Arnold
  Philippi, Mark
BENDIT, Gladys
  Presland, John
BENJAMIN, Lewis S.
  Melville, Lewis
BENNETT, Arnold
  King, Sampson
BENNETT, Dorothy
  Kingsley, Laura
BENNETT, Geoffrey Martin
  Sea-Lion
BENNETT, J. J.
  Jackstaff

BENNETT, William E.
  Armstrong, Warren
BENSON, Michael
  Thomas, Michael
BENTLEY, Edmund Clerihew
  Clerihew, E.
BENTLEY, Frederick Horace
  Wilson, D. M.
BENTLEY, James W. B.
  Claughton-James, James
  Nostalgia
BENTLEY, Phyllis
  Bachelor of Arts, A
BENTON, Peggie
  Burke, Shifty
BERESFORD, Leslie
  Pan
BERGER, Josef
  Digges, Jeremiah
BERMANGE, Maurine J. L.
  Ross, Maggie
BEST, Allena
  Berry, Erick
  Maxton, Anne
BEST, Carol Anne
  Ashe, Susan
  Darlington, Con
  Martin, Ann
  Wayne, Marcia
BEST, Rayleigh Breton Amis
  Amis, Breton
  Bentinck, Ray
  Haddow, Leigh
  Hughes, Terence
  Roberts, Desmond
  Wilde, Leslie

BETHELL, Leonard Arthur
  Cailloux, Pousse
  Severn, Forepoint
BETTANY, F. G.
  N. O. B.
BETTERIDGE, Anne
  Newman, Margaret
  Potter, Margaret
BEUTTLER, Edward I. O.
  Butler, Ivan
BEVAN, Aneurin
  Celticus
BEVAN, Tom
  Bamfylde, Walter
BEYNON, Jane
  Lewis, Lange
BHATIA, June
  Edwards, June
  Rana, J.
BHATTACHARYA, Basudeb
  Acharya, Pundit
  Basudeb, Sree
BICKHAM, Jack Miles
  Clinton, Jeff
  Miles, John
BICKLE, Judith
  Tweedale, J.
BIDWELL, Marjory Elizabeth
Sarah
  Gibbs, Mary Ann
BIERCE, Ambrose
  Bowers, *Mrs* J. Milton
  Herman, William
  Sloluck, J. Milton
BIERMANN, June *and* TOOHEY,
Barbara
  Bennett, Margaret

9

BIGG, Patricia Nina
    Ainsworth, Patricia
BINGHAM, E. A. *and* LA COSTE,
  Guy R.
    Berton, Guy
BINGLEY, David Ernest
    Adams, Bart
    Benson, Adam
    Bridger, Adam
    Canuck, Abe
    Carver, Dave
    Chatham, Larry
    Chesham, Henry
    Coltman, Will
    Coniston, Ed
    Dorman, Luke
    Fallon, George
    Horsley, David
    Jefford, Bat
    Kingston, Syd
    Lynch, Eric
    Martell, James
    North, Colin
    Plummer, Ben
    Prescott, Caleb
    Remington, Mark
    Roberts, John
    Romney, Steve
    Silvester, Frank
    Starr, Henry
    Tucker, Link
    Wigan, Christopher
    Yorke, Roger
BINNS, Ottwell
    Bolt, Ben
BIRCH, Jack Ernest Lionel *and*
  MURRAY, Venetia Pauline
    Flight, Francies

BIRD, Cyril Kenneth
    Fougasse
BIRD, Dennis Leslie
    Noel, John
BIRD, William Henry Fleming
    Fleming, Harry
BIRKENHEAD, Elijah
    Birkenhead, Edward
BIRNEY, Hoffman
    Kent, David
BIRT, Francis Bradley
    Bradley, Shelland
BISHOP, Curtis Kent
    Brandon, Curt
BISHOP, Morris Gilbert
    Johnson, W. Bolingbroke
BISHOP, Stanley
    Edgar, Icarus Walter
BISSET-SMITH, G. T.
    Bizet, George
BLACK, Dorothy
    Black, Kitty
BLACK, Hazleton
    Graham, Scott
BLACK, Ladbroke Lionel Day
    Day, Lionel
    Urquhart, Paul
BLACK, Maureen
    Black, Veronica
    Darby, Catherine
    Peters, Maureen
    Rothmann, Judith
    Whitby, Sharon
BLACK, Oliver
    Black, Jett
BLACKBURN, Barbara
    Grant, Jane

BLACKBURN, James Garford
  Garford, James
BLACKETT, Veronica
  Heath, Veronica
BLACKMORE, Anauta
  Anauta
BLAGBROUGH, Harriet
  Eastertide
BLAIKLOCK, Edward
  Grammaticus
BLAIR, Dorothy
  Bolitho, Ray D.
BLAIR, Dorothy *and* PAGE,
  Evelyn
  Scarlett, Roger
BLAIR, Eric
  Orwell, George
BLAIR, Kathryn
  Brett, Rosalind
  Conway, Celine
BLAIR, Norma Hunter
  Hunter, Alison
BLAIR, Pauline Hunter
  Clare, Helen
  Clarke, Pauline
BLAIR-FISH, Wallace Wilfred
  Blair
BLAKE, George
  Vagabond
BLAKE, Leslie James
  Tabard, Peter
BLAKE, Sally Mirliss
  Sara
BLAKE, Wilfrid Theodore
  Wing Adjutant
BLAKESTON, Oswell *and*
 BURFORD, Roger d'Este
  Simon

BLATCHFORD, Robert
  Nunquam
BLAUTH-MUSZKOWSKI, Peter
  Blauth, Christopher
BLECH, William James
  Blake, William
  Blake, William James
BLIXEN-FINECKE, Karen
 Christence, *Baroness*
  Andrézel, Pierre
  Blixen, Karen
  Dinesen, Isak
BLOFELD, John
  Chu Feng
BLOOD, Marje
  McKenzie, Paige
BLOOM, Jack Don
  Donne, Jack
BLOOM, Ursula
  Burns, Sheila
  Essex, Mary
  Harvey, Rachel
  Mann, Deborah
  Prole, Lozania
  Sloane, Sara
BLOOMER, Arnold
  More, Euston
BLOOMFIELD, Anthony John
 Westgate
  Westgate, John
BLOSSOM, D. Bradford
  Bradford, De Witt
BLUNDELL, Harold
  Bellairs, George
BLUNDELL, V. R.
  Nixon, Kathleen
BLYTH, Harry
  Meredith, Hal

BLYTON, Enid
  Pollock, Mary
BOATFIELD, Jeffrey
  Jeffries, Jeff
BOBIN, John W.
  Ascott, Adelie
  Greenhalgh, Katherine
  Nelson, Gertrude
BODENHAM, Hilda
  Boden, Hilda
BODINGTON, Nancy Hermione
  Smith, Shelley
BOEHM, David Alfred
  Masters, Robert V.
BOGGS, Winifred
  Burke, Edmund
BOLSTER, *Sister* M. Angela
  Bolster, Evelyn
BOLTON, Miriam
  Davis, Stratford
  Sharman, Miriam
BOND, Florence D. F.
  Demarest, Anne
BOND, Gladys Baker
  Mendel, Jo
  Walker, Holly Beth
BOND, Grace
  Todhunter, Philippa
BOON, Violet Mary
  Williams, Violet M.
BOOTH, John Bennion
  Costs
BOOTH, Philip Arthur
  Werner, Peter
BORBOLLA Barbara
  Martyn, Don
BORDEN, Deal
  Borden, Leo

BORG, Philip Anthony John
  Bexar, Phil
  Borg, Jack
  Pickard, John Q.
BORLAND, Harold Glen
  Borland, Hal
  West, Ward
BORNEMAN, Ernest
  McCabe, Cameron
BORNEMANN, Eva
  Geisel, Eva
BOSHELL, Gordon
  Bee
BOSWORTH, Willan George
  Borth, Willan G.
  Leonid
  Worth, Maurice
BOULTON, A. Harding
  Harding, Richard
BOURQUIN, Paul
  Amberley, Richard
BOWDEN, Jean
  Barry, Jocelyn
  Bland, Jennifer
  Curry, Avon
  Dell, Belinda
BOWEN, Reuben
  Kajar
BOWEN-JUDD, Sara Hutton
  Woods, Sara
BOWER, John Graham
  Klaxon
BOWMAN, Gerald
  Magnus, Gerald
BOYD, Elizabeth Orr
  MacCall, Isabel
BOYD, Martin à Beckett
  Mills, Martin

BOYLE, John Howard Jackson
  Dawson, Michael
BRADBURY, Parnell
  Dermott, Stephen
  Lynn, Stephen
BRADBY, Rachel
  Anderson, Rachel
BRADLEY, Ian *and* HOLLOWS,
  Norman F.
  Duplex
BRADLEY, Katherine H. *and*
  COOPER, Edith E.
  Field, Michael
BRADLEY, Marion Z. *and*
  COULSON, Juanita
  Wells, John J.
BRADSHAW-JONES, Malcolm
  Henry
  Jones, Bradshaw
BRADY, Jane Frances
  White, Jane
BRAEME, Charlotte Monica
  Clay, Bertha M.
BRAHAM, Hal
  Colton, Mel
  Trask, Merrill
BRAINERD, Edith *and*
  BRAINERD, J. Chauncey
  Rath, E. J.
BRAITHWAITE, Althea
  Althea
BRAMBLEBY, Ailsa
  Craig, Jennifer
BRAMWELL, James Guy
  Byrom, James
BRAND, Charles Neville
  Lorne, Charles

BRANDENBERG, Alyce
  Christina
  Aliki
BRAUN, Wilbur
  Albert, Ned
  Brandon, Bruce
  Fernway, Peggy
  Ring, Basil
  Warren, Wayne
BRAYBROOKE, Patrick
  P. B.
BRECKENFELD, Vivian Gurney
  Breck, Vivian
BRENAN, Edward Fitzgerald
  Beaton, George
  Brenan, Gerald
— BRENNAN, John
  Welcome, John
BRENT, Peter Ludwig
  Peters, Ludovic
BRESLIN, Howard
  Niall, Michael
BRETHERTON, C. H.
  Algol
BRETON-SMITH, Clare
  Boon, August
  Caldwell, Elinor
  Vernon, Claire
  Wilde, Hilary
BRETT, Leslie Frederick
  Brett, Michael
BRIDGES, Thomas Charles
  Beck, Christopher
  Bridges, Tom
BRIGGS, Phyllis
  Briggs, Philip

13

BRIGHOUSE, Harold *and*
  WALTON, John
    Conway, Olive
BRIGHT, Mary C.
    Egerton, George
BRINSMEAD, Hesba
    Brinsmead, H. F.
    Hurgerford, Pixie
BRINTON, Henry
    Fraser, Alex
BROCK, Alan St. Hill
    Dewdney, Peter
BROCKIES, Enid Florence
    Magriska, Hélène, *Countess*
BRODEY, Jim
    Femora
    Taylor, Ann
BRODIES, John
    Guthrie, John
BRODIE, Julian Paul *and*
  GREEN, Alan Baer
    Denbie, Roger
BROGAN, Colm
    Candidus
BROGAN, Denis
    Barrington, Maurice
BROOKE, Peter
    Carson, Anthony
BROOKES, Ewart Stanley
    Tyler, Clarke
BROOKMAN, Laura L.
    Wilson, Edwina H.
BROOKES, Anne
    Carter, Ann
    Carter, Anne
    Milburn, Cynthia
    Millburn, Cynthia

BROOKS, Collin
    Brook, Barnaby
BROOKS, Edwy Searles
    Comrade, Robert W.
    Gray, Berkely
    Gunn, Victor
BROOKS, Ern
    Orion
BROOKS, Jeremy
    Meikle, Clive
BROOKS, Vivian Collin
    Mills, Osmington
BROSIA, D. M.
    D'Ambrosio, Raymond
BROWN, George Douglas
    Douglas, George
    King, Kennedy
BROWN, Howard,
    Evans, John
BROWN, Ivor
    I. B.
BROWN, John
    Browning, John
BROWN, John Ridley
    Castle, Douglas
BROWN, Kay
    Back-Back
BROWN, L. Rowland
    Grey, Rowland
BROWN, Laurence Oliver
    Oliver, Laurence
BROWN, Margaret Elizabeth
  Snow
    Brown, Marel
BROWN, May
    Blake, Vanessa
    Brown, Mandy

14

BROWN, Morna D.
  Ferrars, E. X.
  Ferrars, Elizabeth
BROWN, Rosalie
  Moore, Rosalie
BROWN, Zenith
  Ford, Leslie
  Frome, David
BROWNE, Charles Farrar
  Ward, Artemus
BROWNE, Harry T.
  John o' the North
BROWNE, Thomas Alexander
  Boldrewood, Rolf
BROWNJOHN, Alan
  Berrington, John
BRUFF, Nancy
  Gardner, Nancy Bruff
BRUNNER, John
  Woodcott, Keith
BRUSTLEIN, Daniel
  Alain
BRUSTLEIN, Janice
  Janice
BRYANT, Baird
  Baron, Willie
BRYSON, Charles
  Barry, Charles
BUCHAN, Anna
  Douglas, O.
BUCHANAN, B. J.
  Shepherd, Joan
BUCKLAND-WRIGHT, Mary
  Hume, Frances
BUCKLEY, Fergus Reid
  Crumpet, Peter

BUDD, John
  Prescot, Julian
BUDD, William John
  Budd, Jackson
  Jackson, Wallace
BUDDEE, Paul
  Richards, Paul
BUGAEV, Boris Nikolaevich
  Biely, Andrey
BUGGIE, Olive M.
  Bugy, Oly
BUITENKANT, Nathan
  Mark, David
BULLEID, H. A. V.
  Collins, D.
BULLETT, Gerald
  Fox, Sebastian
BUMPUS, Doris Marjorie
  Alan, Marjorie
BUNCE, Oliver Bell
  Censor
BUNCH, David R.
  Groupe, Darryl R.
BUNTING, D. G.
  George, Daniel
BURBRIDGE, Edith Joan
  Cockin, Joan
BURDEN, Jean
  Ames, Felicia
BURFORD, Roger d'Este
  East, Roger
BURFORD, Roger d'Este *and*
  BLAKESTON, Oswell
  Simon
BURG, David
  Dolberg, Alexander
BURGE, Milward Rodon Kennedy
  Kennedy, Milward

BURGESS, Thornton W.
  Thornton, W. B.
BURGIN, G. B.
  Smee, Wentworth
BURKE, John Frederick
  Burke, Jonathan
  Esmond, Harriet
  George Jonathan
  Jones, Joanna
  Miall, Robert
  Morris, Sara
  Sands, Martin
BURKHARDT, Eve *and*
  BURKHARDT, Robert
  Ferdinand
  Bliss, Adam
  Eden, Rob
  Jardin, Rex
BURNE, Clendennin Talbot
  Hawkes, John
BURNETT, Hallie
  Hutchinson, Anne
BURNETT, Hugh
  Phelix
BURNETT-SMITH, Annie S.
  Swan, Annie S.
BURNS, Bernard
  Auld, Philip
BURNS, Vincent
  Burns, Bobby
BURROUGHS, William
  Lee, William
BURROWS, Hermann
  Rag Man
BURTON, Alice Elizabeth
  Kerby, Susan Alice
BUSH, Christopher
  Home, Michael

BUSH-FEKETE, Marie Ilona
  Fagyas, Maria
BUSSY, Dorothy
  Olivia
BUTLER, Arthur Ronald
  Butler, Richard
BUTLER, Bill
  Sabbah, Hassan i
BUTLER, Gwendolyn
  Melville, Jennie
BUTLER, Samuel
  Owen, John Pickard
BUTLER, Teresa Mary
  Hooley, Teresa
BUTTERS, Paul
  Williamson, Paul
BUTTERWORTH, Frank Nestle
  Blundell, Peter
BUTTON, Margaret
  Leona
BUXTON, Anne
  Maybury, Anne
  Troy, Katherine
BYERS, Amy
  Barry, Ann
BYFORD-JONES, Wilfred
  Quaestor

Oh Amos Cottle!—
Phoebus what a name
To fill the speaking trump
of future fame.
—Lord Byron. English bards and
Scotch reviewers

CADELL, Elizabeth
  Ainsworth, Harriet

CAESAR, Gene
  Laredo, Johnny
CAESAR, Richard Dynely *and*
  MAYNE, William J. C.
  James, Dynely
CAIN, Arthur Homer
  King, Arthur
CAIN, Paul
  Ruric, Peter
CALDWELL, Janet Taylor *and*
  REBACK, Marcus
  Caldwell, Taylor
  Reiner, Max
CALLAHAN, Claire Wallis
  Hartwell, Nancy
CALLARD, Thomas H.
  Ross, Sutherland
CAMERON, Elizabeth Jane
  Duncan, Jane
CAMERON, William Ernest
  Allerton, Mark
CAMM, Frederick James
  N. I.
  Waysider
CAMPBELL, Alice Ormond
  Ingram, Martin
CAMPBELL, Barbara Mary
  Cam
CAMPBELL, Gabrielle Margaret
  Vere
  Bowen, Marjorie
  Paye, Robert
  Preedy, George
  Preedy, George R.
  Shearing, Joseph
  Winch, John
CAMPBELL, John Lorne
  Chanaidh, Fear

CAMPBELL, John Wood Jr.
  Stuart, Don A.
CAMPBELL, Margaret *and*
  JANSEN, Johanna
  Bayard, Fred
CAMPBELL, R. O.
  Stavely, Robert
CAMPBELL, Sydney George
  Campbell, Stuart
CAMPBELL, Walter Stanley
  Vestal, Stanley
CAMPBELL, William Edward
  March
  March, William
CAMPION, Sidney
  Swayne, Geoffrey
CANADAY, John
  Head, Matthew
CANAWAY, W. H.
  Canaway, Bill
  Hamilton, William
  Hermes
CANNING, Victor
  Gould, Alan
CAPLIN, Alfred Gerald
  Capp, Al
CAPSTICK, Elizabeth
  Scott, Elizabeth
CARAS, Roger
  Sarac, Roger
CARDENA, Clement
  De Laube
CARDIF, Maurice
  Lincoln, John
CAREW, John Mohun
  Carew, Tim
CAREW-SLATER, Harold James
  Carey, James

17

Real names

CAREY, Joyce
  Mallory, Jay
CARLE, C. E. *and* DEAN, M. D.
  Morgan, Michael
CARLISLE, R. H.
  Hawkeye
CARLTON, Grace
  Garth, Cecil
CARNEGIE, Raymond Alexander
  Carnegie, Sacha
CARNEY, Jack
  Eff, B.
CARR, Barbara Irene Veronica
 Comyns
  Comyns, Barbara
CARR, John Dickson
  Dickson, Carr
  Dickson, Carter
CARR, Margaret
  Carroll, Martin
  Kerr, Carole
CARRIER, Robert *and* DICK
 Oliver Lawson
  Oliver, Robert
CARRINGTON, Charles
  Edmonds, Charles
CARRINGTON, Hereward
  Lavington, Hubert
CARTER, Bryan
  Carter, Nick
CARTER, Compton Irving
  Carter, John L.
CARTER, Ernest
  Giffin, Frank
CARTER, Felicity Winifred
  Bonett, Emery
CARTER, John Franklin
  Diplomat

  Franklin, J.
  Unofficial Observer
CARTER, Thomas
  Wood, J. Claverdon
CARUSO, Joseph
  Barnwell, J. O.
CARY, Joyce
  Carey, Arthur
  Joyce, Thomas
CASEMENT, Christina
  Maclean, Christina
CASEY, Michael T. *and* CASEY,
 Rosemary
  Casey, Mart
CASMAN, Frances White
  Keene, Frances W.
CASSELEYR, Camille
  Danvers, Jack
CASSITY, June
  Mo, Manager
CASSON, Frederick
  Beatty, Baden
CASTLE, Brenda
  Ferrand, Georgina
CASTLE, Frances Mundy
  Whitehouse, Peggy
CASTLE, Frank
  Thurman, Steve
CASTLE SMITH, *Mrs* G.
  Brenda
CASWELL, Anne
  Orr, Mary
CATALANI, Victoria
  Haas, Carola
CATHERALL, Arthur
  Channel, A. R.
  Corby, Dan
  Hallard, Peter

18

CATTO, Maxwell Jeffrey
   Catto, Max
   Finkell, Max
   Kent, Simon
CAULFIELD, Max
   McCoy, Malachy
CAVERHILL, William Melville
   Melville, Alan
CHADWICK, Joseph
   Barton, Jack
   Callahan, John
   Conroy, Jim
CHALKE, Herbert
   Blacker, Hereth
CHALLANS, Mary
   Renault, Mary
CHALMERS, Patrick
   P. C.
CHALONER, John Seymour
   Chalon, Jon
CHAMBERS, Aidan
   Blacklin, Malcolm
CHANCE, John Newton
   Chance, Jonathan
   Drummond, John
   Lymington, John
   Newton, David C.
CHANDLER, Arthur
   Whitley, George
CHAPMAN, Mary I. *and*
 CHAPMAN, John Stanton
   Chapman, Mariston
   Selkirk, Jane
CHAPMAN, Raymond
   Nash, Simon
CHAPPELL, George S.
   Traprock, Walter E.

CHARLES, Richard
   Awdry, R. C.
CHARLTON, Joan *and others*
   Heptagon
CHARNOCK, Joan
   Thomson, Joan
CHAUNDLER, Christine
   Martin, Peter
CHEETHAM, James
   Cheetham, Hal
CHESHIRE, Gifford Paul
   Cheshire, Giff
   Merriman, Chad
   Pendleton, Ford
CHESTERTON, G. K.
   Arion
   G. K. C.
CHETHAM-STRODE, Warren
   Douglas, Noel
   Hamilton, Michael
CHEVALIER, Paul Eugene
  George
   George, Eugene
CHEYNE, *Sir* Joseph
   Munroe, R.
CHILD, Philip A. G.
   Wentworth, John
CHIPPERFIELD, Joseph E.
   Craig, John Eland
CHISHOLM, Lilian
   Alan, Jane
   Lorraine, Anne
CHITTY, *Sir* Thomas Willes
   Hinde, Thomas
CHOSACK, Cyril
   Maclean, Barry
CHOVIL, Alfred Harold
   Brook, Peter

CHRISTIE, *Dame* Agatha
  Mallowen, Agatha Christie
  Westmacott, Mary
CHRISTIE, Douglas
  Campbell, Colin
  Durie, Lynn
CHURCH, Elsie
  Parrish, Jean J.
CITOVITCH, Enid
  Baldry, Enid
CLAIR, Colin
  Nicholai, C. L. R.
CLAMP, Helen M. E.
  Leigh, Olivia
CLARK, Alfred Alexander
 Gordon
  Hare, Cyril
CLARK, Charles Heber
  Adeler, Max
CLARK, Dorothy *and*
 McMEEKIN, Isabel
  McMeekin, Clark
CLARK, Douglas
  Ditton, James
CLARK, Frederick Stephen
  Dalton, Clive
CLARK, Mabel Margaret
  Storm, Lesley
CLARK, Maria
  Clark, Mary Lou
CLARK, Marie Catherine Audrey
  Curling, Audrey
CLARK, Mary Elizabeth *and*
 QUIGLEY, M. C.
  Clark, Margery
CLARK, Winifred
  Finley, Scott

CLARKE, Brenda
  Honeyman, Brenda
CLARKE, David
  Waldo, Dave
CLARKE, Dorothy Josephine
  Shaw, Josephine
CLARKE, J. Calvitt
  Addison, Carol
  Grant, Richard
CLARKE, *Lady*
  Fitzgerald, Errol
CLARKE, Percy A.
  Frazer, Martin
  Lander, Dane
  Lytton, Jane
  Nielson, Vernon
CLARKE, Rebecca Sophia
  Sophie, May
CLAYTON, Richard H. M.
  Haggard, William
CLEARY, C. V. H.
  Day, Harvey
  Duncan, A. H.
  Norris, P. E.
CLEAVER, Hylton Reginald
  Crunden, Reginald
CLEGG, Paul
  Vale, Keith
CLEMENS, Brian
  O'Grady, Tony
CLEMENS, Paul
  Cadwallader
CLEMENS, Samuel Langhorne
  Twain, Mark
CLEVELY, Hugh Desmond
 Claymore
  Claymore, Tod

CLINE, Norma
  Klose, Norma Cline
CLOPET, Liliane M. C.
  Bethune, Mary
CLUTTERBUCK, Richard
  Jocelyn, Richard
CLYDE, Leonard Worswick
  Baron, Peter
COAD, Frederick R.
  Sosthenes
COATES, Anthony
  Mandeville, D. E.
COBB, Clayton W.
  Patten, J.
COBB, Ivo Geikie
  Weymouth, Anthony
COCKBURN, Claud
  Helvick, James
  Pitcairn, Frank
COERR, Eleanor Beatrice
  Hicks, Eleanor
  Page, Eleanor
COFFEY, Edward Hope
  Hope, Edward
COFFMAN, Virginia
  Du Vaul, Virginia
COHEN, Morton N.
  Moreton, John
COHEN, Victor
  Caldecott, Veronica
COKE, Desmond
  Blinders, Belinda
COLE, Lois Dwight
  Dudley, Nancy
  Eliot, Anne
COLE, Margaret A.
  Renton, Julia
  Saunders, Ione

COLEMAN, John
  Dexter, John
  Gorman, Ginny
  Hughes, Valerina
  Hughes, Zach
  Kanto, Peter
  Pilgrim, Derral
  Rangely, E. R.
  Rangely, Olivia
  Van Heller, Marcus
COLEMAN, William Lawrence
  Coleman, Lonnie
COLEMAN-COOKE, John C.
  Ford, Langridge
COLES, Albert John
  Stewer, Jan
COLES, Cyril Henry *and*
  MANNING, Adelaide Frances
Oke
  Coles, Manning
  Gaite, Francis
COLES, Phoebe Catherine
  Fraser, Peter
COLEY, Rex
  Ragged Staff
COLLIE, Ruth
  Stitch, Wilhelmina
COLLIN SMITH, Rodney
  Collin, Rodney
COLLINGS, Edwin
  Blackwell, John
COLLINGS, I. J.
  Collings, Jillie
  George, Vicky
COLLINGS, Joan
  Sutherland, Joan
COLLINS, Dale
  Fennimore, Stephen

21

COLLINS, Mildred
  Collins, Joan
COLLINS, Vere Henry
  Tellar, Mark
COLLINSON OWEN, H.
  C. O.
COLLOMS, Brenda
  Cross, Brenda
  Hughes, Brenda
COMBER, Elizabeth
  Han Suyin
COMBER, Lillian
  Beckwith, Lillian
COMBER, Rose
  Star, Elison
COMPTON, D. G.
  Compton, Guy
  Lynch, Frances
CONARAIN, Alice Nina
  Bowyer, Nina
  Conarain, Nina
  Hoy, Elizabeth
CONDON, Madeline B.
  Haefer, Hanna
CONE, Molly
  More, Caroline
CONE, P. C. L.
  Clapp, Patricia
CONLY, Robert Carroll
  O'Brien, Richard C.
CONNOLLY, Cyril
  Palinurus
CONNOR, Joyce Mary
  Marlow, Joyce
CONNOR, *Sir* William
  Cassandra
CONRAD, Isaac
  Conrad, Jack

COOK, Dorothy Mary
  Cameron, D. Y.
  Clare, Elizabeth
COOK, Ida
  Burchell, Mary
COOK, Ramona Graham
  Graham, Ramona
COOK, William Everett
  Cook, Will
  Everett, Wade
  Keene, James
  Peace, Frank
  Riordan, Dan
COOKE, C. H.
  Bickerdyke, John
COOKE, Diana
  Witherby, Diana
COOKSON, Catherine
  Fawcett, Catherine
  Marchant, Catherine
COOLBEAR, Marian H.
  Colbere, Hope
COOMBS, Joyce
  Hales, Joyce
  Scobey, Marion
COOPER, Edith E. *and*
  BRADLEY, Katherine H.
  Field, Michael
COOPER, Edmund
  Avery, Richard
COOPER, Gordon
  Colam, Lance
COOPER, John
  Finch, John
  Lloyd, John
COOPER, John Murray
  Sutherland, William

22

COOPER, Mae Klein *and* KLEIN,
  Grace
  Farewell, Nina
COPE, *Sir* Zachary
  Zeta
COPELAND, Lewis
  Henry, Lewis C.
COPPEL, Alfred
  Gilman, Robert Cham
  Marin, A. C.
  Marin, Alfred
COPPER, Dorothy
  Carter, Diana
  Dickens, Irene
  Grant, Carol
  Green, Linda
CORDES, Theodor K.
  Casey, T.
  Daedalus
  Erskine-Gray
COREY, Jane
  Carew, Jean
  Holden, Joanne
CORK, Barry
  Causeway, Jane
CORLEY, Edwin *and* MURPHY,
  John
  Buchanan, Patrick
  Cornish, Doris Mary
  Lisle, Mary
CORNWELL, David John Moore
  Le Carré, John
CORRALL, Alice Enid
  Glass, Justine
CORTEZ-COLUMBUS, Robert
  Cimabue
  Kennedy, R. C.

COSTA, Gabriel
  Callisthenes
COULSON, John
  Bonett, John
COULSON, Juanita *and*
  BRADLEY, Marion Z.
  Wells, John J.
COULSON, Robert Stratton *and*
  DE WEESE, T. Eugene
  Stratton, Thomas
COULTER, Stephen
  Mayo, James
COURAGE, John
  Goyne, Richard
COURNOS, John
  Courtney, John
  Gault, Mark
COURSE, Pamela
  Becket, Lavinia
  Mansbridge, Pamela
COURTIER, Sidney Hobson
  Chestor, Rui
COURTNEY-BROWNE, Reginald
D. S.
  Browne, Courtney
COUSINS, Margaret
  Johns, Avery
  Masters, William
  Parrish, Mary
COVE, Joseph Walter
  Gibbs, Lewis
COVERT, Alice Lent
  Dale, Maxine
  Lowell, Elaine
COWARD, Noël
  Whittlebot, Hernia

COWLISHAW, Ranson
  Wash, R.
  Woodrook, R. A.
COWPER, Francis
  Roe, Richard
COX, A. B.
  Berkeley, Anthony
  Iles, Francis
COX, Edith Muriel
  Goaman, Muriel
COX, Euphrasia Emeline
  Cox, Lewis
  Parsons, Bridget
COX, John
  Cox, Jack
  Roberts, David
COX, William Robert
  Reeve, Joel
COX, William Trevor
  Trevor, William
COXALL, Jack Arthur
  Dawson, Oliver
CRADOCK, Phyllis Nan Sortain
  Cradock, Fanny
  Dale, Frances
CRADOCK, Phyllis Nan Sortain
 and CRADOCK, John
  Bon Viveur
CRAIG, Edward Anthony
  Carrick, Edward
CRAIGIE, Dorothy M.
  Craigie, David
CRAIGIE, Pearl Mary Teresa
  Hobbes, John Oliver
CRAINE, John Henry
  Jason
CRAWFORD, Phyllis
  Turner, Josie

CRAWFORD, Sallie
  Trotter, Sallie
CREASEY, Clarence Hamilton
  Cressy, Edward
CREASEY, Jeanne
  Crecy, Jeanne
  Williams, J. R.
  Williams, Jeanne
CREASEY, John
  Ashe, Gordon
  Cooke, M. E.
  Cooke, Margaret
  Cooper, Henry St John
  Deane, Norman
  Fecamps, Elise
  Frazer, Robert Caine
  Gill, Patrick
  Halliday, Michael
  Hogarth, Charles
  Hope, Brian
  Hughes, Colin
  Hunt, Kyle
  Mann, Abel
  Manton, Peter
  Marric, J. J.
  Marsden, James
  Martin, Richard
  Mattheson, Rodney
  Morton, Anthony
  Ranger, Ken
  Reilly, William K.
  Riley, Tex
  York, Jeremy
CREBBIN, Edward Horace
  Sea-wrack
CRICHTON, Eleanor
  McGavin, Moyra

CRICHTON, Kyle
  Forsythe, Robert
CRICHTON, Lucilla Matthew
  Andrews, Lucilla
CRICHTON, Michael
  Hudson, Jeffrey
  Lange, John
CRISP, S. E.
  Crispie
CRITCHLOW, Dorothy
  Dawson, Jane
CROCCHIOLA, Stanley Francis
  Louis
  Stanley, F.
CROFT-COOKE, Rupert
  Bruce, Leo
  Croft, Taylor
CROLY, Jane Cunningham
  June, Jenny
CRONIN, Bernard
  Adair, Dennis
  North, Eric
CRONIN, Brendan Leo
  Cronin, Michael
  Miles, David
CROSBIE, Hugh Provan
  Carrick, John
  Crosbie, Provan
CROSS, John Keir
  MacFarlane, Stephen
CROSSEN, Kendell Foster
  Barlay, Bennett
  Chaber, M. E.
  Foster, Richard
  Monig, Christopher
  Richards, Clay
CROUDACE, Glyn
  Monnow, Peter

CROUNSE, Helen Louise
  Jackson, Joyce
CROWE, *Lady*
  Lunn, Peter
CROWLEY, Aleister *see*
  CROWLEY, Edward Alexander
CROWLEY, Edward Alexander
  Abhavananda
  Carr, H. D.
  Crowley, Aleister
  Fénix, *Comte de*
  Frater, Perdurabo
  Gentleman of the University
    of Cambridge
  Khan, Khaled
  St E. A. of M. and S.
  Shivaji, Mahatma Guru Sri
    Paramahansa
  Svareff, *Count* Vladimir
  Therion, The Master
CRYER, Neville
  Fern, Edwin
CUMBERLAND, Marten
  O'Hara, Kevin
CUMMINGS, Bruce Frederick
  Barbellion, W. N. P.
CUMMINS, Mary Warmington
  Melville, Jean
CUNNINGHAM, Virginia Myra
  Mundy
  Mundy, V. M.
CURNOW, Allen
  Whim Wham
CURRIE, *Lady*
  Fane, Violet
CURRY, Thomas Albert
  Jefferis, Jeff

25

CUST, Barbara Kate
    Fanshaw, Caroline
    Ward, Kate
CUTHRELL, Faith Baldwin
    Baldwin, Faith

*A man that should call everything
by its right name would hardly
pass the streets without being
knocked down as a common
enemy.*
—Marquis of Halifax. Works

DA CRUZ, Daniel
    Ballentine, John
    Cross, T. T.
DACHS, David
    Stanley, Dave
DAINTON, William
    Dainton, Courtney
DAKERS, Elaine
    Lane, Jane
DALE, Margaret
    Miller, Margaret J.
DALLY, Ann
    Mullins, Ann
DALRYMPLE-HAY, Barbara *and*
 DALRYMPLE-HAY, John
    Hay, John
DALTON, Gilbert
    Carstairs, Rod
    Norton, Victor
DANIEL, Glyn Edmund
    Rees, Dilwyn

DANIELL, Albert Scott
    Bowood, Richard
    Daniell, David Scott
DANNAY, Frederic
    Nathan, Daniel
DANNAY, Frederic *and* LEE,
 Manfred B.
    Queen, Ellery
    Ross, Barnaby
DANSON, Frank Corse
    Dickson, Frank C.
DAREFF, Hal
    Foley, Scott
DARGAN, Olive
    Burke, Fielding
D'ARLEY, Catherine
    Arley, Catherine
DAUGHTREY, Olive Lydia
    Earle, Olive L.
DAUKES, Sidney Herbert
    Fairway, Sidney
DAVENTRY, Leonard John
    Alexander, Martin
DAVID, Julia
    Draco, F.
DAVIDSON, Edith May
    May, Roberta E.
DAVIDSON, Margaret
    Compere, Mickie
    Davidson, Mickie
DAVIES, Betty Evelyn
    Warwick, Pauline
DAVIES, D. Jacob
    Jacob, Herbert Mathias
DAVIES, David Margerison
    Margerison, David
DAVIES, Edith
    Jay, Joan

DAVIES, Joan Howard
  Drake, Joan
DAVIES, John
  Whitaker, Ray
DAVIES, John Evan Weston
  Mather, Berkely
DAVIES, Leslie Purnell
  Berne, Leo
  Blake, Robert
  Bridgeman, Richard
  Evans, Morgan
  Jefferson, Ian
  Peters, Lawrence
  Philips, Thomas
  Thomas, G. K.
  Vardre, Leslie
  Welch, Rowland
DAVIES, Robertson
  Marchbanks, Samuel
DAVIS, Arthur Hoey
  Rudd, Steele
DAVIS, Burton *and* DAVIS, Clare
  Ogden
  Saunders, Lawrence
DAVIS, Frederick Clyde
  Coombs, Murdo
  Ransome, Stephen
DAVIS, Frederick William
  Campbell, Scott
DAVIS, Hope Hale
  Hale, Hope
DAVIS, Lavinia
  Farmer, Wendell
DAVIS, Lily May *and* DAVIS,
  Rosemary
  Davis, Rosemary L.
DAVIS, Lois Carlile
  Lamplaugh, Lois

DAVIS, Martha Wirt
  Arsdale, Wirt Van
DAVIS, Robert Prunier
  Brandon, Joe
DAVIS, Rosemary *and* DAVIS,
  Lily May
  Davis, Rosemary L.
DAVIS, Will R.
  Wallace, John
DAY, George Harold
  Quince, Peter
— DAY LEWIS, Cecil
  Blake, Nicholas
DE BANZIE, Eric *and* RESSICH,
  John S. M.
  Baxter, Gregory
DE BELLET, Liane
  De Facci, Liane
DE CAIRE, Edwin
  Moodie, Edwin
DE CHAIR, Somerset
  Hon. Member for X
DE CRISTOFORO, R. J.
  Cristy, R. J.
DE FREITAS, Michael
  Michael X
— DE FREYNE, George
  Bridges, Victor
DE JONG, David Cornel
  Breola, Tjalmar
— DE LA MARE, Walter
  Ramal, Walter
DE LA PASTURE, Edmée E. M.
  Delafield, E. M.
DE LAUNAY, André Joseph
  Launay, André
  Launay, Droo
DE LEEUW, Cateau W.
  Hamilton, Kay
  Lyon, Jessica

27

DE MENDELSSOHN, Hilde
  Spiel, Hilde
DE SCHANSCHIEFF, Juliet
 Dymoke
  Dymoke, Juliet
DE VOTO, Bernard Augustine
  August, John
  Hewer, Cady
DE WEESE, T. Eugene *and*
  COULSON, Robert Stratton
  Stratton, Thomas
DEAN, M. D. *and* CARLE, C. E.
  Morgan, Michael
DEAN, Mary
  Mee, Mary
DEAN, Robert George
  Griswold, George
DEE, Stephanie
  Plowman, Stephanie
DEGHY, Guy *and* WATERHOUSE,
 Keith
  Froy, Herald
  Gibb, Lee
DEGRAS, Henry Ernest
  Benney, Mark
DEINDORFER, Robert G.
  Bender, Jay
  Dender, Jay
  Greene, Robert
DEL REY, Lester
  St John, Philip
DELANEY, Mary Murray
  Lane, Mary D.
DELANY, Joseph Francis
  Dane, Joel Y.
DELVES-BROUGHTON, Josephine
  Bryan, John

DEMING, Richard
  Franklin, Max
  Moreno, Nick
DENHOLM, David
  Forrest, David
DENNEY, Diana
  Ross, Diana
DENNIS, Geoffrey Pomeroy
  Browne, Barum
DENNIS-JONES, Harold
  Hamilton, Paul
  Hessing, Dennis
DENNISON, Enid
  Lloyd, Willson
DENNISTON, Elinore
  Allan, Dennis
  Foley, Rae
DENNY, Norman George
  Dale, Norman
DENT, Anthony
  Amplegirth, Anthony
  Lampton, Austen
DENTON, John
  Longley, John
DENVIL, Jane Gaskell
  Gaskell, Jane
DERLETH, August William
  Grendon, Stephen
  Mason, Teddy
DERN, Erolie Pearl
  Courtland, Roberta
  Dern, Peggy
  Gaddis, Peggy
DESMARAIS, Ovide E.
  Demaris, Ovid
DEVANEY, Pauline *and* APPS,
 Edwin
  Wraith, John

DEWAR, Hubert Stephen Lowry
  Wessex Redivivus
DEWEY, Thomas Blanchard
  Brandt, Tom
DICK, Oliver Lawson *and*
  CARRIER, Robert
  Oliver, Robert
DICK-ERIKSON, Cicely Sibyl
 Alexandra
  Dick, Alexandra
  Ericson, Sybil
  Erikson, Charlotte
  Hay, Frances
DICK-HUNTER, Noel
  N. D. H.
DICK-LAUDER, *Sir* George
  Lauder, George Dick
DICKINSON, Anne Hepple
  Hepple, Anne
DIENES, Zoltan
  Zed
DIETZ, Howard
  Freckles
DILCOCK, Noreen
  Christian, Jill
  Ford, Norrey
  Walford, Christian
DILLARD, Polly Hargis
  Hargis, Pauline
  Hargis, Polly
DILLON, E. J.
  Lanin, E. B.
DILNOT, George
  Froest, Frank
DINGLE, Aylward Edward
  Cotterell, Brian
  Sinbad

DINNER, William
  Smith, Surrey
DISCH, Thomas M. *and*
  SLADEK, John Thomas
  Demijohn, Thom
DIVINE, Arthur Durham
  Divine, David
  Rame, David
DIXON, Arthur
  Whye, Felix
DIXON, Ella Hepworth
  Wynman, Margaret
DOANE, Pelagie
  Hoffner, Dorothy
DODGE, Josephine Daskam
  Bacon, J. D.
DOHERTY, Ivy Ruby
  Hardwick, Sylvia
DOLBEY, Ethel M.
  Hawthorne, E. M. D.
DONN-BYRNE, Brian Oswald
  Byrne, Donn
DONNELLY, Augustine
  Bullen Bear
DONSON, Cyril
  Hartford, Via
  Kidd, Russell
  Mackin, Anita
  Pinder, Chuck
DORLING, Henry Taprell
  Taffrail
DORR, Julia Caroline
  Thomas, Caroline
DOUGLAS, Archibald C.
  Nemo
DOUGLAS, Keith
  Hatred, Peter

29

DOUGLAS, Mary
  Tew, Mary
DOUGLAS, Norman *and*
 FITZGIBBON, Elsa
  Normyx
DOUGLASS, Percival Ian
  Bear, I. D.
  Crane, Henry
DOWNEY, Edmund
  Allen, F. M.
DRACKETT, Phil
  King, Paul
DRAGO, Harry Sinclair
  Ermine, Will
  Lomax, Bliss
DRESSER, Davis
  Baker, Asa
  Davis, Don
  Halliday, Brett
  Wayne, Anderson
DRESSER, Davis *and* ROLLINS,
 Kathleen
  Debrett, Hal
DREW, Jane B.
  Fry, Jane
DRIVER, Christopher
  Archestratus
DRUMMOND, Alison
  Schaw, Ruth
DRUMMOND, Cherry
  Evans, Cherry
DRUMMOND, Edith
  Carman, Dulce
DRUMMOND, Humphrey
  Ap Evans, Humphrey
DRYHURST, Michael John
  Darling, V. H.

DU BOIS, Theodora
  McCormick, Theodora
DUDDINGTON, Charles Lionel
  Campbell, Berkeley
  Nightingale, Charles
DUDLEY, Ernest
  Lydecker, J. J.
DUDLEY-SMITH, Trevor
  Black, Mansell
  Burgess, Trevor
  Fitzalan, Roger
  Hall, Adam
  North, Howard
  Rattray, Simon
  Scott, Warwick
  Smith, Caesar
  Trevor, Elleston
DUFF, Charles
  Chernichewski, Vladimir
DUFF, Douglas Valder
  Mainsail
  Savage, Leslie
  Stanhope, Douglas
  Wickloe, Peter
DUFFIELD, Dorothy Dean
  Duffield, Anne
DUFFY, Agnes Mary
  Vox, Agnes Mary
DUGGAN, Denise Valerie
  Egerton, Denise
DUGGLEBY, Jean Colbeck
  Kennedy, Diana
DUGHMAN, John Karl *and*
 DUGHMAN, Frieda Mae
  Churchill, Luanna
DUKE, Anita
  Hewett, Anita

DUKE, Madelaine
  Donne, Maxim
  Duncan, Alex
DUKENFIELD, William Claude
  Bogle, Charles
  Criblecoblis, Otis
  Fields, W. C.
  Jeeves, Mahatma Kane
DUNCAN, Actea
  Thomas, Carolyn
DUNCAN, Kathleen
  Simmons, Catherine
  Simmons, Kim
DUNCAN, Robert Lipscomb
  Roberts, James Hall
DUNCAN, William Murdoch
  Cassells, John
  Dallas, John
  Graham, Neill
  Locke, Martin
  Malloch, Peter
  Marshall, Lovat
DUNK, Margaret
  Duke, Margaret
DUNKERLEY, Elsie Jeanette
  Oxenham, Elsie Jeanette
DUNKERLEY, William Arthur
  Oxenham, John
DUNLOP, Agnes M. R.
  Kyle, Elisabeth
  Ralston, Jan
DUNN, Mary
  Faid, Mary
DUNNE, Finlay Peter
  Dooley, Martin
DUNNETT, Dorothy
  Halliday, Dorothy

DUNSING, Dee
  Mowery, Dorothy
DUPUY-MAZUEL, Henri
  Catalan, Henri
DURBRIDGE, Francis *and*
  MCCONNELL, James Douglas
  Rutherford
  Temple, Paul
DURGNAT, Raymond
  Green, O. O.
DURRELL, Lawrence
  Norden, Charles
DURST, Paul
  Bannon, Peter
  Chelton, John
  Cochran, Jeff
  Shane, John

EAGAN, Frances W.
  Seeker, A
EAGLESTONE, Arthur Archibald
  Dataller, Roger
EAMES, Helen Mary
  Mercury
EARNSHAW, Patricia
  Mann, Patricia
EASTWOOD, Helen B.
  Baxter, Olive
  Ramsay, Fay
EBBETT, Eve
  Burfield, Eva
EBBS, Robert
  Pitchford, Harry Ronald
  Severn, Richard
EBERLE, Irmengarde
  Allen, Allyn
  Carter, Phyllis Ann

31

EBERT, Arthur Frank
  Arthur, Frank
ECCLESHARE, Colin
  O. P.
EDEN, Dorothy
  Paradise, Mary
EDGAR, Alfred
  Lyndon, Barrie
EDGLEY, Leslie
  Bloomfield, Robert
EDGLEY, Leslie *and* EDGLEY,
  Mary
  Hastings, Brook
EDMISTON, Helen J. M.
  Robertson, Helen
EDMONDS, Helen
  Ferguson, Helen
  Kavan, Anna
EDMONDSON, Sybil
  Armstrong, Sybil
EDMUNDSON, Joseph
  Burton, Conrad
  Jody, J. M.
EDWARD, Ann Elizabeth
  West, Anna
EDWARD, Irene
  Barr, Elisabeth
EDWARDS, Florence
  Edwards, Laurence
  Jolly, Susan
EDWARDS, Frederick Anthony
  Edwards, Charman
  Van Dyke, J.
EDWARDS, George Graveley
  Graveley, George
EHRENBORG, *Mrs* C. G.
  Trew, Cecil G.

EHRLICH, Bettina
  Bettina
EIKER, Mathilde
  Evermay, March
EISENSTADT-JELEZNOV,
  Mikhail
  Argus, M. K.
ELDERSHAW, Flora Sydney *and*
  BARNARD, Marjorie Faith
  Eldershaw, M. Barnard
ELGIN, Betty
  Kirby, Kate
ELIADES, David and WEBB,
  Robert Forrest
  Forrest, David
ELLERMAN, Annie Winifred
  Bryher
  Bryher, Winifred
ELLETT, Harold Pincton
  Burnaby, Nigel
ELLIOT, Andrew George
  MacAndrew, Rennie
ELLIOTT-CANNON, Arthur
  Elliott
  Cannon, Elliott
  Forde, Nicholas
  Martyn, Miles
ELLIS, Oliver
  Briony, Henry
ELLISON, James
  Brother Flavius
ELLISON, Joan
  Robertson, Elspeth
ELTING, Mary
  Brewster, Benjamin
  Cole, Davis
  Tatham, Campbell

ELWART, Joan Frances
   Elwart, Joan Potter
   Trawle, Mary Elizabeth
ELY, George Herbert *and*
  L'ESTRANGE, C. James
   Strang, Herbert
EMANUEL, Victor Rousseau
   Rousseau, Victor
EMMS, Dorothy
   Charques, Dorothy
ENGEL, Lyle Kenyon
   Kenyon, Larry
   Kenyon, Paul
ENGLISH, Jean Ellen
   French, Ellen Jean
EPSTEIN, Beryl
   Williams, Beryl
EPSTEIN, Beryl *and* EPSTEIN,
  Samuel
   Allen, Adam
   Coe, Douglas
EPSTEIN, Samuel
   Campbell, Bruce
ESCHERLICH, Elsa Antonie
   Falk, Elsa
ESTRIDGE, Robin
   Loraine, Philip
EVANS, Constance May
   Gray, Jane
   O'Nair, Mairi
EVANS, George
   Geraint, George
EVANS, George *and* EVANS, Kay
   Bird, Brandon
   Evans, Harris
EVANS, Gwynfil Arthur
   Gwynne, Arthur
   Western, Barry

EVANS, Hilary Agard
   Agard, H. E.
EVANS, Hugh Austin
   Austin, Hugh
EVANS, Jean
   Shaw, Jane
EVANS, Julia
   Hobson, Polly
EVANS, Kathleen
   Kaye, Evelyn
EVANS, Kay *and* EVANS, George
   Bird, Brandon
   Evans, Harris
EVANS, Kay *and* EVANS, Stuart
   Tracey, Hugh
EVANS, Marguerite Florence
   Barcynska, Hélène, *Countess*
   Sandys, Oliver
EVANS, Stuart *and* EVANS, Kay
   Tracey, Hugh
EVELYN, John Michael
   Underwood, Michael
EVENS, George Bramwell
   Romany
EVERSON, William Oliver
   Brother Antoninus
EWART, Ernest Andrew
   Cable, Boyd
EWART-BIGGS, Christopher
   Elliott, Charles
EWER, Monica
   Crosbie, Elizabeth
EYERLY, Jeannette *and*
  GRIFFITH, Valeria W.
   Griffith, Jeannette
EYLES, Kathleen Muriel
   Tennant, Catherine

33

EYSSELINCK, Janet Gay
    Burroway, Janet

What are names but air?
—S. T. Coleridge. Names

FABRY, Joseph B.
    Fabrizius, Peter
FADIMAN, Edwin J.
    Mark, Edwina
FAIRBAIRN, R. H.
    R. H. F.
FAIRBURN, Eleanor
    Carfax, Catherine
FAIRCHILD, William
    Cranston, Edward
FAIRFIELD, Cecily Isabel
    West, Rebecca
FAIRLIE, Gerard
    Sapper
FALK, Katherine *and others*
    Heptagon
FALK, Millicent *and others*
    Heptagon
FALL, William E.
    Erimus
FALLA, Frank
    Sarnian
FARGUS, Fredrick John
    Conway, Hugh
FARJEON, Eve
    Jefferson, Sarah
FARJEON, Joseph Jefferson
    Swift, Anthony
FARMERS, Eileen Elizabeth
    Lane, Elizabeth

FARRELL, Anne Elisabeth
    Allaben, Anne E.
FARRIS, John Lee
    Bracken, Steve
FARROW, R.
    Vincent, John
FAST, Howard
    Cunningham, E. V.
    Ericson, Walter
FAST, Julius
    Barnett, Adam
FAUST, Frederick
    Austin, Frank
    Baxter, George Owen
    Bolt, Lee
    Brand, Max
    Butler, Walter C.
    Challis, George
    Dawson, Peter
    Dexter, Martin
    Evan, Evin
    Evans, Evan
    Frederick, John
    Frost, Frederick
    Lawton, Dennis
    M. B.
    Manning, David
    Morland, Peter Henry
    Owen, Hugh
    Silver, Nicholas
    Uriel, Henry
FAY, Judith
    Nicholson, Kate
FEAGLES, Anita MacRae
    Macrae, Travis
FEAR, William H.
    Reynolds, John

FEARING, Kenneth; BEDFORD-
JONES, Henry *and* FRIEDE,
Donald
  Bedford, Donald F.
FEARON, Percy
  Poy
FEEHAN, *Sister* Mary Edward
  Clementia
FEILDING, Dorothy
  Fielding, A. E.
FEIWEL, Raphael Joseph
  Fyvel, T. R.
FELDMAN, Eugene P. R.
  Burroughs, Margaret
FELL, Frederick Victor
  Fredericks, Vic
FELLOWES-GORDON, Ian
  Collier, Douglas
  Gordon, Ian
FELLOWS, Dorothy Alice
  Collyer, Doric
  Hunt, Dorothy
FELSTEIN, Ivor
  Steen, Frank
FELTON, Ronald Oliver
  Welch, Ronald
FENN, Caroline K. *and* MCGREW,
Julia
  McGrew, Fenn
FENN, George Manville
  Manville, George
FENWICK-OWEN, Roderic
  Owen, Roderic
FERGUSON, Marilyn
  Renzelman, Marilyn
FERGUSON, Rachel
  Columbine
  Rachel

FERGUSON, William Blair
Morton
  Morton, William
FERGUSSON HANNAY, *Lady*
  Leslie, Doris
FERNEYHOUGH, Roger Edmund
  Hart, R. W.
FETHERSTONHAUGH, Patrick
William Edward
  Fetherston, Patrick
FETTER, Elizabeth
  Lees, Hannah
FEW, Eunice Beatty
  Few, Betty
FICKLING, Forrest E. *and*
  FICKLING, Gloria
  Fickling, G. G.
FIELD, M. J.
  Freshfield, Mark
FIELDING, Alexander
  Fielding, Xan
FIELDING, Archibald
  Fielding, Dorothy
FIELDING, Molly Hill
  Field, Hill
FINK, Merton
  Finch, Matthew
  Finch, Merton
FINKEL, George
  Pennage, E. M.
FINLAY, Ian
  Philaticus
FINLEY, Martha
  Farquharson, Martha
FINN, *Sister* Mary Paulina
  Pine, M. S.
FINNEY, Jack
  Braden, Walter

FINNIN, Mary
  Hogarth, John
FIRTH, Violet Mary
  Fortune, Dion
FISCHER, Matthias Joseph
  Laurence, Robert
FISH, Robert Lloyd
  Pike, Robert
  Pike, Robert L.
FISHER, Dorothea F. C.
  Canfield, Dorothy
FISHER, Douglas George
  Douglas, George
FISHER, John
  Piper, Roger
FISHER, Stephen Gould
  Gould, Stephen
  Lane, Grant
FISHER, Veronica Suzanne
  Veronique
FITCHETT, W. H.
  Vedette
FITZGERALD, Beryl
  Hoffman, Louise
FITZ-GERALD, S. J. A.
  Hannaford, Justin
FITZGIBBON, Elsa *and*
 DOUGLAS, Norman
  Normyx
FITZHARDINGE, Joan Margaret
  Phipson, Joan
FLACK, Isaac Harvey
  Graham, Harvey
FLAGG, John
  Gearon, John
FLANAGAN, Ellen
  Raskin, Ellen

FLANNER, Janet
  Genêt
FLEISCHER, Anthony
  Hofmeyer, Hans
FLEISHMANN, Helle
  Kuthumi
FLEMING, Ronald
  Fleming, Rhoda
  Frazer, Renee
  Langley, Peter
FLETCHER, Constance
  Fleming, George
FLETCHER, Harry L. Verne
  Fletcher, John
  Garden, John
  Hereford, John
FLEUR, Anne Elizabeth
  Elizabeth, Anne
  Lancaster, A. F.
  Sari
FLEXNER, Stuart
  Fletcher, Adam
FLOREN, Lee
  Austin, Brett
  Franchon, Lisa
  Hall, Claudia
  Hamilton, Wade
  Harding, Matt
  Lang, Grace
  Nelson, Marguerite
  Sterling, Maria Sandra
  Thomas, Lee
  Turner, Len
  Watson, Will
FLUHARTY, Vernon L.
  Carder, Michael
  O'Mara, Jim

FLYNN, *Sir* J. A.
  Oliver, Owen
FLYNN, Mary
  Livingstone, Margaret
FOCKE, E. P. W.
  Ernest, Paul
FOLSOM, Franklin Brewster
  Brewster, Franklin
  Gorham, Michael
  Nesbit, Troy
FOOT, Michael
  Cassius
FOOT, Michael; HOWARD, Peter
  and OWEN, Frank
  Cato
FOOTE, Carol
  Odell, Carol
FOOTE, Carol *and* GILL, Travis
  Odell, Gill
FORBES, Deloris Stanton
  Forbes, Stanton
  Wells, Tobias
FORBES, Marcelle Azra
  Morphy, *Countess*
FORD, Corey
  Riddell, John
FORD, T. Murray
  Le Breton, Thomas
FORD, T. W.
  Clay, Weston
  Shott, Abel
FORDE, Claude Marie
  Claude
FORSYTHE, Robin
  Dingwall, Peter
FORTE, Christine
  Forster, Christine

FOSDICK, Charles Austin
  Castlemon, Harry
FOSTER, Donn
  Saint-Eden, Dennis
FOSTER, George Cecil
  Seaforth
FOSTER, Jess Mary Mardon
  White, Heather
FOSTER, Marian Curtis
  Mariana
FOULDS, Elfrida Vipont
  Vipont, Charles
  Vipont, Elfrida
FOUTS, Edward Lee
  Lee, Edward
FOWKES, Aubrey
  Boy
FOWLER, Eric
  Mardle, Jonathan
FOWLER, Helen
  Foley, Helen
FOWLER, Henry Watson
  Egomet
  Quilibet
  Quillet
FOWLER, Kenneth A.
  Brooker, Clark
FOX, Charles
  Jeremy, Richard
FOX, James
  Holmes, Grant
FOX, Mona Alexis
  Brand, Mona
FOX, Norman Arnold
  Sabin, Mark
FOX, Winifred *and others*
  Heptagon

FOXALL, P. A.
  Vincent, Jim
FRAENKEL, Heinrich
  Assiac
FRANCE-HAYHURST,
  Evangeline
  France, Evangeline
FRANCIS, Arthur Bruce Charles
  Bruce, Charles
FRANCIS, Stephen D.
  Williams, Richard
FRANCK, Frederick S.
  Fredericks, Frank
FRANK, Waldo David
  Search-Light
FRANKAU, Julia Davis
  Danby, Frank
FRANKAU, Pamela
  Naylor, Eliot
FRANKLIN, Cynthia
  Neville, C. J.
FRANKLIN, Stella Maria Sarah
  Miles
  Brent, *of Bin Bin*
FRASER-HARRIS, D.
  Grange, Ellerton
FRAZEE, Steve
  Jennings, D.
FRAZER, James Ian Arbuthnot
  Fraser, Shamus
FREDE, Richard
  Frederics, Jocko
  Macdowell, Frederics
FREEDGOOD, Morton
  Godey, John
FREELING, Nicolas
  Nicolas, F. R. E.

FREEMAN, Kathleen
  Cory, Caroline
  Fitt, Mary
  Wick, Stuart Mary
FREEMAN, R. Austin
  Ashdown, Clifford
FRENCH, Alice
  Thanet, Octave
FREWER, Glyn
  Lewis, Mervyn
FREWIN, Leslie Ronald
  Dupont, Paul
FREY, Charles Weiser
  Findley, Ferguson
FRIEDBERG, Gertrude
  Tonkongy, Gertrude
FRIEDE, Donald; FEARING,
  Kenneth *and* BEDFORD-JONES,
  Henry
  Bedford, Donald F.
FRIEDLANDER, Peter
  French, Fergus
FRIEDMAN, Eve Rosemary
  Tibber, Robert
  Tibber, Rosemary
FRIEND, Oscar Jerome
  Jerome, Owen Fox
FROST, Kathleen Margaret
  Merivale, Margaret
FRY, Clodagh Micaela Gibson
  Gavin, Amanda
FRYEFIELD, Maurice P.
  Brooks, W. A.
  Brooks, William Allan
  Holmes, Arnold W.
FTYARAS, Louis George
  Alexander, L. G.

FULLBROOK, Gladys
  Hutchinson, Patricia
FULLER, Edmund
  Amicus Curiae
FULLER, Harold Edgar
  Fuller, Ed
  Fulman, Al
FULLER, Henry B.
  Page, Stanton
FULLER, James Franklin
  Ignotus
FURLONG, Vivienne
  Welburn, Vivienne
FYTTON ARMSTRONG, T. I.
  Gawsworth, John

GADDIS, Peggy
  Craig, Georgia
GAINES, Robert
  Summerscales, Rowland
GALLAGHER, Frank
  Hogan, David
GALSWORTHY, John
  Sinjohn, John
GANDLEY, Kenneth Royce
  Jacks, Oliver
  Royce, Kenneth
GANTNER, Neilma B.
  Sidney, Neilma
GARBER, Nellia B.
  Berg, Ila
GARD, Joyce
  Reeves, Joyce
GARDINER, Alfred George
  Alpha of the Plough
GARDINER, Dorothea Frances
  Frank, Theodore

GARDNER, Erle Stanley
  Fair, A. A.
  Green, Charles M.
  Kendrake, Carleton
  Kenny, Charles J.
GARDNER, Jerome
  Gilchrist, John
GARFIELD, Brian
  O'Brian, Frank
GARGILL, Morris *and* HEARNE,
  John
  Morris, John
GARNETT, David
  Burke, Leda
GARRATT, Alfred
  Garratt, Teddie
GARRETT, Winifred Selina
  Dean, Lyn
GARRISON, Webb Black
  Webster, Gary
GARRITY, David James
  Garrity
GARROD, John William *and*
  PAYNE, Ronald Charles
  Castle, John
GARVEY, Eric William
  Herne, Eric
GARVIN, J. L.
  Calehas
GARWOOD, Godfrey Thomas
  Thomas, Gough
GASE, Richard
  Gale, John
GASPAROTTI, Elizabeth
  Seifert, Elizabeth
GASTON, William J.
  Bannatyne, Jack

GAUNT, Arthur N.
  Nettleton, Arthur
GAUTIER-SMITH, Peter Claudius
  Conway, Peter
GEEN, Clifford
  Berkley, Tom
GEISEL, Theodor Seuss
  Dr Seuss
  Lesieg, Theo
GELB, Norman
  Mallery, Amos
GEORGE, Peter
  Peters, Bryan
GEORGE, Robert Esmonde
  Gordon
  Sencourt, Robert
GERAHTY, Digby George
  Standish, Robert
GERMANO, Peter
  Cord, Barry
  Kane, Jim
GERSHON, Karen
  Tripp, Karen
GERSON, Noel Bertram
  Edwards, Samuel
  Lewis, Paul
  Phillips, Leon
  Vail, Philip
  Vaughan, Carter A.
GESSNER, Lynne
  Clarke, Merle
GIBBS, Norah
  Boyd, Prudence
  Garland, Lisette
  Ireland, Noelle
  Merrill, Lynne
  Ritchie, Claire
  Shayne, Nina

Wayne, Heather
Whittingham, Sara
GIBSON, Walter Brown
  Brown, Douglas
  Grant, Maxwell
GIBSON, William
  Mass, William
GIFFORD, James Noble
  Noble, Emily
  Saxon, John
GILBERT, Ruth
  Ainsworth, Ruth
GILBERT, William Schwenck
  Bab
  Tomline, F. Latour
GILBERTSON, Mildred
  Gilbert, Nan
  Mendel, Jo
GILCHRIST, Alan
  Cowan, Alan
GILDEN, Katya *and* GILDEN,
  Bert
  Gilden, K. B.
GILDERDALE, Michael
  Flemming, Sarah
GILL, Travis *and* FOOTE, Carol
  Odell, Gill
GILL, Winifred *and others*
  Heptagon
GILLES, Daniel
  Johnson, Marigold
GILLHAM, Elizabeth Wright
  Enright
  Enright, Elizabeth
GILMER, Elizabeth Meriwether
  Dix, Dorothy

GILZEAN, Elizabeth Houghton
  Houghton, Elizabeth
  Hunton, Mary
GIRDLESTON, A. H.
  A. H. G.
GITTINGS, Jo
  Manton, Jo
GLASKIN, G. M.
  Jackson, Neville
GLASSCO, John
  Colman, George
  Okada, Hideki
  Underwood, Miles
GLASSCOCK, Anne Bonner
  Bonner, Michael
GLEADOW, Rupert
  Case, Justin
GLEMSER, Bernard
  Napier, Garaldine
GLEN, Duncan Munro
  Munro, Ronald Eadie
GLENTON, Stella Lennox
  King, Stella
GLIDDEN, Frederick Dilley
  Short, Luke
GLIDDEN, Jonathan H.
  Dawson, Peter
GLOVER, Modwena
  Sedgwick, Modwena
GLUCK, Sinclair
  Danning, Melrod
GOAMAN, Muriel
  Cox, Edith
GODFREY, Frederick M.
  Cronheim, F. G.
GODFREY, Lionel Robert
 Holcombe

Kennedy, Elliott
  Mitchell, Scott
GODLEY, Robert
  James, Franklin
GOETCHEUS, Carolyn
  Lynn, Carol
GOGGAN, John Patrick
  Patrick, John
GOHM, Douglas Charles
  O'Connell, Robert Frank
GOLBERG, Harry
  Grey, Harry
GOLDEN, Dorothy
  Dennison, Dorothy
GOLDFRANK, *Mrs* Herbert
  Kay, Helen
GOLDIE, Kathleen Annie
  Fidler, Kathleen
GOLDING, Louise
  Davies, Louise
GOLDMAN, William
  Longbaugh, Harry
GOLDSTON, Robert
  Conroy, Robert
GOLLER, Celia Margaret
  Fremlin, Celia
GOLSWORTHY, Arnold
  Holcombe, Arnold
  Jingle
GOMPERTZ, Martin Louis Alan
  Ganpat
GOOD, Edward
  Oyved, Moysheh
GOODAVAGE, Joseph F.
  Greystone, Alexander A.
  Savage, Steve

GOODCHILD, George
  Dare, Alan
  Reid, Wallace Q.
  Templeton, Jesse
GOODEY, P. E.
  Condon, Patricia
GOODMAN, George Jerome W.
  Smith, Adam
GOODMAN, George Jerome *and*
  KNOWLTON, Winthrop
  Goodman, Winthrop
GOODWIN, Geoffrey
  Gemini
  Telstar
  Topicus
GOODWIN, Harold Leland *and*
  HARKINS, Peter J.
  Blaine, John
GOODYEAR, Stephen Frederick
  Taylor, Sam
GOODYKOONTZ, William F.
  Goode, Bill
GORDON, Alan Bacchus
  Ordon, A. Lang
GORDON, Charles William
  Connor, Ralph
GORDON, Jan
  Gore, William
GORDON, Robert I.
  London, Anne
  London, Robert
GOREY, Edward St John
  Blutig, Eduard
GOSLING, Veronica
  Henriques, Veronica
GOSSMAN, Oliver
  Clyde, Craig
GOTTLIEBSEN, Ralph Joseph
  Scott, O. R.

GOTTSCHALK, Laura Riding
  Riding, Laura
GOVAN, Mary Christine
  Allerton, Mary
  Darby, J. N.
GOWING, Sidney Floyd
  Goodwin, John
GOYDER, Margot *and* JOSKE,
  Neville
  Neville, Margot
GOYNE, Richard
  Courage, John
GRABER, George Alexander
  Cordell, Alexander
GRAHAM, Charles
  Montrose, David
GRAHAM, James Maxtone
  Anstruther, James
GRAHAM, Maude Fitzgerald
  Graham, Susan
GRAINGER, Francis Edward
  Hill, Headon
GRANT, Donald *and* WILSON,
  William
  Ness, K. T.
GRANT, Hilda Kay
  Grant, Kay
  Hilliard, Jan
GRANT, M. H.
  Linesman
  Scolopax
GRANT, *Lady* Sybil
  Scot, Neil
GRANT, William
  Onlooker
GRAVELEY, G. C.
  Grayson, Daphne

GRAVES, Clotilda Inez Mary
  Dehan, Richard
GRAVES, Robert
  Doyle, John
GRAY, Dorothy K.
  Haynes, Dorothy K.
GRAY, K. E.
  Grant, Eve
GRAY, Lindsay Russell Nixon
  Lemon, Grey
GRAY, Simon
  Reade, Hamish
GRAY, Terence J. S.
  Wei Wu Wei
GRAYDON, William Murray
  Gordon, William Murray
  Murray, William
GRAYLAND, Valerie M.
  Belvedere, Lee
  Subond, Valerie

A good name is better than
precious ointment.
Bible. Ecclesiastes, 7.1.

GREALEY, Tom
  Southworth, Louis
GREAVES, Michael
  Callum, Michael
GREEN, Alan Baer *and* BRODIE,
  Julian Paul
  Denbie, Roger
GREEN, Charles Henry
  Sandhurst, B. G.
GREEN, Dorothy
  Auchterlonie, Dorothy

GREEN, Elisabeth Sara
  Tresilian, Liz
GREEN, Evelyn Everett
  Adair, Cecil
GREEN, Lalage Isobel
  March, Hilary
  Pulvertaft, Lalage
GREEN, Maxwell
  Cabby with camera
GREEN, Peter
  Delaney, Denis
GREEN, T.
  Ramsey, Michael
GREENAWAY, Gladys
  Manners, Julia
GREENBERG, Jack
  Greenhill, Jack
GREENE, Sigrid
  De Lima, Sigrid
GREENE, Ward
  Dudley, Frank
GREENER, William Oliver
  Gerrare, Wirt
GREENHILL, Elizabeth Ann
  Giffard, Ann
GREENLAND, W. K.
  King, W. Scott
GREENWOOD, Augustus George
  Archer, Owen
GREENWOOD, Julia E. C.
  Askham, Francis
GREENWOOD, T. E.
  McCabe, Rory
GREGG, Hilda
  Grier, Sydney C.
GREIG, Maysie
  Ames, Jennifer
  Barclay, Ann

Thompson, Madeline
Warren, Mary D.
GRESHAM, Elizabeth F.
Grey, Robin
GRIBBEN, James
James, Vincent
GRIBBLE, Leonard Reginald
Cody, Stetson
Denver, Lee
Grant, Landon
Grex, Leo
Grey, Louis
Marlowe, Piers
Muir, Dexter
Sanders, Bruce
GRIERSON, Walter
Enquiring Layman
GRIEVE, Alexander Haig
Glanville
Glanville, Alec
GRIEVE, Christopher Murray
MacDiarmid, Hugh
GRIEVESON, Mildred
Flemming, Cardine
Mather, Anne
GRIFFIN, Jonathan
Thurlow, Robert
GRIFFIN, Vivian Cory
Crosse, Victoria
GRIFFITH, Valeria W. *and*
EYERLY, Jeannette
Griffith, Jeannette
GRIFFITHS, Aileen Esther
Passmore, Aileen E.
GRIFFITHS, Charles
Bold, Ralph
GRIFFITHS, Jack
Griffith, Jack

GRIMSTEAD, Hettie
Manning, Marsha
GRINDAL, Richard
Grayson, Richard
GRINGHUIS, Richard H.
Gringhuis, Dirk
GROSSMAN, Judith
Hamilton, Ernest
Merril, Judith
Sharon, Rose
Thorstein, Eric
GROSSMAN, Judith *and*
KORNBLUTH, Cyril M.
Judd, Cyril
GRUBER, Frank
Acre, Stephen
Boston, Charles K.
Vedder, John K.
GUARIENTO, Ronald
Parks, Ron
GUEST, Enid
Quin, Shirland
GUEST, Francis Harold
Spenser, James
GUGGISBERG, *Sir* F. G.
Ubique
GUIGO, Ernest Philip
Holt, E. Carleton
GUINNESS, Maurice
Brewer, Mike
Gale, Newton
GUIRDHAM, Arthur
Eaglesfield, Francis
GULICK, Grover C.
Gulick, Bill
GUNN, John Angus Lancaster
Hall, B.

GUTHRIE, P. R.
  Pain, Barry
GUTHRIE, Thomas Anstey
  Anstey, F.
GUYONVARCH, Irene
  Pearl, Irene
GWINN, Christine M.
  Kelway, Christine
GWINN, William R.
  Randall, William
GWYNN, Audrey
  Thomson, Audrey
GWYNN, Ursula Grace
  Leigh, Ursula
GYE, Harold Frederick Neville
  Gye, Hal
  Hackston, James

HAARER, Alec Ernest
  Shanwa
HADFIELD, Alan
  Dale, Robin
HAGAN, Stelia F.
  Hawkins, John
HALDANE, Robert Aylmer
  Square, Charlotte
HALE, Kathleen
  McClean, Kathleen
HALE, Sylvia
  Barnard, Nancy
HALEY, W. J.
  Sell, Joseph
HALL, Bennie Caroline
  Hall, Bennet
HALL, Emma L.
  St Claire, Yvonne
HALL, Frederick
  Hall, Patrick

HALL, Irene
  Gough, Irene
HALL, Josef Washington
  Close, Upton
HALL, Marie
  Boas, Marie
HALL, Oakley Maxwell
  Manor, Jason
HAMBLETON, Phyllis MacVean
  Vane, Phillipa
HAMILTON, Alex
  Pooter
HAMILTON, Cecily
  Hamilton, Max
  Rae, Scott
HAMILTON, Charles Harold St
John
  Clifford, Martin
  Conquest, Owen
  Redway, Ralph
  Richards, Frank
  Richards, Hilda
HAMILTON, *Sir* George
Rostrevor
  Rostrevor, George
HAMILTON, Leigh Brackett
  Brackett, Leigh
HAMILTON, Mary A. A.
  Iconoclast
HAMILTON, Mary Margaret Kaye
  Kaye, Mary Margaret
HAMILTON-WILKES, Edwin
  Hamilton-Wilkes, Monty
  Uncle Monty
HAMMERTON, J. A.
  J. A. H.
HAMMETT, Dashiell
  Collinson, Peter

HAMMOND, Lawrence
   Francis, Victor
HAMMOND-INNES, Ralph
   Hammond, Ralph
   Innes, Hammond
HAMON, Louis *Count*
   Cheiro
HAMPDEN, John
   Montagu, Robert
HANKINSON, Charles J.
   Holland, Clive
HANLEY, Clifford
   Calvin, Henry
HANLEY, James
   Bentley, James
   Shone, Patric
HANNA, Frances
   Nichols, Fan
HANNAY, James Owen
   Birmingham, George A.
HANZELON, Robert M.
   De Hart, Robert
HARBAGE, Alfred
   Kyd, Thomas
HARBAUGH, Thomas Chalmers
   Holmes, *Captain* Howard
HARBINSON-BRYANS, Robert
   Bryans, Robin
   Harbinson, Robert
HARDINGE, George
   Milner, George
HARDINGE, Rex
   Capstan
HARDISON, O. B.
   Bennett, H. O.
HARDWICK, Richard
   Holmes, Rick
   Honeycutt, Richard

HARDY, Jane
   Boileau, Marie
HARDY, Marjorie
   Hardy, Bobbie
HARE, Walter B.
   Burns, Mary
HARKINS, Peter
   Adams, Andy
HARKINS, Peter J. *and*
  GOODWIN, Harold Leland
   Blaine, John
HARKNETT, Terry
   Gilman, George G.
   Hardy, Adam
   Pike, Charles R.
HARLAND, Henry
   Luska, Sidney
HARMAN, Richard
   Martin, Richard
HARPER, Edith
   Flamank, E.
HARRELL, Irene Burk
   Amor, Amos
   Waylan, Mildred
HARRIS, Ida Fraser
   Proctor, Ida
HARRIS, Joel Chandler
   Uncle Remus
HARRIS, John
   Hebden, Mark
HARRIS, John Wyndham Parkes
  Lucas Beynon
   Beynon, John
   Harris, John Beynon
   Parkes, Lucas
   Wyndham, John
HARRIS, Marion Rose
   Young, Rose

HARRIS, Mark
  Wiggen, Henry W.
HARRIS, Pamela
  Meinikoff, Pamela
HARRIS, Polly Anne Colver
  Colver, Anne
  Harris, Colver
HARRIS, William
  Harris, Peter
HARRISON, Chester William
  Hickok, Will
HARRISON, Constance Cary
  Refugitta
HARRISON, Elizabeth C.
  Cavanna, Betty
  Headley, Elizabeth
HARRISON, J. H.
  Wynyard, John
HARRISON, John Gilbert
  Gilbert, John
HARRISON, Julia
  Richmond, Fiona
HARRISON, Michael
  Downes, Quentin
HARRISON, Philip
  Carmichael, Philip
HARRISON, Richard Motte
  Motte, Peter
HART, Caroline Horowitz
  Winters, Mary K.
HARTHOORN, Susanne
  Hart, Susanne
HARTIGAN, Patrick Joseph
  O'Brien, John
HARTLEY, Ellen R.
  Raphael, Ellen
HARTMANN, Helmut Henry
  Seymour, Henry

HARVEY, Charles
  Willoughby, Hugh
HARVEY, Margaret Susan Janet
  Michelmore, Susan
HARVEY, Peter Noel
  Day, Adrian
  Peters, Noel
HARVEY, William
  Denovan, Saunders
HASSON, James
  De Salignac, Charles
HASWELL, C. J. D.
  Foster, George
  Haswell, Jock
HAUCK, Louise Platt
  Landon, Louise
HAUSMAN, Leon Augustus
  Poe, Bernard
HAWKINS, *Sir* Anthony Hope
  A. H.
  Hope, Anthony
HAWTON, Hector
  Curzon, Virginia
HAYNES, John Harold
  Wake, G. B.
HAYNES DIXON, Margaret
  Rumer
  Godden, Rumer
HAYS, Peter
  Jefferies, Ian
HAZLEWOOD, Rex
  Delta
  Keneu
HEADLEY, Elizabeth
  Allen, Betsy
HEAL, Edith
  Page, Eileen
  Powers, Margaret

47

HEARD, Henry Fitzgerald
  Heard, Gerald
HEARNE, John *and* GARGILL,
  Morris
  Morris, John
HEAVEN, Constance
  Fecher, Constance
HEBERDEN, Mary Violet
  Leonard, Charles L.
HECTOR, Barbara
  Barrie, Hester
HEELIS, Beatrix
  Potter, Beatrix
HEILBRUN, Carolyn
  Cross, Amanda
HEINEY, Donald William
  Harris, Macdonald
HEINLEIN, Robert A.
  Macdonald, Anson
HEISS, John Stanger
  Asche, Oscar
HEITNER, Iris
  James, Robert
HEMING, Dempster E.
  Dempster, Guy
HEMING, Jack C. W.
  Western-Holt, J. C.
HENDERSON, Archibald
  Steele, Erskine
HENDERSON, Donald Landels
  Bridgwater, Donald
  Landels, D. H.
  Landels, Stephanie
HENDERSON, James Leal
  Currier, Jay L.
HENDERSON, James Maddock
  Danvers, Peter
  Jordan, Bryn

HENDERSON, Le Grand
  Le Grand
HENDRY, Frank Coutts
  Shalimar
HENHAM, E. J.
  Trevena, John
HENKLE, Henrietta
  Buckmaster, Henrietta
HENLEY, Art
  Eric, Kenneth
  Jones, Webb
HENNISSART, Martha *and*
  LATIS, Mary J.
  Dominic, R. B.
  Lathen, Emma
HEPBURN, Thomas Nicoll
  Setoun, Gabriel
HEPPELL, Mary
  Clare, Marguerite
  Heppell, Blanche
HERBERT, *Sir* Alan Patrick
  A. P. H.
  Haddock, Albert
HERBERT, John
  Simple, Peter
HERN, Anthony
  Hope, Andrew
HERNDEN, Beryl *and*
  BALFOUR, Eve
  Hearnden, Balfour
HERRON, Elsie Ellerington
  Elsey, J. J.
HERTZBERG, Nancy
  Keesing, Nancy
HETHERINGTON, Keith James
  Conway, Keith
  Keith, James

HEUMAN, William
  Kramer, George
HEWETSON, Sara
  Dicant, V. L.
HEWISON, Robert John Petrie
  Petrie, John
HEWITT, Cecil Rolph
  Rolph, C. H.
HEWITT, Kathleen Douglas
  Martin, Dorothea
HEWSON, Irene Dale
  Ross, Jean
HEYER, Georgette
  Martin, Stella
HIBBERT, Eleanor Alice Burford
  Burford, Eleanor
  Carr, Philippa
  Ford, Elbur
  Holt, Victoria
  Kellow, Kathleen
  Plaidy, Jean
  Tate, Ellalice
HIBBS, John
  Blyth, John
HICKEN, Una
  Kindler, Asta
HICKEY, Madelyn E.
  De Lacy, Louise
  Eastlund, Madelyn
  Hickey, Lyn
  Sullivan, Eric Harrison
HICKS, Tyler Gregory
  Murphy, Louis J.
HIGGINBOTHAM, Anne D.
  Higginbotham, Anne T.
  McIntosh, Ann T.
HIGGINS, Charles
  Dall, Ian

HIGGINS, Margaret
  O'Brien, Bernadette
HIGGINSON, Henry Clive
  Theta, Eric Mark
HIGGS, Alec S.
  Stansbury, Alec
HIGHSMITH, Patricia
  Morgan, Claire
HILL, Brian
  Magill, Marcus
HILL, Douglas
  Hillman, Martin
HILL, Grace
  MacDonald, Marcia
HILL, John Alexander
  Skeever, Jim
HILLS, Frances E.
  Mercer, Frances
HILLSTROM, Joseph
  Hill, Joe
HILLYARD, Mary Dorothea
  Kellway, Mary D.
HILTON, James
  Trevor, Glen
HILTON, John Buxton
  Stanley, Warwick
HINCKS, Cyril Malcolm
  Coulsdon, John
  Dayle, Malcolm
  Gee, Osman
  Howard, John M.
  Malcolm, Charles
  Malcolm, Ronald
HINES, Dorothea
  De Culwen, Dorothea
HIRD, Neville
  Meyer, Henry J.

HIRST, Gillian
  Baxter, Gillian
HISCOCK, Eric
  E. H.
  Whitefriar
HISCOCK, Leslie
  Marsh, Patrick
HITCHENS, Dolores
  Birkley, Dolan
  Burke, Noel
  Olsen, D. B.
HITCHIN, Martin
  Mewburn, Martin
HOAR, Peter
  Amberley, Simon
HOAR, Roger Sherman
  Farley, Ralph Milne
HOBSBAWM, E. J.
  Newton, Francis
HODDER-WILLIAMS,
 Christopher
  Brogan, James
HODGE, Horace Emerton
  Hodge, Merton
HODGES, Barbara K.
  Cambridge, Elizabeth
HODGES, Doris Marjorie
  Hunt, Charlotte
HOFDORP, Pim
  Geerlink, Will
HOFF, Harry Summerfield
  Cooper, William
HOFFENBERG, Mason
  Drake, Hamilton
  Perez, Faustino
HOFFENBERG, Mason *and*
 SOUTHERN, Terry
  Kenton, Maxwell

HOFFMAN, Anita
  Fettsman, Ann
HOGAN, Ray
  Ringold, Clay
HOGAN, Robert Jasper
  Cantrell, Wade B.
  Jasper, Bob
HOGARTH, Grace
  Gay, Amelia
HOGARTH, Grace *and* NORTON,
 Alice Mary
  Weston, Allen
HOGBEN, Lancelot Thomas
  Calvin, Kenneth
HOGBIN, Herbert
  Hogbin, Ian
HOGG, Beth
  Grey, Elizabeth
HOGG, Michael
  Simple, Peter
HOGUE, Wilbur Owings
  Shannon, Carl
HOKE, Helen L.
  Sterling, Helen
  Troy, Alan
HOLBECHE, Philippa
  Shore, Philippa
HOLDAWAY, Marjorie F.
  Japonica
HOLDAWAY, Neville Aldridge
  Temple-Ellis, N. A.
HOLDEN, J. R.
  Joystick
HOLDEN, Raymond
  Peckham, Richard
HOLLEY, Marietta
  Jemyma
  Josiah Allen's Wife

HOLLIDAY, Joseph
  Bosco, Jack
  Dale, Jack
HOLLIDAY, Robert Cortes
  Hill, Murray
HOLLOWS, Norman F. *and*
  BRADLEY, Ian
  Duplex
HOLMES, Charles Henry
  Adams, Clayton
HOLMES, Daniel Henry
  Henry, Daniel Jr
HOLMES, Llewellyn Perry
  Hardin, Dave
  Stuart, Matt
HOLMES, Peter
  Fenwick, Peter
HOLMSTROM, John Eric
  Gellert, Roger
HOLROYD, Ethel Mary
  Cookridge, John Michael
  Marshall, Beverley
HOLT, Henry
  Hopkins, Stanley
HOLT, Margaret Van Vechten
  Holt, Rackham
HOME-GALL, Edward Reginald
  Clive, Clifford
  Dale, Edwin
  Hall, Rupert
  Home-Gall, Reginald
HOMERSHAM, Basil Henry
  Manningham, Basil
HOOD, Torrey
  Bevans, Torre
  Torrey, Marjorie
HOOK, Alfred Samuel
  Colton, A. J.

HOOK, H. Clarke
  Harvey, Ross
HOOKE, Charles W.
  Fielding, Howard
HOPE, Charles Evelyn Graham
  Pelham, Anthony
HOPE, Essex
  Smith, Essex
HOPKINS, Robert Sydney
  Rostand, Robert
HOPLEY-WOOLRICH, Cornell
  George
  Hopley, George
  Irish, William
  Woolrich, Cornell
HOPP, Signe
  Zinken
HOPSON, William L.
  Sims, John
HORKAN, Nelle Irwin
  Edwards, Ellen
HORLER, Sydney
  Cavendish, Peter
  Heritage, Martin
  Standish, J. O.
HORNBY, John W.
  Brent, Calvin
  Grace, Joseph
  Summers, Gordon
HORNBY, Lesley
  Twiggy
HORNE, Geoffrey
  North, Gil
HOSIE, Stanley William
  Stanley, Michael
HOSKEN, Alice Cecil Seymour
  Stanton, Coralie

51

HOSKEN, Clifford James Wheeler
  Keverne, Richard
HOSKIN, Cyril Henry
  Rampa, T. Lobsang
HOUGH, Richard Alexander
  Carter, Bruce
HOUGH, Stanley Bennett
  Gordon, Rex
  Stanley, Bennett
HOUNSFIELD, Joan
  Wheezy
HOUSEMAN, Lorna
  Westall, Lorna
HOVICK, Rose Louise
  Lee, Gypsy Rose
HOWARD, Felicity
  Longfield, Jo
HOWARD, Herbert Edmund
  Philmore, R.
HOWARD, James Arch
  Fisher, Laine
HOWARD, Munroe
  St Clair, Philip
HOWARD, Peter; FOOT, Michael
 and OWEN, Frank
  Cato
HOWARTH, Patrick John Fielding
  Francis, C. D. E.
HOWE, Doris
  Munro, Mary
  Nash, Newlyn
HOWELL, Douglas Nayler
  Hancock, Robert
HOWITT, John Leslie Despard
  Despard, Leslie
HOYT, Edwin Palmer Jr
  Martin, Christopher

HUBBARD, Clifford Lionel Barry
  Canis
HUBBARD, Elbert
  Fra Elbertus
HUBBARD, Frank McKinney
  Hubbard, Kin
  Martin, Abe
HUBBARD, L. Ron
  Elron
  Esterbrook, Tom
  La Fayette, Rene
  Northrop, *Captain* B. A.
  Rachen, Kurt von
HUDSON, H. Lindsay
  Lindsay, H.
HUDSON, William Henry
  Harford, Henry
HUEFFER, Ford Madox
  Ford, Ford Madox
HUFF, Darrell
  Hough, Don
  Nelson, Chris
  West, Mark
HUGGETT, Berthe
  Brook, Esther
HUGHES, Ivy
  Hay, Catherine
HUGHES, Valerie Anne
  Carrington, V.
HUGHES, Walter Dudley
  Derventio
HUGHES, Walter Llewellyn
  Walters, Hugh
HUGHES, William
  Northerner
HUGILL, John Anthony
 Crawford
  Crawford, Anthony

HUGILL, Robert
  Gill, Hugh
HULBERT, Joan
  Rostron, Primrose
HULL, Richard
  Sampson, Richard Henry
HUMPHREYS, Eliza M. J.
  Rita
HUMPHRIES, Adelaide
  Harris, Kathleen
  Way, Wayne
  West, Token
HUMPHRIES, Barry
  Barry
HUMPHRIES, Elsie Mary
  Forrester, Mary
HUMPHRIES, Sydney
  Vane, Michael
HUMPHRYS, Leslie George
  Condray, Bruno
  Humphrys, Geoffrey
HUNT, E. Howard
  Baxter, John
  Davis, Gordon
  Dietrich, Robert
  St John, David
HUNT, Katherine Chandler
  Nash, Chandler
HUNT-BODE, Gisele
  Hunt, Diana
HUNTER, Alfred John
  Addiscombe, John
  Brenning, L. H.
  Dax, Anthony
  Drummond, Anthony
  Hunter, Jean
  Hunter, John

HUNTER, Bluebell Matilda
  Guildford, John
HUNTER, Christine
  Hunter, John
  Steer, Charlotte
HUNTER, Eileen
  Clements, E. H.
  Laura
HUNTER, Elizabeth
  Chace, Isobel
HUNTER, Evan
  Cannon, Curt
  Collins, Hunt
  McBain, Ed
  Marsten, Richard
HUNTER, William R.
  Hagen, Brett
HUNTER BLAIR, Pauline *see*
  BLAIR, Pauline Hunter
HUNTINGTON, Helen
  Lynde, H. H.
HURREN, Bernard
  Nott, Barry
HURT, Edwin Franklin
  Franklin, E.
HURWOOD, Bernhardt J.
  Knight, Mallory
HUSKINSON, Richard King
  King, Richard
HUTCHINSON, Barbara Beatrice
  Fearn, Roberta
HUTCHINSON, Juliet Mary Fox
  Phoenice, J.
HUTCHINSON, Robert Hare
  Hare, Robert
HUTCHISON, Graham, Seton
  Seton, Graham

HUTTON, Andrew Nielson
  Olympic
HUXLEY, Julian Sorell
  Balbus
HUXTABLE, Marjorie
  Dare, Simon
  Stewart, Marjorie
HYDE, Edmund Errol Claude
  Rejje, E.
HYDE, Lavender Beryl
  Ashe, Elizabeth
HYMERS, Laura M.
  West, Laura M.
HYNDMAN, Jane Andrews
  Wyndham, Lee
HYNDMAN, Robert Utley
  Wyndham, Robert

IBBOTT, Arthur Pearson
  Bertram, Arthur
IDELL, Albert Edward
  Rogers, Phillips
INGAMELLS, F. G.
  Home Guard
INGRAM-MOORE, Erica
  Marsden, June
IRISH, Betty M.
  Arthur, Elisabeth
  Bell, Nancy
IRVING, John Treat
  Quod, John
IRWIN, Constance
  Frick, C. H.
IVISON, Elizabeth
  Towers, Tricia
  Wilson, Elizabeth

*Sam Johnson is hardly a name
for a great writer.
—George Bernard Shaw.*

JACKSON, Ada Acraman
  Ajax
JACKSON, Caary Paul
  Lochions, Colin
  Paulson, Jack
JACKSON, Kathryn
  Hubbard, Joan
JACOB, Naomi
  Gray, Ellington
JACOB, Piers Anthony
  Anthony, Piers
JACOBS, Charles
  Humana, Charles
JACOBS, Helen Hull
  Hull, H. Braxton
JACOBS, Thomas Curtis Hicks
  Carstairs, Kathleen
  Curtis, Tom
  Dower, Penn
  Howard, Helen
  Pender, Marilyn
  Pendower, Jacques
  Penn, Ann
JACOT DE BOLNOD, B. L.
  Jacot, Bernard
JAFFE, Gabriel
  Poole, Vivian
JAMES, Charles
  Coronet
JAMES, Florence Alice Price
  Warden, Florence

JAMES, Godfrey Warden
  Broome, Adam
JAMES, J. W. G.
  Norham, Gerald
JAMESON, Annie Edith
  Buckrose, J. E.
JAMIESON, Kathleen Florence
  Janes, Kathleen
  Janes, Kathleen F.
JANIFER, Laurence M.
  Harris, Larry M
JANNER, Greville
  Mitchell, Ewan
JANSEN, Johanna *and*
  CAMPBELL, Margaret
  Bayard, Fred
JANVIER, Margaret Thomson
  Vandegrift, Margaret
JANVIER, Thomas Allibone
  Black, Ivory
JAQUES, Edward Tyrell
  Tearle, Christian
JARRETT, Cora
  Keene, Faraday
JAY, Geraldine
  Jay, Charlotte
JAY, Marion
  Spalding, Lucille
JEFFERIES, Greg
  Collins, Geoffrey
JEFFERIES, Ira
  Morris, Ira J.
JEFFERY, Graham
  Brother Graham
JEFFREY-SMITH, May
  Aunt Maysie
  Thornton, Maimee

JEFFRIES, Bruce Graham
    Montague
  Bourne, Peter
  Graeme, Bruce
  Graeme, David
JEFFRIES, Gay
  Graeme, Linda
JEFFRIES, Roderic Graeme
  Ashford, Jeffrey
  Graeme, Roderic
JELLY, Oliver
  Fosse, Alfred
JENKINS, Alan Charles
  Bancroft, John
JENKINS, Sara Lucile
  Sargent, Joan
JENKINS, William Fitzgerald
  Leinster, Murray
JENNINGS, E. C.
  Jay
JENNINGS, Hilda *and others*
  Heptagon
JENNINGS, John Edward
  Baldwin, Bates
  Williams, Joel
JEROME, Owen Fox
  Friend, Oscar Jerome
JERVIS, Vera Murdock Stuart
  England, Jane
JEWETT, Sarah Orne
  Eliot, Alice C.
JOHN, Owen
  Bourne, John
JOHNSON, Annabel I. *and*
  JOHNSON, Edgar R.
  Johnson, A. E.
JOHNSON, H.
  Robertson, Muirhead

55

JOHNSON, Henry T.
  Thomson, Neil
JOHNSON, Lilian Beatrice
  Johnson, Lee
JOHNSON, Marion
  Masson, Georgina
JOHNSON, Nancy Marr
  Marr, Nancy J.
JOHNSON, Pamela Hansford *and*
 STEWART, Neil
  Lombard, Nap
JOHNSON, Victor
  Bell, John
JOHNSON, Virginia Wales
  Cousin Virginia
JOHNSTON, George Henry
  Shane, Martin
JOHNSTON, Robert Thomson
  Forsyth, R. A.
JONES, A. Miles
  Bullingham, Ann
JONES, Frank H.
  Mentor
JONES, Harry Austin
  Jons, Hal
JONES, Jack
  Reynolds, Jack
JONES, Judith Anastasia
  Maro, Judith
JONES, *Lady* Roderick
  Bagnold, Enid
  Lady of Quality
JONES, Le Roi
  Baraka, Imamu Amiri
JONES, Maynard Benedict
  Jones, Nard
JONES, P. D.
  Denham, Peter

JONES, Robert Maynard
  Jones, Bobi
  Probert, Lowri
  Siôn, Mari
JONES, Susan Carleton
  Carleton, S.
JORDAN, June
  Meyer, June
JORDAN, Robert Furneaux
  Player, Robert
JOSCELYN, Archie Lynn
  Archer, A. A.
  Cody, A. R.
  Cody, Al
  McKenna, Evelyn
  Westland, Lynn
JOSKE, Neville *and* GOYDER,
 Margot
  Neville, Margot
JOURDAIN, Eleanor F.
  Lamont, Frances
JUDD, Frederick
  Lester-Rands, A.
JUDD, Harrison
  Garrett, Truman
JUDSON, Jeanne
  Hancock, Frances Deane

KAGEY, Rudolf
  Steel, Kurt
KAHANE, Jack
  Barr, Cecil
  Carr, Basil
KAHN, H. S.
  Sackerman, Henry
KALISCH, A.
  Crescendo

KAMPF, Harold Bertram
  Kaye, Harold B.
KANE, Frank
  Boyd, Frank
KANE, Henry
  McCall, Anthony
KAPLAN, Jean Caryl
  Caryl, Jean
KAPP, Yvonne
  Cloud, Yvonne
KARIG, Walter
  Patrick, Keats
KATCHAMAKOFF, Atanas
  Shannon, Monica
KATZIN, Olga
  Sagittarius
KAUFMAN, Louis
  Keller, Dan
KAY, Ernest
  Ludlow, George
  Random, Alan
KAY, Frederic George
  Gee, Kenneth F.
  Howard, George
KAYE, Barrington
  Kaye, Tom
KAYE, Mary Margaret
  Hamilton, Mollie
KAYSER, Ronal
  Clark, Dale
KEANE, Mary Nesta
  Farrell, M. J.
KEATING, Lawrence Alfred
  Bassett, John Keith
  Thomas, H. C.
KEATLEY, Sheila
  Avon, Margaret

KECK, Maud *and* ORBISON,
 Roy
  Orbison, Keck
KEDDIE, Margaret Manson
  Auntie Margaret
KEEGAN, Mary Constance
  Heathcott, Mary
  Raymond, Mary
KEELE, Kenneth David
  Cassils, Peter
KEELING, Jill Annette
  Shaw, Jill A.
KEEVILL, Henry John
  Allison, Clay
  Alvord, Burt
  Bonney, Bill
  Earp, Virgil
  Harding, Wes
  McLowery, Frank
  Mossman, Burt
  Reno, Mark
  Ringo, Johnny
KELLEY, Audrey *and* ROOS,
 William
  Roos, Kelley
KELLIHER, Dan T. *and*
 SECRIST, W. G.
  Secrist, Kelliher
KELLY, Elizabeth
  Kellier, Elizabeth
  Stevenson, Christine
KELLY, Harold Ernest
  Carson, Lance
  Glinto, Darcy
  Toler, Buck
KEMPF, Pat
  Hunter, Pat

KENNEDY, H. A.
  H. A. K.
KENNEDY, Joseph Charles
  Kennedy, X. J.
KENNINGTON, Gilbert Alan
  Grant, Alan
  Kennington, Alan
KENSDALE, W. E. N.
  Norwood, Elliott
KENT, Arthur
  Boswell, James
  Bradwell, James
  Du Bois, M.
  Granados, Paul
  Stamper, Alex
  Vane, Brett
KENWARD, Betty
  Jennifer
KENYON, Fred
  Cumberland, Gerald
KERR, D.
  Colt, Russ
KERR, Doris Boake
  Boake, Capel
KERR, James Lennox
  Dawlish, Peter
  Kerr, Lennox
KERSHAW, John H. D.
  D'Allenger, Hugh
KETCHUM, Philip
  Saunders, Carl McK.
KETTLE, Jocelyn
  Kettle, Pamela
KIDD, Walter E.
  Pendleton, Conrad
KIEFER, Warren *and*
  MIDDLETON, Harry
  Kiefer, Middleton

KIMBRO, John
  Ashton, Ann
  Bramwell, Charlotte
  Kimbro, Jean
  Kimbrough, Katheryn
KING, Albert
  Albion, Ken
  Bannon, Mark
  Brennan, Walt
  Brent, Catherine
  Bronson, Wade
  Cleveland, Jim
  Conrad, Paul
  Cooper, Craig
  Creedi, Joel
  Dallas, Steve
  Doan, Reece
  Driscoll, Eli
  Ford, Wallace
  Foreman, Lee
  Foster, Evan
  Gibson, Floyd
  Gifford, Matt
  Girty, Simon
  Hammond, Brad
  Harlan, Ross
  Harmon, Gil
  Hoffman, Art
  Holland, Tom
  Howell, Scott
  Hoyt, Nelson
  Kane, Mark
  Kelsey, Janice
  Kimber, Lee
  King, Ames
  King, Berta
  King, Christopher
  Mason, Carl

Muller, Paul
Ogden, Clint
Owen, Ray
Prender, Bart
Ripley, Alvin
Santee, Walt
Scott, Grover
Shelby, Cole
Taggart, Dean
Tyler, Ellis
Waldron, Simon
Wallace, Agnes
Wetzel, Lewis
Yarbo, Steve
KING, Francis
Cauldwell, Frank
KING, Frank
Conrad, Clive
KING, James Clifford
Fry, Pete
King, Clifford
KING, John
Boswell, John
Kildare, John
KING, Kay
Holt, Elizabeth
KING-HALL, Stephen
Etienne
KINGSLEY, Mary
Malet, Lucas
KIRK, Richard Edmund
Church, Jeffrey
KIRKHAM, Nellie
Myatt, Nellie
KIRKUP, James
James, Andrew
Terahata, Jun
Tsuyuki Shigeru

KIRKWOOD, Joyce
Corlett, Joyce I.
KIRWAN, Molly
Morrow, Charlotte
KIRWAN-WARD, Bernard
Ward, Kirwan
KITCHIN, F. H.
Copplestone, Bennet
KLASS, Philip
Tenn, William
KLEIN, Grace *and* COOPER,
May Klein
Farewell, Nina
KLEINHAUS, Theodore John
Littlejohn, Jon R.
KNAPP, Clarence
Glutz, Ambrose
KNIGHT, Bernard
Picton, Bernard
KNIGHT, Eric
Hallas, Richard
KNIGHT, Francis Edgar
Salter, Cedric
KNIGHT, Kathleen Moore
Amos, Alan
KNIGHTS, Leslie
Leslie, Val
KNIPE, Emilie
Benson, Thérèse
KNIPSCHEER, James M. W.
Fox, James M.
Holmes, Grant
KNOTT, William Cecil
Carol, Bill J.
Knott, Bill
St Giraud
KNOWLES, Mabel Winifred
Wynne, May

KNOWLTON, Edward Rogers
 Rogers, Kerk
KNOWLTON, Winthrop *and*
 GOODMAN, George Jerome
 Goodman, Winthrop
KNOX, E. V.
 Evoe
KNUDSEN, Margrethe
 Knudsen, Greta
KOESTLER, Arthur
 Costler, *Dr* A.
KOFFLER, Camilla
 Ylla
KOHLS, Olive N. Allen
 Allen, Dixie
KONINGSBERGER, Hans
 Koning, Hans
KOONTZ, Dean R.
 Coffey, Brian
KÖRMENDI, Ferenc
 Julian, Peter
KORNBLUTH, Cyril M.
 Park, Jordon
KORNBLUTH, Cyril M. *and*
 GROSSMAN, Judith
 Judd, Cyril
KORNBLUTH, Cyril M. *and*
 POHL, Frederick
 Gottesman, S. D.
KORZENIOWSKI, Jessie
 Conrad, Jessie
KORZENIOWSKI, Teodor Josef
 Konrad
 Conrad, Joseph
KOSINSKI, Jerzy
 Novak, Joseph
KOVAR, Edith May
 Lowe, Edith

KRASNEY, Samuel A.
 Curzon, Sam
KRAUS, Robert
 Hippopotamus, Eugene H.
KRECHNIAK, Joseph Marshall
 Marshall, Joseph
KRISHNAMURTI, Jiddu
 Alcyone
KRONMILLER, Hildegarde
 Lawrence, Hilda
KUBIS, Patricia Lou
 Scott, Casey
KUMMER, Frederick Arnold
 Fredericks, Arnold
KURNITZ, Harry
 Page, Marco
KUSKIN, Karla Seidman
 Charles, Nicholas
KUTTNER, Henry
 Garth, Will
 Padgett, Lewis
 Vance, Jack

LA COSTE, Guy R. *and*
 BINGHAM, E. A.
 Berton, Guy
LAFFEATY, Christina
 Carstens, Netta
 Fortina, Martha
LAFFIN, John
 Dekker, Carl
 Napier, Mark
 Sabre, Dirk
LAIDLER, Graham
 Pont
LAKE, Joe Barry
 Barry, Joe

LAKE, Kenneth Robert
  Boyer, Robert
  King, Arthur
  Roberts, Ken
  Soutter, Fred
LAKRITZ, Esther
  Collingswood, Frederick
  Marion, S. T.
LAMB, Antonia
  Hellerlamb, Toni
LAMB, Elizabeth Searle
  Mitchell, K. L.
LAMB, Geoffrey Frederick
  Balaam
LAMB, Mary Montgomerie *see*
  CURRIE, *Lady*
LAMBERT, Hubert Steel
  Marle, T. B.
LAMBERT, Leslie Harrison
  Alan, A. J
LAMBOT, Isobel Mary
  Ingham, Daniel
  Turner, Mary
LAMBURN, John Bettersby
  Crompton
  Crompton, John
LAMBURN, Richmal Crompton
  Crompton, Richmal
L'AMOUR, Louis
  Burns, Tex
LAMPMAN, Evelyn
  Bronson, Lynn
LANDELLS, Anne
  Sibley, Lee
LANDELLS, Richard
  Baron, Paul
  Dryden, Keith
  Gaunt, Richard

  Lanzol, Cesare
  Pelham, Randolph
LANDON, Melville de Lancy
  Lan
  Perkins, Eli
LANDWIRTH, Heinz
  Lind, Jakov
LANE, Kenneth Westmacott
  West, Keith
LANE, *Sir* Ralph Norman Angell
  Angell, Norman
LANES, Selma G.
  Gordon, Selma
LANGBEHN, Theo
  Lang, Theo
  Piper, Peter
LANGDON, John
  Gannold, John
LANGDON-DAVIES, John
  James, John
  Nada, John
  Stanhope, John
LANGLEY, Sarah
  Langley, Lee
LANGMAID, Kenneth Joseph
  Robb
  Graham, Peter
  Laing, Kenneth
LANGNER, Lawrence
  Child, Alan
LARBALESTIER, Phillip George
  Archer, G. Scott
LARCOMBE, Jennifer Geraldine
  Rees, J. Larcombe
LARIAR, Lawrence
  Knight, Adam
  Stark, Michael

61

LARKINS, William
  Long, Gerry
LARRALDE, Romulo
  Brent, Romney
LASH, William Quinlan
  Quinlan, William
LASKI, Marghanita
  Russell, Sarah
LASKY, Jesse L.
  Love, David
  Smeed, Frances
LATHAM, Alison *and* LATHAM,
  Esther
  Latham, Murray
LATHROP, Lorin Andrews
  Gambier, Kenyon
LATIS, Mary J. *and*
 HENISSART, Martha
  Dominic, R. B.
  Lathen, Emma
LAUGHLIN, Virginia Carli
  Clarke, John
  Laklan, Carli
LAVENDER, David Sievert
  Catlin, Ralph
LAW, Michael
  Kreuzenau, Michael
LAWLOR, Patrick
  Penn, Christopher
LAWRENCE, D. H.
  Davison, Lawrence H.
LAWRENCE, Dulcie
  Hamilton, Judith
  Mace, Margaret
LAWRENCE, Elizabeth
  Bradburne, E. S.
LAWRENCE, James Duncan
  Lancer, Jack

LAWRENCE, T. E.
  C. D.
  C. J. G.
  J. C.
  Ross, J. H.
  Shaw, T. E.
LAWSON, Alfred
  Torroll, G. D.
LAZENBY, Norman
  Norton, Jed
LE GALLIENNE, Richard
  Logroller
LE RICHE, P. J.
  Kish
LEAF, Munro
  Calvert, John
  Mun
LEDERER, Esther Pauline
  Landers, Ann
LEE, Austin
  Austwick, John
  Callender, Julian
LEE, Henry David Cook
  Parios
LEE, Manfred B. *and* DANNAY,
  Frederic
  Queen, Ellery
  Ross, Barnaby
LEE, Manning de Villeneuve
  Hatch, Robert
LEE, Marion Van Der Veer
  Lee, Babs
LEE, Maureen
  Northe, Maggie
LEE, Norman
  Armstrong, Raymond
  Corrigan, Mark
  Hobart, Robertson

LEE HOWARD, L. A.
  Howard, Leigh
  Krislov, Alexander
LEE-RICHARDSON, James
  Dunne, Desmond
LEEMING, Jill
  Chaney
LEFFINGWELL, Albert
  Chambers, Dana
  Jackson, Giles
LEHMAN, Paul Evan
  Evan, Paul
LEHRBURGER, Egon
  Larsen, Egon
LEIBER, Fritz
  Lathrop, Francis
LEISK, David
  Johnson, Crockett
LEITE, George Thurston *and*
 SCOTT, Jody
  Scott, Thurston
LEMIEUX, Kenneth
  Orvis, Kenneth
LEMMON, Laura Lee
  Wilson, Lee
LENANTON, *Lady*
  Lenanton, C.
  Oman, Carola
LENT, Blair
  Small, Ernest
LEON, Henry Cecil
  Cecil, Henry
  Maxwell, Clifford
LEONARD, Lionel Frederick
  Lonsdale, Frederick
LESLEY, Peter
  Allen, John W. Jr
  Lesley, J. P.

LESLIE, Cecilie
  Macadam, Eve
LESLIE, Henrietta
  Mendl, Gladys
LESLIE, Josephine A. C.
  Dick, R. A.
LESSER, Milton
  Marlowe, Stephen
L'ESTRANGE, C. James *and*
 ELY, George Herbert
  Strang, Herbert
LEVIN, Abraham
  George, G. S.
LEVIN, Bernard
  Battle, Felix
  Cherryman, A. E.
  Taper
LEVINE, William
  Levinrew, Will
LEVY, Newman
  Flaccus
LEWIN, Michael Sultan
  Furber, Douglas
LEWING, Anthony
  Bannerman, Mark
LEWIS, Alfred Henry
  Quin, Dan
LEWIS, Charles Bertrand
  Quad, M.
LEWIS, Clifford *and* LEWIS,
 Judith Mary
  Berrisford, Judith
LEWIS, Clive Staples
  Hamilton, Clive
LEWIS, Mary Christianna
  Berrisford, Mary
  Brand, Christianna

Roland, Mary
Thompson, China
LEWIS, Mildred
De Witt, James
LEWIS, Roy
Lewis, J. B.
Springfield, David
LEY, Willy
Willey, Robert
LEYLAND, Eric
Cleaver, Denis
Felmersham, Michael
Fielding, Anthony
Grant, Nesta
Little, Sylvia
Lodge, John
Patterson, Duke
Strangeway, Mark
Tarrant, Elizabeth
Wyatt, Escott
LIDDELOW, Marjorie Joan
Law, Marjorie J.
LIEBERS, Arthur
Love, Arthur
LIEBLER, Jean Mayer
Mather, Virginia
LIGHTNER, A. M.
Hopf, Alice L.
LILIENTHAL, David Jr
Ely, David
LILLEY, Peter *and*
STANSFIELD, Anthony
Buckingham, Bruce
LILLIE, Gordon W.
Pawnee Bill
LINDHOLM, Anna Chandler
Fay, Dorothy

LINDSAY, Barbara *and*
STERNE, E. G.
James, Josephine
LINDSAY, Jack
Preston, Richard
LINDSAY, Kathleen
Cameron, Margaret
Richmond, Mary
LINDSAY, Maurice
Brock, Gavin
LININGTON, Elizabeth
Blaisdell, Anne
Egan, Lesley
O'Neill, Egan
Shannon, Dell
LIPKIND, William
Will
LIPPINCOTT, Sara Jane
Greenwood, Grace
LIPSCHITZ, *Rabbi* Chaim
Yerushalmi, Chaim
LIST, Ilka Katherine
Macduff, Ilka
Obolensky, Ilka
LITTLE, Constance *and* LITTLE,
Gwenyth
Little, Conyth
LITTLE, D. F.
Wessex, Martin
LITTLE, Gwenyth *and* LITTLE,
Constance
Little, Conyth
LITTLE, Malcolm
Malcolm X
LIVERTON, Joan
Medhurst, Joan
LIVINGSTON, A. D.
Delano, Al

LLOYD, Richard Dafydd Vivian
  Llewellyn
  Llewellyn, Richard
LOADER, William
  Nash, Daniel
LOBAUGH, Elma K.
  Lowe, Kenneth
LOBLEY, Robert
  Nong
LOCK, Arnold Charles Cooper
  Cooper, Charles
LOCKIE, Isobel
  Knight, Isobel
LOCKRIDGE, Frances Louise *and*
  LOCKRIDGE, Richard
  Richards, Francis
LOCKWOOD, Frank
  Circumlibra
LOEWENGARD, Heidi H. F.
  Albrand, Martha
  Holland, Katrin
  Lambert, Christine
LOFTS, Norah
  Astley, Juliet
  Curtis, Peter
LOGAN, Olive
  Chroniqueuse
LOGUE, Christopher
  Vicarion, *Count* Palmiro
LONG, Amelia
  Laing, Patrick
  Reynolds, Adrian
  Reynolds, Peter
LONG, Amelia *and* McHUGH,
  Edna
  Coxe, Kathleen Buddington
LONG, Gladys
  Beaton, Jane

LONG, Leonard
  Long, Shirley
LONG, Lily Augusta
  Doubleday, Roman
LONG, Lois
  Lipstick
LONGRIGG, Roger Erskine
  Drummond, Ivor
  Erskine, Rosalind
LONGSTREET, Stephen
  Burton, Thomas
  Haggard, Paul
  Ormsbee, David
  Weiner, Henri
LOOKER, Samuel Joseph
  Game Cock
  Pundit, Ephraim
  Wade, Thomas
LOOMIS, Noel Miller
  Miller, Frank
  Water, Silas
LORD, Doreen Mildred Douglas
  Ireland, Doreen
  Lord, Douglas
LORD, Phillips H.
  Parker, Seth
LORD, William Wilberforce
  Langstaff, Tristram
LORDE, Andre Geraldin
  Domini, Rey
LORENZ, Frederic
  Holden, Larry
LORING, Emilie
  Story, Josephine
LOTHROP, Harriet Mulford
  Sidney, Margaret
LOTTICH, Kenneth
  Conrad, Kenneth

LOW, Lois
  Paxton, Lois
LOWELL, Jan *and* LOWELL,
  Robert
  Lowell, J. R.
LOWNDES, Marie Adelaide Belloc
  Curtin, Philip
LU KUAN YU
  Luk, Charles
LUARD. William Blaine
  Luard, L.
LUCAS, Beryl Llewellyn
  Llewellyn
LUCAS, E. V.
  E. V. L.
  V. V. V.
LUCAS, Edgar Ernest
  Goodson, Bill
LUCCHETTI, Anthony
  Prescott, John
LUCCOCK, Halford Edward
  Stylites, Simeon
LUCEY, James D.
  James, Matthew
LUM, Bettina Peter
  Lum, Peter
LUMSDEN, Jean
  Swift, Rachelle
LUNN, *Sir* Arnold
  Croft, Sutton
  Rubicon
LUNN, Hugh Kingsmill
  Kingsmill, Hugh
LUTYENS, Mary
  Wyndham, Esther
LUXMORE, Robert
  Fesenmeyer

LYBURN, Eric Frederic St John
  Toller
LYLE-SMYTHE, Alan
  Caillou, Alan
LYND, Robert
  Y. Y.
LYNDS, Dennis
  Arden, William
  Collins, Michael
  Crowe, John
LYNE, Charles
  De Castro, Lyne
LYNES, Daisy Elfreda
  Glyn-Forest, D.
LYNN, Elwyn
  Augustus
LYONS, John Benignus
  Fitzwilliam, Michael
LYTTLETON, Edith Joan
  Lancaster, G. B.

How public, like a frog
To tell your name the livelong day
To an admiring bog.
--Emily Dickinson. Collected
poems.

MACALLISTER, Alister
  Brock, Lynn
  Wharton, Anthony
McALMON, Robert
  Urquhart, Guy
McBRIDE, Robert Medill
  Medill, Robert
  Reid, Marshall

McCALL, Virginia
  Nielson, Virginia
MACCARTHY, *Sir* Desmond
  Hawk, Affable
McCARTHY, Shaun
  Callas, Theo
  Cory, Desmond
McCARTNEY, R. J.
  Scott, Bruce
McCHESNEY, Mary F.
  Rayter, Joe
McCLINTOCK, Marshall
  Duncan, Gregory
  Marshall, Douglas
  Starret, William
MACCLURE, Victor
  Craig, Peter
McCONNELL, James Douglas
  Rutherford
  Rutherford, Douglas
McCONNELL, James Douglas
  Rutherford *and* DURBRIDGE,
  Francis
  Temple, Paul
McCORMICK, George
  Deacon, Richard
McCORQUODALE, Barbara
  Hamilton
  Cartland, Barbara
McCUE, Lillian Bueno
  De la Torre, Lillian
McCULLEY, Johnston
  Brien, Raley
  McAlpin, Grant
McCULLOCH, Derek
  Uncle Mac
McCULLOCH, Joseph
  Michaelhouse, John

McCUTCHAN, Philip D.
  Galway, Robert Conington
  MacNeil, Duncan
  Wigg, T. I. G.
McDERMOTT, John Richard
  Ryan, J. M.
McDONALD, Margaret Josephine
  McDonald, Jo
MACDONALD, Philip
  Fleming, Oliver
  Lawless, Anthony
  Porlock, Martin
MACDONALD, Susanne
  MacFarland, Anne
MACDONNELL, A. G.
  Cameron, John
  Gordon, Neil
MACDONNELL, James Edmond
  Macnell, James
McELFRESH, Adeline
  Cleveland, John
  Scott, Jane
  Wesley, Elizabeth
McEVOY, Marjorie
  Bond, Gillian
  Harte, Marjorie
McFARLANE, David
  Tyson, Teilo
MACFARLANE, George Gordon
  Miller, Patrick
McFAUL, Frances Elizabeth
  Grand, Sarah
McGAUGHY, Dudley Dean
  Dean, Dudley
  Owen, Dean
McGEOGH, Andrew
  Paul, Adrian

McGIVERN, William Peter
  Peters, Bill
MACGLASHAN, John
  Glashan, John
McGLOIN, Joseph Thaddeus
  O'Finn, Thaddeus
MACGREGOR, James Murdoch
  McIntosh, J. T.
MACGREGOR, Miriam
  Pegden, Helen
McGREW, Julia *and* FENN,
  Caroline K.
  McGrew, Fenn
McGUINNESS, Bernard
  McGuinness, Brian
McHARGUE, Georgess
  Chase, Alice
  Usher, Margo Scegge
MACHEN, Arthur
  Siluriensis, Leolinus
MACHLIN, Milton
  Jason, William
  Roberts, McLean
McILWAIN, David
  Maine, Charles Eric
  Rayner, Richard
  Wade, Robert
McILWRAITH, Maureen Mollie
  Hunter
  Hunter, Mollie
MACINTOSH, Joan
  Blaike, Avona
McINTOSH, Kinn Hamilton
  Aird, Catherine
MACINTYRE, John
  Brandane, John
MACINTYRE, John Thomas
  O'Neil, Kerry

MACK, Elsie Frances
  Moore, Frances Sarah
MACK, J. C. O.
  Callum Beg
MACKAY, Fulton
  MacBride, Aeneas
MACKAY, James Alexander
  Angus, Ian
MACKAY, Lewis
  Matheson, Hugh
MACKAY, Minnie
  Corelli, Marie
MACKENZIE, Joan
  Finnigan, Joan
MACKEOWN, N. R.
  Giles, Norman
MACKESY, Leonora Dorothy
  Rivers
  Starr, Leonora
McKIBBON, John
  Probyn, Elise
MACKIE, Albert David
  Macnib
McKILLOP, Norman
  Beg, Toram
MACKINLAY, Lelia A. S.
  Grey, Brenda
MACKINNON, Charles Roy
  Conte, Charles
  Donald, Vivian
  Macalpin, Rory
  Montrose, Graham
  Rose, Hilary
  Stuart, Charles
  Torr, Iain
MACKINTOSH, Elizabeth
  Daviot, Gordon
  Tey, Josephine

McLACHLAN, Dan
  McMud, Dok
MACLAREN, James Paterson
  Medicus
McLAREN, Moray David Shaw
  Murray, Michael
MACLEAN, Alistair
  Stuart, Ian
McLEAN, Kathryn
  Forbes, Kathryn
MACLEOD, Charlotte
  Hughes, Matilda
MACLEOD, Ellen
  Anderson, Ella
MACLEOD, Jean Sutherland
  Airlie, Catherine
MACLEOD, Joseph Todd Gordon
  Drinan, Adam
MACLEOD, Robert
  Knox, Bill
MACLEOD-SMITH, D.
  Mariner, David
McMEEKIN, Isabel *and* CLARK,
  Dorothy
  McMeekin, Clark
McMILLAN, Donald
  Stuart, John Roy
MACMILLAN, Douglas
  Cary, D. M.
McMILLAN, James
  Coriolanus
McMORDIE, John Andrew
  Shan
MACMULLAN, Charles W.
  Kirkpatrick
  Munro, C. K.
McNALLY, Mary Elizabeth
  O'Brien, Deirdre

McNAMARA, Barbara Willard
  O'Conner, Elizabeth
McNAMARA, Lena
  Mack, Evalina
McNAUGHT, Ann Boyce
  Gilmour, Ann
MACNEICE, Louis
  Malone, Louis
McNEILE, H. C.
  Sapper
McNEILLIE, John
  Niall, Ian
McNEILLY, Wilfred
  Ballinger, W. A.
McNEILLY, Wilfred *and*
  BAKER, William Howard
  Ballinger, W. A.
MACPHERSON, Jessie
  Kennie, Jessie
MACQUARRIE, Hector
  Cameron, Hector
MACQUEEN, James William
  Edwards, James G.
MACRORY, Patrick
  Greer, Patrick
MACVEAN, Phyllis
  Greaves, Gillian
  Hambledon, Phyllis
MADDISON, Angela Mary
  Banner, Angela
MAGEE, James
  Taylor, John
MAGEE, William Kirkpatrick
  Eglinton, John
MAGRAW, Beatrice
  Padeson, Mary
MAGRILL, David S.
  Dalheath, David

69

MAGUIRE, Robert A. J.
  Taaffe, Robert
MAHONEY, Elizabeth
  Mara, Thalia
MAIDEN, Cecil
  Cecil, Edward
MAINPRIZE, Don
  Rock, Richard
MAINWARING, Daniel
  Homes, Geoffrey
MAIR, George Brown
  Macdouall, Robertson
MAIZEL, Clarice Louise
  Maizel, Leah
MALLESON, Joan Graeme
  Medica
MALLESON, Lucy
  Gilbert, Anthony
  Meredith, Anne
MANFRED, Frederick Feikema
  Feikema, Feike
MANN, George
  Schwarz, Bruno
MANN, Violet Vivian
  Allen, Barbara
  Stuart, Alex
  Stuart, Vivian
MANNES, Marya
  Sec
MANNING, Adelaide Frances Oke
  and COLES, Cyril Henry
  Coles, Manning
  Gaite, Francis
MANNING, Frederic
  Private 19022
MANNING, Rosemary
  Voyle, Mary

MANNOCK, Laura
  Adair, Sally
  Mannock, Jennifer
  Whetter, Laura
MANNON, Martha *and*
 MANNON, Mary Ellen
  Mannon, M. M.
MANTIBAND, James
  Keystone, Oliver
MANTLE, Winifred Langford
  Fellowes, Anne
  Lang, Frances
  Langford, Jane
MAREK, Kurt W.
  Ceram, C. W.
MARLOWE, Stephen
  Less, Milton
MARQUAND, John Phillips
  Phillips, John
MARQUAND, Leopold
  Burger, John
MARQUES, Susan Lowndes
  Lowndes, Susan
MARRECO, Anne
  Acland, Alice
MARRISON, Leslie William
  Dowley, D. M
MARSH, John
  Davis, Julia
  Elton, John
  Harley, John
  Lawrence, Irene
  Marsh, Joan
  Richmond, Grace
  Sawley, Petra
  Ware, Monica
  Woodward, Lillian

MARSHALL, Arthur Hammond
   Marshall, Archibald
MARSHALL, Charles Hunt *and*
   YATES, George Worthing
   Hunt, Peter
MARSHALL, Christabel
   St John, Christopher
MARSHALL, Edison
   Hunter, Hall
MARSHALL, Evelyn
   Marsh, Jean
MARSHALL, Marjorie
   March, Stella
MARSTON, J. E.
   Jeffrey, E. Jeffrey
MARTEAU, F. A.
   Bride, Jack
   Rameaut, Maurice
MARTENS, Anne Louise
   Kendall, Jane
MARTIN, Charles Morris
   Martin, Chuck
MARTIN, Kingsley
   Critic
MARTIN, Malachi
   Serafian, Michael
MARTIN, Netta
   Ashton, Lucy
MARTIN, Patricia Miles
   Miles, Miska
MARTIN, Reginald Alec
   Cameron, Brett
   Dixon, Rex
   Eliott, E. C.
   McCoy, Hank
   Martin, Rex
   Martin, Robert
   Martin, Scott

MARTIN, Robert Bernard
   Bernard, Robert
MARTIN, Robert Lee
   Roberts, Lee
MARTIN, *Sir* Theodore
   Bon Gaultier
MARTIN, Timothy
   Tim
MARTIN, Violet Florence
   Ross
   Ross, Martin
MARTINEZ-DELGADO, Luis
   Luimardel
MARTING, Ruth Lenore
   Bailey, Hilea
MARTINN, Paul
   Plaut, Martin
MARTYN, Wyndham
   Grenvil, William
MASCHLER, Tom *and*
   RAPHAEL, Frederic
   Caine, Mark
MASCHWITZ, Eric
   Marvel, Holt
MASON, Arthur Charles
   Scrope, Mason
MASON, Douglas Rankine
   Rankine, Douglas
MASON, F. Van Wyck
   Coffin, Geoffrey
   Mason, Frank W.
   Weaver, Ward
MASON, Michael
   Blake, Cameron
MASON, Philip
   Woodruff, Philip
MASON, Sydney Charles
   Carr, Charles

Carr, Elaine
Hatton, Cliff
Hayes, Clanton
Henderson, Colt
Holmes, Caroline
Horn, Chester
Langley, John
Ledgard, Jake
Lee, Jesse
Lomax, Jeff
Maddern, Stan
Maine, Sterling
Mann, Stanley
Marlow, Phyllis
Masters, Steve
Merrick, Spencer
Stanley, Margaret
MASTERS, Kelly
Ball, Zachary
MATHERS, Edward Powys
Torquemada
MATHESON, Donald H.
Harmston, Donald
MATHEWS, Albert
Siogvolk, Paul
MATTHEWMAN, Phyllis
Surrey, Kathryn
MATTHEWS, Clayton
Moore, Arthur
MATTHEWS, Edwin, J.
Saxon
MATTHEWS, James Brander
Matthews, Brander
Penn, Arthur
MATTHEWS, Margaret Bryan
Goodyear, Susan
MATUSOW, Harvey Marshall
Allenby, Gordon

Matusow, Marshall
Muldoon, Omar
Sadballs, John
MAUGHAM, Robert Cecil
Romer *Viscount*
Maugham, Robin
MAVOR, Osborne Henry
Bridie, James
MAXFIELD, Prudence
Hill, Prudence
MAXTONE-GRAHAM, Joyce
Struther, Jan
MAXWELL, Patricia Anne
Trehearne, Elizabeth
MAXWELL, Violet S.
Maxwell, C. Bede
MAY, John
Duffer, Allan
MAYER, Jane *and* SPIEGEL,
Clara E.
Jaynes, Clare
MAYNE, Ethel Colburn
Huntly, Frances E.
MAYNE, William J. C. *and*
CAESAR, Richard Dynely
James, Dynely
MAZURE, Alfred Leonardus
Cullner, Lenard
Maz
MAZZOCCO, Edward
Maze, Edward
MEAD, Martha Norburn
Norburn, Martha
MEAD, Sidney
Moko
MEAKER, Marijane
Kerr, M. E.
Packer, Vin

MEANS, Mary *and*
  SAUNDERS, Theodore
    Scott, Denis
MEARES, John Willoughby
  Uncut Cavendish
MEARES, Leonard F.
  Grover, Marshall
  McCoy, Marshall
MEE, Arthur
  Idris
MEGAW, Arthur Stanley
  Stanley, Arthur
MEGROZ, R. L.
  Cumberland, Roy
  Dimsdale, C. D.
MEHTA, Rustam
  Hartman, Roger
  Martin, R. J.
MEIGS, Cornelia Lynde
  Aldon, Adair
MEINZER, Helen Abbott
  Abbott, A. C.
MELIDES, Nicholas
  Macguire, Nicolas
MELLETT, John Calvin
  Brooks, Jonathan
MELLING, Leonard
  Lummins
MELONEY, William
  Frenken-Meloney
  Grant, Margaret
MENZEL, Donald H.
  Howard, Don
MERCER, Cecil William
  Yates, Dornford
MEREDITH, Kenneth Lincoln
  Mayo, Arnold

MERTZ, Barbara G.
  Michaels, Barbara
  Peters, Elizabeth
METHOLD, Kenneth
  Cade, Alexander
MEYER, Harold Albert
  Merrick, Hugh
MEYER, Jerome Sydney
  Jennings, S. M.
MEYERS, Roy
  Lethbridge, Rex
MEYNELL, Esther H.
  Moorhouse, E. Hallam
MEYNELL, Laurence Walter
  Baxter, Valerie
  Eton, Robert
  Ludlow, Geoffrey
  Tring, A. Stephen
MEYNELL, Shirley Ruth
  Darbyshire, Shirley
MEYNELL, Wilfred
  Oldcastle, John
MIDDLETON, Harry *and*
  KIEFER, Warren
    Kiefer, Middleton
MIDDLETON, Henry Clement
  Simplex, Simon
MIDDLETON, Maud Barbara
  Walker, Barbara
MIERS, Earl Schenk
  Meredith, David William
MILAM, Lorenzo W.
  Allworthy, A. W.
MILKOMANE, George Alexis
  Milkomanovich
  Bankoff, George
  Borodin, George
  Braddon, George

Conway, Peter
Redwood, Alec
Sava, George
MILLAR, Kenneth
Macdonald, John
Macdonald, John Ross
Macdonald, Ross
MILLAR, Minna
Collier, Joy
MILLARD, Christopher S.
Mason, Stuart
MILLAY, Edna St Vincent
Boyd, Nancy
MILLER, Albert
Mills, Alan
MILLER, Charles Dean
Von Mueller, Karl
MILLER, Cincinnatus H.
Miller, Joaquin
MILLER, Harriet
Miller, Olive Thorne
MILLER, J. A.
Pook, Peter
MILLER, Mary
Durack, Mary
MILLER, Mary Britton
Bolton, Isabel
MILLER, Warren
Vail, Amanda
MILLER, William *and* WADE, Robert
Masterson, Whit
Miller, Wade
Wilmer, Dale
MILLER, Wright
North, Mark
MILLETT, Nigel
Oke, Richard

MILLIGAN, Elsie
Burr, Elsie
MILLS, Algernon Victor
Latimer, Rupert
MILLS, Hugh Travers
Travers, Hugh
MILLS, Janet Melanie Ailsa
Challoner, H. K.
MILLWARD, Pamela
Midling, Perspicacity
MILNE, Charles
Milne, Ewart
MILNER, Marion
Field, Joanna
MILTON, Gladys Alexandra
Carlyle, Anthony
M'ILWRAITH, Jean N.
Forsyth, Jean
MINTO, Frances
Cowen, Frances
Hyde, Eleanor
Munthe, Frances
MINTO, Mary
Macqueen, Jay
MITCHELL, Clare May
Canfield, Cleve
MITCHELL, Donald Grant
Marvel, Ik
Timon, John
MITCHELL, Gladys
Hockaby, Stephen
Torrie, Malcolm
MITCHELL, Isabel
Plain, Josephine
MITCHELL, James
Munro, James
MITCHELL, James Leslie
Gibbon, Lewis Grassic

MITCHELL, John
  Slater, Patrick
MIZNER, Elizabeth Howard
  Howard, Elizabeth
MOBERLY, Charlotte Anne
  Elizabeth
  Morison, Elizabeth
MOCKLER, Gretchen
  Travis, Gretchen
MODELL, Merriam
  Piper, Evelyn
MOFFATT, James
  More, J. J.
MOGRIDGE, Stephen
  Stevens, Jill
MOHAN, Josephine
  Jemonte
MOLESWORTH, *Mrs* Mary Louisa
  Stewart
  Graham, Ennis
MOLLOY, Edward
  Jamieson, Thomas
  Jones, H. S.
  Ward, Herbert B. S.
MONGER, Ifor
  Manngian, Peter
  Richards, Peter
MONRO-HIGGS, Gertrude
  Monro, Gavin
MONROE, Donald *and* MONROE,
  Keith
  Keith, Donald
MONTGOMERY, Leslie Alexander
  Doyle, Lynn
MONTGOMERY, Robert Bruce
  Crispin, Edmund
MONTGOMERY, Rutherford
  George

Avery, Al
  Proctor, Everitt
MOORE, Bertha B.
  Cannon, Brenda
MOORE, Doris Langley
  Gentlewoman, A
MOORE, Harold William
  Roome, Holdar
MOORE, John
  Trotwood, John
MOORE, Mary McLeod
  Pandora
MOORHOUSE, Herbert Joseph
  Moorhouse, Hopkins
MOORHOUSE, Hilda
  Vansittart, Jane
MOORHOUSE, Sydney
  Langdale, Stanley
  Lyndale, Sydney M.
MORDAUNT, Evelyn May
  Mordaunt, Elinor
  Riposte, A
MOREAU, David
  Merlin, David
MORETTI, Ugo
  Drug, Victor
  Gouttier, Maurice
  Sherman, George
MOREWOOD, Sarah L.
  Hope, Noel
MORGAN, Brian Stanford
  Morgan, Bryan
MORGAN, Charles
  Menander
MORGAN, Diana
  Blaine, Sara
MORGAN, Murray C.
  Murray, Cromwell

75

Real names

MORGAN, Thomas Christopher
   Muir, John
MORIN, Claire
   France, Claire
MORISON, John
   Clergyman, A
MORLAND, Nigel
   Dane, Mary
   Donavan, John
   Forrest, Norman
   Garnett, Roger
   McCall, Vincent
   Shepherd, Neal
MORLEY, Leslie Reginald William
   Hutchins, Anthony
MORRIS, David
   Hall, Martyn T.
MORRIS, Jean
   O'Hara, Kenneth
MORRIS, John
   McGaw, J. W.
MORRISON, Arthur
   Hewitt, Martin
MORRISON, Eula A.
   Delmonico, Andrea
MORRISON, Margaret Mackie
   Cost, March
   Morrison, Peggy
MORRISON, Thomas
   Muir, Alan
MORSE, Anne Christenson
   Head, Ann
MORSE, Martha
   Wilson, Martha
MORTIMER, John
   Lincoln, Geoffrey
MORTIMER, Penelope
   Temple, Ann

MORTON, A. Q.
   Kew, Andrew
MORTON, Guy Mainwaring
   Traill, Peter
MORTON, J. B.
   Beachcomber
MOSS, Robert Alfred
   Moss, Nancy
   Moss, Roberta
MOSTYN, Anita Mary
   Fielding, Ann Mary
MOTT, Edward Spencer
   Gubbins, Nathaniel
MOTT, J. Moldon
   Blackburn, John
MOTTRAM, Ralph Hale
   Marjoram, J.
MOUNT, Thomas Ernest
   Cody, Stone
   King, Oliver
MOUNTBATTEN, *Lord* Louis
   Marco
MOUNTFIELD, David
   Grant, Neil
MUDDOCK, Joyce Emerson
   Donovan, Dick
MUGGESON, Margaret
   Dickinson, Margaret
   Jackson, Everatt
MUIR, Edwin
   Moore, Edward
MUIR, Marie
   Blake, Monica
   Kaye, Barbara
MUIR, Wilhelmina Johnstone
   Muir, Willa
   Scott, Agnes Neill

MULHEARN, Winifred
  Grandma
MUMFORD, A. H.
  Videns
MUNBY, Arthur Joseph
  Brown, Jones
MUNRO, Hector Hugh
  Saki
MUNRO, Hugh
  Jason
MURFREE, Mary Noailles
  Craddock, Charles Egbert
  Dembry, R. Emmet
MURIEL, John
  Dewes, Simon
  Lindsey, John
MURPHY, Charlotte *and*
  MURPHY, Lawrence
  Murphy, C. L.
MURPHY, John *and* CORLEY,
  Edwin
  Buchanan, Patrick
MURPHY, Lawrence *and*
  MURPHY, Charlotte
  Murphy, C. L.
MURPHY, Lawrence D.
  Lawrence, Steven C.
MURRAY, Andrew Nicholas
  Islay, Nicholas
MURRAY, Blanche
  Murray, Geraldine
MURRAY, Joan
  Blood, Joan Wilde
MURRAY, Ruth Hilary
  Finnegan, Ruth
MURRAY, Venetia Pauline *and*
  BIRCH, Jack Ernest Lionel
  Flight, Francies

MURRY, John Middleton Jr
  Cowper, Richard
  Murry, Colin
  Murry, Colin Middleton
MURRY, Violet
  Arden, Mary
MUSKETT, Netta Rachel
  Hill, Anne
MUSSI, Mary
  Edgar, Josephine
  Howard, Mary
MUSTO, Barry
  Simon, Robert
MYERS, Mary
  Borer, Mary Cathcart
MYSTERY WRITERS OF
  AMERICA INC:CALIFORNIA
  CHAPTER
  Durrant, Theo

NAIR, K. K.
  Chaitanya, Krishna
NEAL, Adeline Phyllis
  Grey, A. F.
NELMS, Henning
  Talbot, Hake
NELSON, Ethel
  Nina
NELSON, Lawrence
  Trent, Peter
NERNEY, Patrick W.
  Nudnick
NETTELL, Richard
  Kenneggy, Richard
NETTZ, Julie
  Julie
NEUBAUER, William Arthur
  Arthur, William

Garrison, Joan
Marsh, Rebecca
Newcomb, Norma
NEVILLE, Alison
Candy, Edward
NEVILLE, Derek
Salt, Jonathan
NEWELL, Robert Henry
Kerr, Orpheus C.
NEWLIN, Margaret
Rudd, Margaret
NEWMAN, Bernard
Betteridge, Don
NEWMAN, James Roy
Stryfe, Paul
NEWMAN, Lyn Lloyd
Irvine, Lyn
NEWMAN, Mona A. J.
Fitzgerald, Barbara
Stewart, Jean
NEWMAN, Terence
O'Connor, Dermot
NEWNHAM, Don
Eden, Matthew
NEWTON, Dwight Bennett
Bennett, Dwight
NEWTON, H. Chance
Gawain
NEWTON, William Simpson
Mitcham, Gilroy
Newton, Macdonald
NICHOLS, *Captain* G. H. F.
Quex
NICHOLS, Mary Eudora
Brown, Eve
NICHOLSON, Joan
Craig, Alison
Weir, Jonnet

NICHOLSON, Margaret Beda
Yorke, Margaret
NICHOLSON, Violet
Hope, Lawrence
NICKSON, Arthur
Hodson, Arthur
Peters, Roy
Saunders, John
Winstan, Matt
NICOL, Eric Patrick
Jabez
NICOLE, Christopher
Cade, Robin
Grange, Peter
Logan, Mark
York, Andrew
NICOLL, *Sir* William Robertson
Clear, Claudius
Wace, W. E.
NIELSON, Helen Berniece
Giles, Kris
NILSON, Annabel
Nilson, Bee
NISBET, Ulric
Callaway, Hugh
NISOT, Mavis Elizabeth
Penmare, William
NOCK, Albert Jay
Historicus
Journeyman
NOLAN, Cynthia
Reed, Cynthia
NOLAN, Frederick
Christian, Frederick H.
NOLAN, William F.
Anmar, Frank
Cahill, Mike
Edwards, F. E.

NOONAN, Robert
  Tressall, Robert
  Tressell, Robert
NORGATE, Walter
  Le Grys, Walter
NORTH, William
  Rodd, Ralph
NORTHAM, Lois Edgell
  Nelson, Lois
NORTHCOTT, Cecil
  Miller, Mary
NORTON, Alice Mary
  North, Andrew
  Norton, André
NORTON, Alice Mary *and*
  HOGARTH, Grace
  Weston, Allen
NORTON, Marjorie
  Ellison, Marjorie
NORTON, Olive Marion
  Neal, Hilary
  Noon, T. R.
  Norton, Bess
  Norway, Kate
NORWAY, Nevil Shute
  Shute, Nevil
NORWOOD, Victor George
 Charles
  Banton, Coy
  Baxter, Shane V.
  Bowie, Jim
  Brand, Clay
  Cody, Walt
  Corteen, Craig
  Corteen, Wes
  Dangerfield, Clint
  Destry, Vince
  Fargo, Doone

  McCord, Whip
  Rand, Brett
  Russell, Shane
  Shane, Rhondo
  Tressidy, Jim
NOWELL, Elizabeth Cameron
  Clemons, Elizabeth
NUMANO, Allen
  Corenanda, A. L. A.
NURSE, Malcolm Ivan Meredith
  Padmore, George
NUTT, David
  Brand, David
NUTT, Lily Clive
  Arden, Clive
NUTTALL, Anthony
  Allyson, Alan
  Bardsley, Michael
  Curtis, Spencer
  Lenton, Anthony
  Tracey, Grant
  Trent, Lee
  Wells, Tracey
NYE, Nelson Coral
  Colt, Clem
  Denver, Drake C.

OAKESHOTT, Edna
  Peters, Jocelyn
OAKLEY, Eric Gilbert
  Capon, Peter
  Gregson, Paul
  Scott-Morley, A.
OBENCHAIN, Eliza Caroline
  Hall, Eliza Calvert
O'BRIEN, Conor Cruise
  O'Donnell, Donat

O'CONNOR, Patrick
 Nanky Poo
O'CONNOR, Patrick Joseph
 Fiacc, Padraic
O'CONNOR, Richard
 Archer, Frank
 Wayland, Patrick
O'CONNOR, T. P.
 T. P.
O'DONOGHUE, Elinor Mary
 Oddie, E. M.
O'DONOVAN, Michael Francis
 O'Connor, Frank
O'FARRELL, William
 Grew, William
OGNALL, Leopold Horace
 Carmichael, Harry
 Howard, Hartley
O'GRADY, John P.
 Culotta, Nino
 O'Grada, Sean
OLD, Phyllis Muriel Elizabeth
 Shiel-Martin
OLD COYOTE, Elnora A.
 Old Coyote, Sally
 Wright, Elnora A.
 Wright, Sally
OLDFIELD, Claude Houghton
 Houghton, Claude
OLDMEADOW, Ernest James
 Downman, Francis
OLIVER, Amy Roberta
 Onions, Berta
 Ruck, Berta
OLIVER, Doris M.
 Hughes, Alison
OLIVER, George
 Onions, Oliver

OLIVER, John Rathbone
 Roland, John
OLNEY, Ellen Warner
 Hayes, Henry
OLSEN, Theodore Victor
 Stark, Joshua
OLSON, Herbert Vincent
 Olsen, Herb
O'MAHONY, Charles Kingston
 Kingston, Charles
O'MALLEY, *Lady*
 Bridge, Ann
O'MORE, Peggy
 Bowman, Jeanne
O'NEILL, Herbert Charles
 Strategicus
O'NEILL, Rose Ceci
 Latham, O'Neill
O'NOLAN, Brian
 Knowall, George
 Na gCopaleen, Myles
 O'Brien, Flann
OPPENHEIM, E. Phillips
 Partridge, Anthony
OPPENHEIMER, Carlota
 Carlota
ORBISON, Roy *and* KECK,
Maud
 Orbison, Keck
ORDE-WARD, F. W.
 Williams, F. Harald
ORGA, Irfan
 Riza, Ali
O'RIORDAN, Conal O'Connell
 Connell, Norreys
ORME, Eve
 Day, Irene

O'ROURKE, Frank
  O'Malley, Frank
ORTON, Thora
  Colson, Thora
OSBERT, Reuben
  Osborn, Reuben
OSBORNE, Dorothy Gladys
  Arthur, Gladys
O'SHAUGHNESSY, Marjorie
  Shaw, Adelaide
OSLER, Eric Richard
  Dick, T.
OSTERGAARD, Geoffrey
  Gerard, Gaston
OSTLERE, Gordon Stanley
  Gordon, Richard
OSTLERE, Mary
  Gordon, Mary
OSTRANDER, Isabel Egerton
  Chipperfield, Robert Orr
  Fox, David
  Grant, Douglas
OURSLER, Fulton
  Abbot, Anthony
OURSLER, William Charles
  Gallagher, Gale
OVERHOLSER, Wayne D.
  Daniels, John S.
  Leighton, Lee
  Stevens, Dan J.
  Wayne, Joseph
OVERY, Jillian P. J.
  Martin, Gil
  Overy, Martin
ØVSTEDAL, Barbara
  Laker, Rosalind
  Paul, Barbara

OWEN, Dilys
  Edwards, Olwen
OWEN, Frank; FOOT, Michael
  and HOWARD, Peter
  Cato
OWEN, Jack
  Dykes, Jack
OWENS, Iris
  Daimler, Harriet
OXMAN, Philip
  Peachum, Thomas
OZAKI, Milton K.
  Saber, Robert O.

My name is legion: for we are many.
—Bible. Mark, 5.9

PADGETT, Ron
  Dangerfield, Harlan
  Veitch, Tom
PADLEY, Arthur
  Winn, Patrick
PADLEY, Walter
  Marcus Aurelius
PAGE, Evelyn *and* BLAIR, Dorothy
  Scarlett, Roger
PAGE, P. K.
  Cape, Judith
PAGET, Violet
  Lee, Vernon
PAINE, Lauran Bosworth
  Ainsworthy, Roy
  Allen, Clay
  Almonte, Rosa

81

Andrews, A. A.
Armour, John
Bartlett, Kathleen
Batchelor, Reg
Beck, Harry
Bedford, Kenneth
Benton, Will
Bosworth, Frank
Bradford, Will
Bradley, Concho
Brennan, Will
Carrel, Mark
Carter, Nevada
Cassady, Claude
Clarke, Richard
Clarke, Robert
Custer, Clint
Dana, Amber
Dana, Richard
Davis, Audrey
Drexler, J. F.
Duchesne, Antoinette
Durham, John
Fisher, Margot
Fleck, Betty
Frost, Joni
Glendenning, Donn
Glenn, James
Gordon, Angela
Gorman, Beth
Hart, Francis
Hayden, Jay
Holt, Helen
Houston, Will
Howard, Elizabeth
Howard, Troy
Hunt, John
Ingersol, Jared

Kelley, Ray
Ketchum, Jack
Kilgore, John
Liggett, Hunter
Lucas, J. K.
Lyon, Buck
Martin, Bruce
Martin, Tom
Morgan, Angela
Morgan, Arlene
Morgan, Frank
Morgan, John
Morgan, Valerie
O'Connor, Clint
Pindell, Jon
St George, Arthur
Sharp, Helen
Slaughter, Jim
Standish, Buck
Stuart, Margaret
Thompson, Buck
Thompson, Russ
Thorn, Barbara
Undine, P. F.
PAINTING, Norman
   Milna, Bruno
PALESTRANT, Simon
   Edward, Stephen
   Stevens, S. P.
   Strand, Paul E.
PALMER, Cecil
   Ludlow, John
PALMER, John Leslie
   Haddon, Christopher
PALMER, John Leslie *and*
SAUNDERS, Hilary Aidan
   St George

Beeding, Francis
Pilgrim, David
PALMER, John Williamson
Coventry, John
PALMER, Madelyn
Peters, Geoffrey
PALMER, Paul
Downing, Century
PALMER, Stuart
Stewart, Jay
PANIKKAR, Kavalam
Putra, Kerala
PANOWSKI, Eileen Janet
Thompson, Eileen
PARCELL, Norman Howe
Nicholson, John
PARES, Marion
Campbell, Judith
PARGETER, Edith Mary
Peters, Ellis
PARKER, Dorothy
Constant Reader
PARKER, Marion
Dominic, *Sister* Mary
PARKES, Frank
Dompo, Kwesi
PARKES, James, W.
Hadham, John
PARKES, Terence
Larry
PARKHILL, Forbes
Martinez, J. D.
Vloto, Otto
PARR, Olive Katherine
Chase, Beatrice
PARRIS, John
Lascelles, Alison

PARRY, Hugh J.
Cross, James
PARRY, Margaret G.
Glyn, Megan
PARSONS, Anthony
Nicholls, Anthony
PARSONS, Charles P.
Craven Hill
PARTRIDGE, Bellamy
Bailey, Thomas
PARTRIDGE, Eric
Vigilans
PATERSON, W. R.
Swift, Benjamin
PATRICK, Keats
Karig, Walter
PATRY, M. *and* WILLIAMS,
D. F.
Williams, Patry
PATTEN, Gilbert
Standish, Burt L.
PATTERSON, Henry
Fallon, Martin
Graham, James
Higgins, Jack
Marlowe, Hugh
Patterson, Harry
PATTERSON, Isabella Innis
Patterson, Innis
PATTINSON, James
Ryder, James
PATTINSON, Lee
Holland, Rosemary
Maxwell, Ann
Miller, Ellen
PATTINSON, Nancy
Asquith, Nan

PATTISON, Andrew Seth P.
    Seth, Andrew
PATTISON, Ruth
    Abbey, Ruth
PAUL, Elliot Harold
    Rutledge, Brett
PAUL, Maury
    Benedict, Billy
    Knickerbocker, Cholly
    Madison, Dolly
    Stuyvesant, Polly
PAXTON, Lois
    Low, Dorothy Mackie
PAYNE, Charles J.
    Snaffles
PAYNE, Donald Gordon
    Cameron, Ian
    Gordon, Donald
    Marshall, James Vance
PAYNE, Eileen Mary
    Mansell, C. R.
PAYNE, Pierre Stephen Robert
    Cargoe, Richard
    Horne, Howard
    Payne, Robert
    Young, Robert
PAYNE, Ronald Charles *and*
 GARROD, John William
    Castle, John
PAZ, Magdeleine
    Marx, Magdeleine
PEACH, Edward C.
    Ophiel
PEARCE, Brian
    Hussey, Leonard
    Redman, Joseph
PEARCE, Melville Chaning
    Nicodemus

PEARCE, Raymond
    Maplesden, Ray
PEARSON, Denise Naomi
    Gray, Harriet
PECHEY, Archibald Thomas
    Cross, Mark
    Valentine
PECK, Leonard
    Brain, Leonard
PEDLAR, Ann
    Stafford, Ann
PEDRICK-HARVEY, Gale
    Pedrick, Gale
PEED, William Bartlett
    Peek, Bill
PEEL, Frederick *and* SIDDLE,
 Charles
    Slingsby, Rufus
PEEL, Hazel
    Hayman, Hazel
    Peel, Wallis
PEEPLES, Samuel Anthony
    Ward, Brad
PEERS, Edgar Allison
    Truscot, Bruce
PEMBER, William Leonard
    Monmouth, Jack
PEMBER-DEVEREUX, Margaret
 R. R.
    Devereux, Roy
PENNER, Manola J.
    Alexander, Jean
PENWARDEN, Helen
    Smith, Jessica
PEOPLE, Granville Church
    Church, Granville
PEPPER, Joan
    Alexander, Joan

84

PERELMAN, S. J.
  Namlerep, Sidney
PERKINS, Kenneth
  Phillips, King
PERRY, Clair Willard
  Perry, Clay
PERRY, Martin
  Martyn, Henry
PERRY, Robert
  Marquis, Don
PETERS, Arthur A.
  Peters, Fritz
PETERS, Robert Louis
  Bridge, John
PETERSON, Corinna
  Cochrane, Corinna
PETERSON, Margaret
  Green, Glint
PETRIE, Rhona
  Duell, Eileen-Marie
PETRONE, Jane Gertrude
  Muir, Jane
PEYTON, Kathleen Wendy *and*
 PEYTON, Michael
  Peyton, K. M
PHILIPS, Judson Pentecost
  Pentecost, Hugh
PHILLIPS, David Graham
  Graham, John
PHILLIPS, Dennis John Andrew
  Challis, Simon
  Chambers, Peter
  Chester, Peter
PHILLIPS, Gerald William
  Huntingdon, John
PHILLIPS, Horace
  Stanton, Marjorie

PHILLIPS, Hubert
  Caliban
  Dogberry
  Ninespot
PHILLIPS, Hugh
  Hughes, Philip
PHILLIPS, James Atlee
  Atlee, Philip
PHILLIPS, Olga
  Olga
PHILLIPS, Pauline
  Van Buren, Abigail
PHILLPOTTS, Eden
  Hext, Harrington
PHILPOT, Joseph H.
  Lafargue, Philip
PHILPOTT, Alexis Robert
  Pantopuck
PHYSICK, Edward Harold
  Visiak, E. H.
PICKEN, Mary
  Wells, Jane Warren
PIERCE, Mary Cunningham
  Cunningham, Mary
PIGGOTT, William
  Wales, Hubert
PIKE, Mary Hayden
  Langdon, Mary
  Story, Sydney A. J.
PILCHER, Rosamunde
  Fraser, Jane
PILLEY, Phil
  Lindley, Gerard
PINTO, Jacqueline
  Blairman, Jacqueline
PIPER, David Towry
  Towry, Peter

PIPER, Evelyn
  Modell, Merriam
PLACE, Marian Templeton
  White, Dale
  Whitinger, R. D.
PLATH, Sylvia
  Lucas, Victoria
PLATT, Edward
  Trent, Paul
PLOMER, William
  D'Arfey, William
PLUMLEY, Ernest F.
  Clevedon, John
PLUMMER, Clare
  Emsley, Clare
PLUMMER, Thomas Arthur
  Sarne, Michael
POCOCK, Tom
  Allcot, Guy
POHL, Frederik
  McCann, Edson
  MacCreigh, James
POHL, Frederik *and*
 KORNBLUTH, Cyril M
  Gottesman, S. D.
POLAND, Dorothy E. H.
  Farely, Alison
  Hammond, Jane
POLANSKY, Abraham *and*
 WILLSON, Mitchell A.
 Hogarth, Emmett
POLLEY, Judith Anne
  Hagar, Judith
  Luellen, Valentina
PONSONBY, Doris Almon
  Rybot, Doris
POOLE, Reginald Heber
  Heber, Austin

Heber, Reginald
  Poole, Michael
PORN, Alice
  Ali-Mar
PORTER, Barbara Conney
  Conney, Barbara
PORTER, Eleanor
  Stewart, Eleanor
PORTER, Harold Everett
  Hall, Holworthy
PORTER, Maurice
  Mouthpiece
PORTER, William Sydney
  Henry, O.
POSNER, David Louis
  Bourchier, Jules
POSNER, Jacob D.
  Dean, Gregory
POSSELT, Eric
  Palmer, Edgar A.
POTTER, George William
  Withers, E. L.
POTTER, Heather
  Jenner, Heather
POTTER, Margaret
  Betteridge, Anne
POU, Genevieve
  Holden, Genevieve
POUND, Ezra
  Adkins, M. D.
  Atheling, William
  B. L.
  Hall, John
  Helmholtz, Bastien von
  J. L.
  Janus, Hiram
  Llewmys, Weston

Maria, Hermann Karl Georg
  Jesus
Saunders, Abel
T. J. V.
Venison, Alfred
POWELL, Talmage
  McCready, Jack
POWELL-SMITH, Vincent
  Elphinstone, Francis
  Justiciar
  Santa Maria
POWLEY, *Mrs* A. A.
  Gene, Marta
PRAFULLA, Das
  Subhadra-Nandan
PRATHER, Richard S.
  Knight, David
  Ring, Douglas
PRATT, E. B. Atkinson
  Blake, Eleanor
PRATT, Fletcher
  Fletcher, George U.
PRATT, John
  Winton, John
PRATT, Theodore
  Brace, Timothy
PRATT, William Henry
  Karloff, Boris
PRESLAND, John
  Bendit, Gladys
PREVOST-BATTERSBY, H. F.
  Prevost, Francis
PRICE, Beverly Joan
  Randell, Beverly
PRICE, Florence Alice
  Warden, Florence
PRICE, Jeremie
  Lane, Marvyn

PRICE, Olive
  Cherryholmes, Anne
PRIESTLEY, Clive Ryland
  Ryland, Clive
PRIESTLEY, John Boynton
  Goldsmith, Peter
PRIOR, Mollie
  Roscoe, Janet
PRITCHARD, William Thomas
  Dexter, William
PUDDEPHA, Derek
  Quill
PUECHNER, Ray
  Haddo, Oliver
  Victor, Charles B.
PULLEIN-THOMPSON, Christine
  Keir, Christine
PULLEIN-THOMPSON, Dennis
  Cannan, Denis
PULLEIN-THOMPSON,
  Josephine
  Cannan, Joanna
PULLEN, George
  Culpeper, Martin
PULLING, Albert Van Siclen
  Pulling, Pierre
PUNNETT, Margaret *and*
  PUNNETT, Ivor
  Simons, Peter
  Simons, Roger
PURCELL, Victor W. W. S.
  Buttle, Myra
PURDY, Ken
  Prentiss, Karl
PURVES, Frederick
  Lloyd, Joseph M.

QUENTIN, Dorothy
  Beverly, Linda
QUIBELL, Agatha
  Pearce, A. H.
QUIGLEY, Aileen
  Fabian, Ruth
  Lindley, Erica
QUIGLY, Elizabeth Pauline
  Elisabeth
QUILLER-COUCH, *Sir* Arthur
  Q.

RADCLIFFE, Garnett
  Travers, Stephen
RADETZBY von RADETZ,
  Countess
  Harding, Bertita
RADFORD, Ruby Lorraine
  Bailey, Matilda
  Ford, Marcia
RAE, Hugh Cranford
  Crawford, Robert
  Houston, R. B.
RAGG, Thomas Murray
  Thomas, Murray
RALEIGH-KING, Robin Victor
  Lethbridge
  Graham, Robin
  King, Robin
RAMAGE, Jennifer
  Mason, Howard
RAME, Maria Louise
  Ouida
RAMSKILL, Valerie
  Brooke, Carol
RANDOLPH, Lowell King
  Ran, Kip

RANSFORD, Oliver
  Wylcotes, John
RANSOME, L. E.
  Chester, Elizabeth
  Melbourne, Ida
  Ransome, Barbara
  Stirling, Stella
RAPHAEL, Chaim
  Davey, Jocelyn
RAPHAEL, Frederic *and*
  MASCHLER, Tom
  Caine, Mark
RASH, Dora
  Wallace, Doreen
RAUBENHEIMER, George H.
  Harding, George
RAVENSCROFT, John R.
  Ravenscroft, Rosanne
RAWLEY, Callman
  Rakosi, Carl
RAWLINS, Eustace
  Eustace, Robert
RAWSON, Clayton
  Merlini, The Great
  Towne, Stuart
— RAYMOND, Rene
  Chase, James Hadley
  Docherty, James L.
  Grant, Ambrose
  Marshall, Raymond
RAYMOND, Walter
  Cobbleigh, Tom
RAYNER, Augustus Alfred
  Hall, Whyte
— RAYNER, Claire
  Brandon, Sheila
  Lynton, Ann
  Martin, Ruth

REACH, James
  Manning, Roy
  West, Tom
READ, Anthony
  Ferguson, Anthony
READ, James
  Bacon, Jeremy
READ, John
  Jan
REAGAN, Thomas B.
  Thomas, Jim
REANEY, James
  Spoonhill
REBACK, Marcus *and*
  CALDWELL, Janet Taylor
  Caldwell, Taylor
  Reiner, Max
REDMAN, Ben Ray
  Lord, Jeremy
REDMON, Lois
  Rogers, Rachel
REECE, Alys
  Wingfield, Susan
REED, Alexander Wyclif
  Harlequin
REED, Blair
  Ring, Adam
REEMAN, Douglas
  Kent, Alexander
REES, Helen
  Oliver, Jane
REES, Joan
  Avery, June
  Bedford, Ann
  Strong, Susan
REEVE-JONES, Alan
  Lunchbasket, Roger

REEVES, John Morris
  Reeves, James
REID, John
  Caliban
REID, Whitelaw
  Agate
REILLY, Helen K.
  Abbey, Kieran
REINFELD, Fred
  Young, Edward
RENFREW, A.
  Patterson, Shott
RENNIE, James Alan
  Denver, Boone
RENTOUL, T. Laurence
  Gage, Gervais
RESSICH, John S. M. *and*
  DE BANZIE, Eric
  Baxter, Gregory
REY, Hans Augusto
  Uncle Gus
REYNOLDS, Helen Mary
  Greenwood Dickson
  Reynolds, Dickson
REYNOLDS, John E.
  Dexter, Ross
RICCI, Lewis Anselm da Costa
  Bartimeus
RICE, Brian Keith
  Vigilans
RICE, Craig
  Sanders, Daphne
  Venning, Michael
RICE, Dorothy
  Borne, D.
  Vicary, Dorothy
RICE, Joan
  Hallam, Jay

89

RICHARDS, Allen
   Rosenthal, Richard A.
RICHARDS, James
   Cladpole, Jim
RICHARDS, Ronald C. W.
   Saddler, K. Allen
RICHARDSON, Eileen
   Shane
RICHARDSON, Gladwell
   Blacksnake, George
   Jones, Calico
   Kent, Pete
   Kildare, Maurice
   O'Riley, Warren
   Warner, Frank
   Winslowe, John R.
RICHARDSON, Mary Kathleen
   Norton, S. H.
RIDDOLLS, Brenda H.
   English, Brenda H.
RIDEAUX, Charles
   Chancellor, John
RIDGE, William Pett
   Simpson, Warwick
RIGONI, Orlando Joseph
   Ames, Leslie
   Wesley, James
RIGSBY, Howard
   Howard, Vechel
RILEY, James Whitcomb
   Johnson, Benjamin F.
RIMANOCZY, A.
   Eland, Charles
RISTER, Claude
   Billings, Buck
   Holt, Tex

RIVETT, Edith Caroline
   Carnac, Carol
   Lorac, E. C. R.
ROARK, Garland
   Garland, George
ROBBINS, Clarence Aaron
   Robbins, Ted
ROBERTS, Cecil
   Beresford, Russell
ROBERTS, Dorothy James
   Mortimer, Peter
ROBERTS, Eric
   Robin
ROBERTS, Irene
   Carr, Roberta
   Harle, Elizabeth
   Roberts, Ivor
   Rowland, Iris
   Shaw, Irene
ROBERTS, James
   Horton, Robert J.
ROBERTS, Keith J. K.
   Bevan, Alistair
ROBERTS, Ursula
   Miles, Susan
ROBERTSHAW, James Denis
   Gaunt, Michael
ROBERTSON, Constance Noyes
   Scott, Dana
ROBERTSON, Eileen Arbuthnot
   Robertson, E. Arnot
ROBERTSON, Frank Chester
   Crane, Robert
   Field, Frank Chester
   Hill, King
ROBERTSON, James Logie
   Haliburton, Hugh

ROBERTSON, James Robin
  Connell, John
ROBERTSON, Keith
  Keith, Carlton
ROBERTSON, Margery Ellen
  Thorp, Ellen
  Thorp, Morwenna
ROBERTSON, Walter George
  Werrerson, Talbot
ROBEY, Timothy Lester
 Townsend
  Townsend, Timothy
ROBINS, Denise
  French, Ashley
  Gray, Harriet
  Kane, Julia
ROBINS, Elizabeth
  Raimond, C. E.
ROBINSON, H.
  Madeoc
ROBINSON, Joan Gale
  Thomas, Joan Gale
ROBINSON, Julien Louis
  Vedey, Julien
ROBINSON, Lewis George
  Limnelius, George
ROBINSON, Patricia *and*
 STEVENSON, Ferdinan
  Macomber, Daria
ROBINSON, Richard Blundell
  Leaderman, George
ROBSON, Norman
  Robb, John
ROCHE, Thomas
  Yes Tor
ROCHESTER, George Ernest
  Gaunt, Jeffrey

ROCKEY, Howard
  Panbourne, Oliver
RODDA, Charles
  Holt, Gavin
RODDA, Charles *and* AMBLER,
 Eric
  Reed, Eliot
ROE, Eric
  Roe, Tig
ROE, Ivan
  Savage, Richard
ROGERS, Ruth
  Alexander, Ruth
ROGERSON, James
  Hamilton, Roger
ROLFE, Edwin
  Fuller, Lester
ROLFE, Frederick
  Corvo, *Baron*
ROLLINS, Kathleen *and*
 DRESSER, Davis
  Debrett, Hal
ROLLINS, William
  Stacy, O'Connor
ROMANOFF, Alexander
 Nicholayevitch
  Abdullah, Achmed
ROOME, Gerald Antony
  Leslie, Colin
ROOS, William
  Rand, William
ROOS, William *and* KELLEY,
 Audrey
  Roos, Kelley
ROSCOE, John *and* RUSO,
 Michael
  Roscoe, Mike

ROSE, Alvin Emmanuel
  Pruitt, Alan
ROSE, Elizabeth Jane
  Elizabeth
ROSE, Graham
  Graham, John
ROSE, Ian
  Rose, Robert
ROSE, Mary H.
  Maizie
ROSEN, Michael
  Landgrave of Hesse
ROSENBERG, Ethel
  Clifford, Eth
  Penn, Ruth Bonn
ROSENBERG, Henrietta
  Keating, Walter S.
ROSENKRANTZ, Linda
  Damiano, Laila
ROSENQUIST, Fingal
  Südorf, Fingal von
ROSENTHAL, Michael D. H.
  Ross, Michael D. H.
ROSMAN, Alice Grant
  Rosna
ROSS, Dan
  Ross, Clarissa
  Ross, Marilyn
ROSS, Frank Xavier
  Frank, R. Jr.
ROSS, Isaac
  Ross, George
ROSS, William Edward Daniel
  Ames, Leslie
  Dana, Rose
  Gilmer, Ann
  McCormack, Charlotte

  Randolph, Ellen
  Rossiter, Jane
ROSS, Zola Helen
  Arre, Helen
  Iles, Bert
ROSSITER, John
  Ross, Jonathan
ROSSNER, Robert
  Ross, Ivan T.
ROSTEN, Leo C.
  Ross, Leonard Q.
ROTH, Arthur
  McGurk, Slater
ROTH, Holly
  Ballard, K. G.
  Merrill, P. J.
ROTHERAY, Geoffrey Neville
  Rooke, Dennis
ROTHWELL, Henry Talbot
  Talbot, Henry
ROUSSEAU, Leon
  Strydom, Len
ROWE, John Gabriel
  Rowe, Alice E.
  Walters, T. B.
ROWLAND, Donald Sydney
  Adams, Annette
  Bassett, Jack
  Baxter, Hazel
  Benton, Karla
  Berry, Helen
  Brant, Lewis
  Bray, Alison
  Brayce, William
  Brockley, Fenton
  Bronson, Oliver
  Buchanan, Chuck
  Caley, Rod

Carlton, Roger
Cleve, Janita
Court, Sharon
Craig, Vera
Craile, Wesley
Dryden, John
Fenton, Freda
Field, Charles
Kroll, Burt
Langley, Helen
Lansing, Henry
Lant, Harvey
Lynn, Irene
McHugh, Stuart
Madison, Hank
Mason, Chuck
Murray, Edna
Page, Lorna
Patterson, Olive
Porter, Alvin
Random, Alex
Rimmer, W. J.
Rix, Donna
Rockwell, Matt
Roscoe, Charles
Scott, Norford
Scott, Valerie
Segundo, Bart
Shaul, Frank
Spurr, Clinton
Stan, Roland
Stevens, J. D.
Suttling, Mark
Talbot, Kay
Travers, Will
Vinson, Elaine
Walters, Rick
Webb, Neil

RUBEL, James Lyon
  Hayes, Timothy
  Macrae, Mason
RUBENSTEIN, Stanley Jack
  Ar, Esjay
RUBINS, Harold
  Robbins, Harold
RUCHLIS, Hyman
  Barrow, George
RUDNYCKYJ, Jaroslav B.
  Bij-Bijchenko
RUMBOLD-GIBBS, Henry St
  John C.
  Gibbs, Henry
  Harvester, Simon
  Saxon, John
RUNBECK, Margaret Lee
  McKinley, Karen
RUNDLE, Anne
  Lamont, Marianne
  Marshall, Joanne
  Sanders, Jeanne
RUSH, Noel
  Garnett, David S.
  Lee, David
RUSO, Michael *and* ROSCOE,
  John
  Roscoe, Mike
RUSSELL, Elizabeth Mary
  Countess
  Elizabeth
RUSSELL, George William
  A. E.
RUSSELL, Henry George
  Minicam
RUSSELL, Shirley
  King, Stephanie
  Vernon, Marjorie

RUSSELL, Ursula D'Ivry
   D'Ivry, Ursula
RUSTERHOLTZ, Winsome Lucy
   Turvey, Winsome
RUTLEDGE, Nancy
   Bryson, Leigh
RYALL, William Bolitho
   Bolitho, William
RYAN, John D.
   Brother Ernest
RYAN, Paul William
   Finnegan, Robert
RYDBERG, Ernie
   Brouillette, Emil
   McCary, Reed
RYDER, M. L.
   Lawson, Michael
RYDER, Vera
   Cook, Vera
   Mortimer, June
RYNNE, Alice
   Curtayne, Alice
RYWELL, Martin
   Hemingway, Taylor
   Sears, Deane

SAINT, Dora Jessie
   Read, Miss
SAINT-HILAIRE, P. B.
   Pavitra
ST JOHN, Wylly Folk
   Fox, Eleanor
   Larson, Eve
   Pierce, Katherine
   Vincent, Mary Keith
   Williams, Michael
SAKLATVALA, Beram
   Marsh, Henry

SALMON, Annie Elizabeth
   Ashley, Elizabeth
   Martin, Nancy
SALMON, Geraldine Gordon
   Sarasin, J. G.
SALMON, P. R.
   Panlake, Richard
SALSBURY, Nate
   Ireland, Baron
SALTZMANN, Sigmund
   Salten, Felix
SAMACHSON, Joseph
   Miller, John
   Morrison, William
SAMBROT, William Anthony
   Ayes, Anthony
SAMMAN, Fern
   Powell, Fern
SAMPSON, Richard Henry
   Hull, Richard
SANDERSON, Douglas
   Brett, Martin
   Douglas, Malcolm
SANDFORD, Matthew
   Matt
SANDOZ, Mari
   Macumber, Mari
SANDS, Leo G.
   Craig, Lee
   Helmi, Jack
   Herman, Jack
   Meuron, Skip
SASSOON, Siegfried
   Kain, Saul
   Lyre, Pinchbeck
   S. S.
   Sigma Sashûn

SATHERLEY, David *and*
  WHITEHAND, James
    Whitehand, Satherley
SAUNDERS, Ann Loreille
  Cox-Johnson, Ann
SAUNDERS, Hilary Aidan St
  George *and* PALMER, John
  Leslie
    Beeding, Francis
    Pilgrim, David
SAUNDERS, Jean
  Innes, Jean
SAUNDERS, Margaret Marshall
  Saunders, Marshall
SAUNDERS, Theodore *and*
  MEANS, Mary
    Scott, Denis
SAVAGE, Lee
  Stewart, Logan
SAVAGE, Mildred
  Barrie, Jane
SAWKINS, Raymond Harold
  Forbes, Colin
  Raine, Richard
SAXON, Sophia
  Jarrett, Kay
SAYER, Nancy Margetts
  Bradfield, Nancy
SAYER, Walter William
  Quiroule, Pierre
SAYERS, Dorothy L.
  Leigh, Johanna
SAYERS, James D.
  James, Dan
SCHAAF, M. B.
  Goffstein, M. B.
SCHIFF, Sydney
  Hudson, Stephen

SCHISGALL, Oscar
  Hardy, Stuart
SCHMIDT, James Norman
  Norman, James
SCHNEIDER, Daniel Edward
  Taylor, Daniel
SCHOENFELD, Eugene L.
  Pocrates, *Dr* Hip
SCHOFIELD, Sylvia Anne
  Matheson, Sylvia A.
  Mundy, Max
SCHONFIELD, Hugh Joseph
  Hegesippus
SCHUBE, Purcell G.
  Mee
SCHÜTZE, Gladys Henrietta
  Leslie, Henrietta
  Mendl, Gladys
SCOBIE, Stephen Arthur Cross
  Waverley, John
SCOTT, Evelyn
  Souza, Ernest
SCOTT, Hilda R.
  Smith, Harriet
SCOTT, Hugh Stowell
  Merriman, Henry Seton
SCOTT, Jody *and* LEITE, George
  Thurston
    Scott, Thurston
SCOTT, Leslie
  Cole, Jackson
  Leslie, A.
  Leslie, A. Scott
  Scott, Bradford
SCOTT, Marian Gallagher
  Oliver, Gail
SCOTT, Mary E.
  Graham, Jean

SCOTT, Peter Dale
  Greene, Adam
  Sproston, John
SCOTT, Rose Laure
  Buckley, Eunice
SCOTT, Winifred Mary
  Wynne, Pamela
SCOTT-HANSEN, Olive
  Murrell, Shirley
SCROGGIE, Marcus Graham
  Cathode Ray
SEAMAN, Elizabeth C.
  Bly, Nellie
SEAMAN, *Sir* Owen
  Nauticus
  O. S.
SEAVER, Richard
  Mole, Oscar
SEAWELL, Molly Elliot
  Davis, Foxcroft
SEBENTHALL, Roberta
  Kruger, Paul
SEBLEY, Frances Rae
  Jeffs, Rae
SECRIST, W. G. *and* KELLIHER,
  Dan T.
  Secrist, Kelliher
SEEDO, Sonia
  Fuchs, Sonia
SEID, Ruth
  Sinclair, Jo
SELCAMM, George
  Machlis, Joseph
SELDES, Gilbert Vivian
  Johns, Foster
SELDON TRUSS, Leslie
  Selmark, George

SERAILLIER, Anne
  Rogers, Anne
SERNER, Gunnar
  Heller, Frank
SERVADIO, Gaia
  Mostyn-Owen, Gaia
SEUFFERT, Muriel
  Faulkner, Mary
  Seuffert, Muir
SHACKLETON, Edith
  Heald, Edith
SHAFFER, Anthony *and*
 SHAFFER, Peter
  Anthony, Peter
SHAMBROOK, Rona
  Randall, Rona
SHANN, Renée
  Gaye, Carol
  Pent, Katherine
SHARP, *Sir* Henry
  Ainsworth, Oliver
SHARP, William
  Macleod, Fiona
SHAW, Charles
  Singer, Bant
SHAW, George Bernard
  Corno di Bassetto
  G. B. S.
SHAW, Howard
  Howard, Colin
SHAW, Jane
  Gillespie, Jane
SHEA, Patrick
  Laughlin, P. S.
SHELDON, Peter
  Gaddes, Peter

SHELLABARGER, Samuel
  Esteven, John
  Loring, Peter
SHEPPARD, John Hamilton
 George
  Creek, Nathan
SHERIDAN, Elsie Lee
  Cromwell, Elsie
  Gordon, Jane
  Lee, Elsie
SHERIDAN, H. B.
  Sherry, Gordon
SHERMAN, Frank Dempster
  Carmen, Felix
SHIEL, M. P. *and* TRACY, Louis
  Holmes, Gordon
SHIELDS, George Oliver
  Coquina
SHIPMAN, Natalie
  Arthur, Phyllis
SHIRREFFS, Gordon D.
  Donalds, Gordon
  Gordon, Stewart
  Maclean, Art
SHOLL, Anna McClure
  Corson, Geoffrey
SHORTT, Charles Rushton
  Rushton, Charles
SIDDLE, Charles *and* PEEL,
 Frederick
  Slingsby, Rufus
SIEGEL, Doris
  Wells, Susan
SILVERBERG, Robert
  Chapman, Walker
  Drummond, Walter
  Jorgenson, Ivar
  Knox, Calvin

  Osborne, David
  Sebastian, Lee
SILVETTE, Herbert
  Dogbolt, Barnaby
SIM, Katharine Phyllis
  Nuraini
SIMMONDS, Michael Charles
  Essex, Frank
  Simmonds, Mike
SIMMONS, J. S. A.
  Cromie, Stanley
  Montgomery, Derek
SIMONS, Katherine Drayton
 Mayrant
  Mayrant, Drayton
SIMPSON, Bertram L.
  Weale, B. Putnam
SIMPSON, Evan John
  John, Evan
SIMPSON, John Frederick
 Norman Hampson
  Hampson, John
SIMPSON, Keith
  Bailey, Guy
SIMS, George Robert
  Dagonet
SIMSON, Eric Andrew
  Kirk, Laurence
SINCLAIR, Bertha Muzzy
  Bower, B. M.
SINCLAIR, Kathleen Henrietta
  Knight, Brigid
SINGER, James Hyman
  Singer, Burns
SINGH, Gopal
  Dardi
SKIDELSKY, Simon Jasha
  Simon, S. J.

SKINNER, Conrad Arthur
    Maurice, Michael
SKINNER, June O'Grady
    O'Grady, Rohan
SKUES, Goerge Edward
    Mackenzie
    Seaforth
SLADEK, John Thomas *and*
  DISCH, Thomas M.
    Demijohn, Thom
SLANEY, George Wilson
    Woden, George
SLATER, Ernest
    Gwynne, Paul
SLATER, Montagu
    Johns, Richard
SLAUGHTER, Frank Gill
    Terry, C. V.
SLAVITT, David
    Sutton, Henry
SLESAR, Henry
    Leslie, O. H.
SLOGGETT, Nellie
    Cornwall, Nellie
SMALL, Austin J.
    Seamark
SMITH, Alfred Aloysius
    Horn, Trader
SMITH, Charles H.
    Arp, Bill
SMITH, Dorothy Gladys
    Anthony, C. L.
    Smith, Dodie
SMITH, Edgar
    Mason, Michael
SMITH, Edward Ernest
    Lindall, Edward

SMITH, Edward Percy
    Percy, Edward
SMITH, Ernest Bramah
    Bramah, Ernest
SMITH, Florence Margaret
    Smith, Stevie
SMITH, Frances C.
    Smith, Jean
SMITH, Frank E.
    Craig, Jonathan
SMITH, Frederick E.
    Farrell, David
SMITH, Goldwin
    Bystander, A
SMITH, H. Everard
    Everard, Henry
SMITH, Helen Zenna
    Price, Evadne
SMITH, June Johns
    Johns, June
SMITH, Lillian M.
    Warner, Leigh
SMITH, Lily
    Wanderer
SMITH, Margaret Ruth
    Seranne, Ann
SMITH, Marjorie Seymour
    Fearn, Elena
SMITH, Mary
    Drewery, Mary
SMITH, Norman Edward Mace
    Sheraton, Neil
    Shore, Norman
SMITH, Robert
    Chattan, Robert
SMITH, Robert Charles
    Charles, Robert
    Leader, Charles

SMITH, Rodney Collin *see*
  COLLIN SMITH, Rodney
SMITH, Sidney Wallace
  Brodie, Gordon
SMITH, Walter Chalmers
  Knott, Hermann
  Orwell
SMITHELLS, Doreen
  Boscawen, Linda
SMITHERS, Muriel
  Redmayne, Barbara
SMITHIES, Muriel
  Howe, Muriel
SMITTER, Eliott-Burton
  Hadley, Leila
SNODGRASS, W. D.
  Gardons, S. S.
  McConnell, Will
  Prutkov, Kozma
SNOW, Donald Clifford
  Fall, Thomas
SNOW, Charles Horace
  Averill, H. C.
  Ballew, Charles
  Hardy, Russ
  Lee, Ranger
  Marshall, Gary
  Smith, Wade
  Wills, Chester
SNOW, Helen Foster
  Wales, Nym
SNYDER, Louis Leo
  Nordicus
SODERBERG, Percy Measday
  Archer, S. E.
SOLOMON, Samuel
  Moolson, Melusa

SOMERVILLE, Edith Oenone
  Graham, Viva
  Herring, Geilles
  Somerville
SOUTER, Helen Greig
  Aunt Kate
SOUTHERN, Terry *and*
  HOFFENBERG, Mason
  Kenton, Maxwell
SOUTHWOLD, Stephen
  Bell, Neil
  Martens, Paul
  Miles
SPECK, Gerald Eugene
  Kepps, Gerald
  Science Investigator
  Stone, Eugene
SPEICHER, Helen Ross
  Abbott, Alice
SPENCE, William
  Bowden, Jim
  Ford, Kirk
  Rogers, Floyd
  Spence, Duncan
SPENDER, Stephen
  S. H. S.
SPEWACK, Samuel
  Abbott, A. A.
SPICER, Bart *and* SPICER,
  Betty Coe
  Barbette, Jay
SPIEGEL, Clara E. *and* MAYER,
  Jane
  Jaynes, Clare
SPILLANE, Frank Morrison
  Spillane, Mickey
SPINELLI, Grace
  Spinelli, Marcos

SPIRO, Edward H.
  Cookridge, E. H.
SPOONER, Peter Alan
  Mellor, Michael
  Peters, Alan
  Rennie, Jack
  Underwood, Keith
SPRATLING, Walter Norman
  Sparlin, W.
SPRIGG, Christopher St John
  Caudwell, Christopher
SPROAT, Iain Macdonald
  Penn, Richard
SPROULE, Howard
  Sproule, Wesley
SQUIBBS, H. W. Q.
  Quirk
SQUIRE, *Sir* John Collings
  Eagle, Solomon
STACEY, P. M. de Cosqueville
  De Cosqueville, Pierre
  Shelton, Michael
STAFFORD, Muriel
  Sauer, Muriel S.
STAMP, Roger
  Mingston, R. Gresham
STANIER, Maida
  Culex
STANLEY, Nora Kathleen Begbie
  Stange, Nora K.
STANNARD, Eliza Vaughan
  Winter, John Strange
STANSFIELD, Anthony *and*
  LILLEY, Peter
  Buckingham, Bruce
STANTON-HOPE, W. E.
  Hope, Stanton

STAPLES, Reginald Thomas
  Brewster, Robin
STARK, Raymond
  Norwood, John
STARKEY, James Sullivan
  O'Sullivan, Seumas
STARR, Richard
  Essex, Richard
  Richards, Stella
STATON-BEVAN, William
  Norman
  Abbey, Staton
STEARN, John Theodor
  Stern, John
STEARNS, Myron Morris
  Amid, John
STEELE, Mary Quintard Govan
  Gage, Wilson
STEELE, Patricia M. V.
  Joudry, Patricia
STEELE, Robert V. P.
  Thomas, Lately
STEFFAN, Alice Jacqueline
  Steffan, Jack
STEFFENS, Arthur Joseph
  Hardy, Arthur S.
STEIN, Aaron Marc
  Bagby, George
  Bagby, George A.
  Stone, Hampton
STEIN, Gertrude
  Toklas, Alice B.
STEPHEN, Joyce Alice
  Thomas, J. Bissell
STEPHENS, Donald Ryder
  Sinderby, Donald
STEPHENS, Eve
  Anthony, Evelyn

STEPHENS, James
  Esse, James
STERN, David
  Sterling, Peter
STERN, Elisabeth Gertrude
  Morton, Leah
STERN, Frederick Martin
  Martin, Frederick
STERN, James
  St James, Andrew
STERN, Philip Van Doren
  Storme, Peter
STERNE, E. G.
  Broun, Emily
STERNE, E. G. *and* LINDSAY,
  Barbara
  James, Josephine
STEVENS, Frances Moyer
  Hale, Christopher
STEVENS, Henry Charles
  Garry, Stephen
  Mann, John
STEVENSON, Ferdinan *and*
  ROBINSON, Patricia
  Macomber, Daria
STEVENSON, James Patrick
  Radyr, Tomos
STEWART, Alfred Walter
  Connington, J. J.
STEWART, Dorothy Mary
  Elgin, Mary
STEWART, John Innes
  Mackintosh
  Innes, Michael
STEWART, Kenneth Livingston
  Livingston, Kenneth

STEWART, Neil *and* JOHNSON,
  Pamela Hansford
  Lombard, Nap
STICKLAND, Louise Annie
  Beatrice
  Somers, J. L.
STICKLAND, M. E.
  Stand, Marguerite
STINE, George Harry
  Correy, Lee
STITT, James M.
  Brunswick, James
STOCKS, Mary *and others*
  Heptagon
STODDARD, Charles Warren
  Pepperwood, Pip
STODDARD, William Osborn
  Forrest, *Colonel* Cris
STODDART, Jane T.
  Lorna
STOE, M.
  Bazagonov, M. S.
STOFFER, Edith G.
  Ross, Deborah
STOKER, Alan
  Evans, Alan
STOKES, Francis William
  Everton, Francis
STOKES, Manning Lee
  Ludwell, Bernice
  Manning, Lee
STOLL, Dennis Gray
  Craig, Denys
STONE, Grace Zaring
  Vance, Ethel
STONE, Irving
  Tennenbaum, Irving

STONEBRAKER, Florence
   Shepard, Fern
   Stuart, Florence
STONEHAM, Charles Thurley
   Thurley, Norgrove
STONOR, Oliver
   Bishop, Morchard
STORY, Rosamund Mary
   Jeskins, Richard
   Lee, Charles H.
   Lindsay, Josephine
   Tracy, Catherine
   Woods, Ross
STOUTENBURG, Adrien
   Kendall, Lace
STRACHAN, Gladys Elizabeth
   Bill
STRAITON, Edward Cornock
   Vet, T. V.
STRATEMEYER, Edward
   Bonehill, Ralph
   Winfield, Allen
   Winfield, Arthur M.
STREATFEILD, Noel
   Scarlett, Susan
STREET, Cecil John Charles
   Rhode, John
STRONG, Anna Louise
   Anise
STRONG, Charles Stanley
   Stanley, Chuck
   Stoddard, Charles
STRUNSKY, Simeon
   Patient Observer, The
STUART, Dorothy Margaret
   D. M. S.
STUART-HEATON, Peter
   Heaton, Peter

STUART-JERVIS, Charles Edward
   Coysh, Edward
STUBBS, Harry Clement
   Clement, Hal
STUBBS, Jean
   Darby, Emma
   March, Emma
STUDDERT, Annie
   Rixon, Annie
STURE-VASA, Mary
   O'Hara, Mary
STURGES, Mary d'Este
   Virakam, Soror
STURGIS, Justin
   Burgess, Gelett
STURT, George
   Bourne, George
STURTZEL, Howard Allison
   Annixter, Paul
STURTZEL, Jane L.
   Annixter, Jane
STYLES, Showell
   Carr, Glyn

*What song the Syrens sang, or
what name Achilles assumed,
though puzzling questions, are
not beyond all conjecture.*
—*Sir Thomas Browne. Urn burial*

SUDDABY, William Donald
   Griff, Alan
SULLIVAN, Edward Alan
   Murray, Sinclair
SUMMERS, Hollis
   Hollis, Jim

SUMMERTON, Margaret
  Roffman, Jan
SUTTON, Graham
  Marsden, Anthony
SUTTON, Margaret
  Sutton, Rachel B.
SUTTON, Phyllis Mary
  Riches, Phyllis
SVEINSSON, Solveig
  Rivers, Ronda
SWAN, Annie S.
  Lyall, David
  Orchard, Evelyn
SWARD, Robert S.
  Dr Soft
SWATRIDGE, Irene M. M.
  Chandos, Fay
  Lance, Leslie
  Mossop, Irene
  Storm, Virginia
  Tempest, Jan
SWEET, John
  Kim
SWETENHAM, Violet Hilda
  Drummond, Violet Hilda
SWINNERTON, Frank
  Pure, Simon
SYMINGTON, David
  Halliday, James
SYMONDS, E. M.
  Paston, George
SYMONS, Dorothy G.
  Groves, Georgina

TABER, Clarence Wilbur
  Job, Modern

TABORI, Paul
  Stafford, Peter
  Stevens, Christopher
TAIT, Dorothy
  Fairburn, Ann
TAIT, Euphemia Margaret
  Ironside, John
TAIT, George, B.
  Barclay, Alan
TAMES, Richard Lawrence
  Lawrence, James
TANNER, Edward Everett
  Dennis, Patrick
  Rowans, Virginia
TATE, George
  Armstrong, George
TATHAM, Laura
  Martin, John
  Phipps, Margaret
TATTERSALL, Muriel Joyce
  Wand, Elizabeth
TAYLOR, Bert Leston
  B. L. T.
TAYLOR, Constance Lindsay
  Cullingford, Guy
TAYLOR, Deems
  Smeed
TAYLOR, Kamala
  Markandaya, Kamala
TAYLOR, Phoebe Atwood
  Tilton, Alice
TAYLOR, Stephana Vere
  Benson, S. Vere
TEAGUE, John Jessop
  Gerard, Morice
TEGNER, Henry
  Northumbrian Gentleman
  Ruffles

TEILHET, Darwin le Ora
  Fisher, Cyrus
  Fisher, Cyrus T.
TELENGA, Suzette
  Yorke, Susan
TELLER, Neville
  Owen, Edmund
TENNYSON, Margaret
  Forrest, Carol
TERHUNE, Mary Virginia
  Harland, Marion
TERKEL, Louis
  Terkel, Studs
TETTMAR, Betty Eileen
  Spence, Betty E.
THAYER, Tiffany Ellsworth
  Doe, John
  Ellsworth, Eliner
THIMBLETHORPE, June
  Thorpe, Sylvia
THOM, William Albert Strang
  Morrison, J. Strang
THOMAS, Edward
  Eastaway, Edward
THOMAS, Ernest Lewys
  Vaughan, Richard
THOMAS, Eugene
  Grey, Donald
THOMAS, John Oram
  Oram, John
THOMAS, Mary
  Thomas, Tay
THOMAS, Reg
  Preston, Jane
THOMAS, Ronald Wills
  Wills, Ronald
THOMAS, Ross
  Bleeck, Oliver

THOMAS, Stanley A. C.
  Wyandotte, Steve
THOMAS, Walter Dill Jr
  Dill, Walter
THOMASHOWER, Dorothy
  Thomas, Dorothy
THOMPSON, A. M.
  Dangle
THOMPSON, Antony Allert
  Alban, Antony
THOMPSON, Arthur Leonard
  Bell
  Clifford, Francis
THOMPSON, Edward Anthony
  Lejeune, Anthony
THOMPSON, George Selden
  Selden, George
THOMPSON, Harlan
  Holt, Stephen
THOMPSON, J. W. M.
  Quince, Peter
THOMPSON, Phyllis
  Morgan, Phyllis
  Rose, Phyllis
THOMSON, Christine Campbell
  Alexander, Dair
THOMSON, Daisy
  Roe, M. S.
  Thomson, Jon H.
THORNE, Isabel Mary
  Villiers, Elizabeth
THORNETT, Ernest Basil
  Charles
  Penny, Rupert
THORP, Joseph
  T.
THORPE, John
  Campbell, Duncan

Centaur
  Scott, Douglas
THORPE-CLARK, Mavis
  Latham, Mavis
TIERNEY, John
  James, Brian
TILLETT, Dorothy Stockbridge
  Strange, John Stephen
TILLEY, E. D.
  Tilley, Gene
TILSLEY, Frank
  X. Y. Z.
TITUS, Eve
  Lord, Nancy
TODD, Barbara Euphan
  Euphan
TODD, John Murray
  Fox, John
TODD, Ruthven Campbell
  Campbell, R. T.
TOFANI, Louise E.
  Theophany
TOMLIN, Eric
  Stuart, Frederick
TOMLINSON, Joshua Leonard
  Linson
TONKIN, C. B.
  Pledger, P. J.
TOOHEY, Barbara *and*
 BIERMANN, June
  Bennett, Margaret
TORDAY, Ursula
  Allardyce, Paula
  Blackstock, Charity
  Blackstock, Lee
  Keppel, Charlotte
TORREY, Ware
  Crosby, Lee

TORSVAN, Traven
  Traven, B.
TOWNSEND, George Alfred
  Gath
TOWNSEND, Joan
  Pomfret, Joan
TOWNSEND, Mary Ashley
  Ashley, Mary
  Xariffa
TRACY, Donald Fiske
  Fuller, Roger
TRACY, Louis *and* SHIEL, M. P.
  Holmes, Gordon
TRALINS, S. Robert
  O'Shea, Sean
TRANTER, Nigel
  Treadgold, Nye
TRENT, Ann
  Carlton, Ann
  Crosse, Elaine
  Desana, Dorothy
  Sernicoli, Davide
TREWIN, J. C.
  J. C. T.
TRIEM, Paul Ellsworth
  Ellsworth, Paul
TRIMBLE, Chloe Maria
  Gartner, Chloe
TRIMBLE, Louis
  Brock, Stuart
  Travis, Gerry
TRIMMER, Eric
  Jameson, Eric
TRIPP, Kathleen
  Loewenthal, Karen
TRIPP, Miles Barton
  Brett, John Michael

TRIPPE, Peter
 Peters, Geoffrey
TROCCHI, Alexander
 De Las Lunas, Carmencita
 Lengel, Frances
TROUBETZKOI, *Princess*
 Rives, Amelia
TROWBRIDGE, John Townsend
 Creyton, Paul
TRUAX, Rhoda
 Wyngard, Rhoda
TRUMAN, Marcus George
 Beckett, Mark
TRUMBO, Dalton
 Abbott, *Dr* John
 Demaine, C. F.
 Doyle, Emmett
 Fincher, Beth
 Flexman, Theodore
 Jackson, Sam
 Rich, Robert
TRUPO, Anthony
 Norvell, Anthony
TRUSS, Leslie Seldon *see*
 SELDON TRUSS, Leslie
TUCK, John Erskine
 Erskine, John T.
TUCKER, Agnes
 Carruth, Agnes K.
TUCKER, James
 Craig, David
TULLETT, Denis John
 Dee, John
 Melmoth
 Sutton, John
TUNLEY, Roul
 Boyd, Edward

TURNBULL, Dora Amy
 Wentworth, Patricia
TURNER, John Victor
 Hume, David
TURNER, Lida Larrimore
 Larrimore, Lida
TURNER, Philip
 Chance, Stephen
TURNGREN, Annette
 Hopkins, A. T.
TURTON-JONES, Edith
 Gillespie, Susan
TUTE, Warren
 Warren, Andrew
TYLER-WHITTLE, Michael
 Sidney
 Whittle, Sidney

UHR, Elizabeth
 Stern, Elizabeth
ULLYETT, Kenneth
 Bentley, W. J.
UNDERWOOD, Mavis Eileen
 Kilpatrick, Sarah
UNETT, John
 Preston, James
UNWIN, David Storr
 Severn, David
UPCHURCH, Boyd
 Boyd, John
UPWARD, Edward Falaise
 Chalmers, Allen
URELL, William Francis
 Francis, William
UREN, Malcolm
 Malcolm, John
 Matelot

URIS, Auren
  Auren, Paul
URQUHART, Macgregor
  Hart, Max
USHER, Frank Hugh
  Franklin, Charles
  Lester, Frank
USHER, John Gray
  Gray, Christopher

VACZEK, Louis C.
  Hardin, Peter
VAHEY, John George Haslette
  Clandon, Henrietta
  Haslette, John
  Lang, Anthony
  Lodern, Vernon
  Mowbray, John
  Proudfoot, Walter
VAN DEVENTER, Emma M.
  Lynch, Lawrence
VAN ESSEN, W.
  Serjeant, Richard
VAN SILLER, Hilda
  Siller, Van
VAN ZELLER, Claud H.
  Brother Choleric
  Venning, Hugh
VANN, Gerald
  Oke, Simon
VAUGHAN, *Lady* Auriel
  Malet, Oriel
VAUGHAN, Owen
  Rhoscomyl, Owen
VEITCH, Thomas
  Kentigern, John

VENABLES, Terry *and*
  WILLIAMS, Gordon Maclean
  Yuill, P. B.
VENN, Mary Eleanor
  Adrian, Mary
VERNER, Christopher Stuart
  Chase, Lesley
VERNON, Kathleen Rose
  Dixon, Lesley
  Vernon, Kay
VERWER, Johanne
  Johanson, Elizabeth
  Verwer, Hans
VESEY, Ernest Blakeman
  Lewis, Ernest
VICKERS, Roy
  Spencer, John
VIDAL, Gore
  Box, Edgar
VIERECK, George Sylvester
  Corners, George F.
VILLIERS, David Hugh
  Buckingham, David
VINING, Charles A. M.
  R. T. L.
VINING, Elizabeth Gray
  Gray, Elizabeth Janet
VIVIAN, Evelyn C. H.
  Cannell, Charles
VLASTO, John Alexander
  Alexander, John
  Remenham, John
VOELKER, John Donaldson
  Traver, Robert
VOLK, Gordon
  Knotts, Raymond

VULLIAMY, Colwyn Edward
   Rolls, Anthony
   Teg, Twm

WACE, M. A.
   Golden Gorse
WADDEL, Charles Carey
   Carey, Charles
WADDELL, Martin
   Sefton, Catherine
WADDELL, Samuel
   Mayne, Rutherford
WADDINGTON, Miriam
   Merritt, E. B.
WADE, Arthur Sarsfield
   Rohmer, Sax
WADE, Robert *and* MILLER,
  William
   Masterson, Whit
   Miller, Wade
WADE, Rosalind
   Carr, Catharine
WAGENKNECHT, Edward
  Charles
   Forrest, Julian
WAGNER, Margaret Dale
   Wagner, Peggy
WAINHOUSE, Austryn
   Audiart
   Casavini, Pieralissandro
WAINWRIGHT, Gordon Ray
   Gordon, Ray
WALDRON, Corbin A.
   Cal, Dakota
WALKER, David Esdaile
   Esdaile, David

WALKER, Edith
   Trafford, Jean
   Walker, Jean Brown
WALKER, Emily Kathleen
   Ash, Pauline
   Barry, Eileen
   Devon, Sara
   Foster, Delia
   Lawson, Christine
   Lester, Jane
   Mayne, Cora
   Murray, Jill
   Tilbury, Quenna
   Treves, Kathleen
   Vincent, Heather
   Vincent, Honor
   Winchester, Kay
WALKER, Irma Ruth
   Walker, Ira
WALKER, John
   Thirlmere, Rowland
WALKER, Kenneth Macfarlane
   Macfarlane, Kenneth
WALKER, Lucy
   Sanders, Dorothy Lucy
WALKER, Peter Norman
   Coram, Christopher
   Ferris, Tom
   Manton, Paul
WALKER, Rowland
   Kenworthy, Hugh
WALKER, Roy
   Oliver, Roy
WALKER, Stella Archer
   Archer-Batten, S.
WALKER, W. Sylvester
   Coo-ee

WALKERLEY, Rodney L. de
  Burgh
    Athos
WALL, John W.
    Sarban
WALLACE, Elizabeth Virginia
    Wallace, Betty
WALLACE, Henry
    Uncle Henry
WALLER, Leslie
    Cody, C. S.
    Mann, Patrick
WALLIS, Geraldine
    Campbell, Hope
WALMSLEY, Arnold
    Roland, Nicholas
WALSH, James Morgan
    Hill, H. Haverstock
WALTER, Dorothy Blake
    Blake, Katherine
    Blake, Kay
    Ross, Katherine
    Walter, Katherine
    Walter, Kay
WALTON, John *and*
  BRIGHOUSE, Harold
    Conway, Olive
WALZ, Audrey
    Bonnamy, Francis
WARBURG, James Paul
    Paul, James
WARD, Robert Spencer
    King, Evan
WARE, Eugene Fitch
    Ironquill
WARREN, John Russell
    Coverack, Gilbert

WARRINER, Thurman
    Kersey, John
    Troy, Simon
WATERHOUSE, Keith *and*
  DEGHY, Guy
    Froy, Herald
    Gibb, Lee
WATFORD, Joel
    Essex, Jon
WATKINS, Alex
    Linklater, Lane
WATKINS-PITCHFORD, Denys
  James
    B. B.
WATNEY, Bernard
    Dolley, Marcus J.
WATSON, Albert Ernest
    Watson, Andrew
WATSON, Elliot Grant
    Lovegood, John
WATSON, Jack Charles Wauchope
    Chrystie, Edward M.
WATSON, John
    Maclaren, Ian
WATSON, Julia
    De Vere, Jane
    Hamilton, Julia
WATSON, R. A.
    Cromarty, Deas
WATT, Alexander Peter Fordham
    Fraser, Peter
WATT, Esme
    Jeans, Angela
WATTS, Edgar John Palmer
    Palmer, John
WATTS, Peter Christopher
    Chisholm, Matt

James, Cy
Owen, Tom
WAUGH, Hillary Baldwin
Taylor, H. Baldwin
Walker, Harry
WAY, Elizabeth Fenwick
Fenwick, Elizabeth
WAYE, Ellen
Jose, Ellen J.
WEALE, Anne
Blake, Andrea
WEAVER, Harriet Shaw
Wright, Josephine
WEBB, Charles Henry
Paul, John
WEBB, Dorothy Anna
March, Jermyn
WEBB, Godfrey E. C.
England, Norman
Godfrey, Charles
WEBB, Jack
Farr, John
Grady, Tex
WEBB, Jean Frances
Hamill, Ethel
WEBB, Richard Wilson *and*
WHEELER, Hugh Callingham
Patrick, Q.
Quentin, Patrick
Stagge, Jonathan
WEBB, Robert Forrest *and*
ELIADES, David
Forrest, David
WEBB, Ruth Enid
Morris, Ruth
WEBBE, Gale Dudley
Cole, Stephen

WEBSTER, Alice Jane Chandler
Webster, Jean
WEBSTER, Owen
Pilgrim, Adam
WEEKES, Agnes Russell
Pryde, Anthony
WEES, Frances Shelley
Shelley, Frances
WEI, Rex
Williams, Rex
WEIGHTMAN, Archibald John
Stuart, Alan
WEINBAUM, Stanley Grauman
Jessel, John
Stanley, Marge
WEINER, Margery
Lake, Sarah
WEINSTEIN, Nathan Wallenstein
West, Nathanael
WEIR, Rosemary
Bell, Catherine
Green, R.
WELCH, Colin
Simple, Peter
WELDON, A. E.
Macnamara, Brinsley
WELLS, Carolyn
Wright, Rowland
WELLS, H. G.
Bliss, Reginald
WELLS, Helen
Lewis, Francine
WELLS, Lee Edwin
Poole, Richard
WERNER, Elsa Jane
Bedford, A. N.
Bedford, Annie North
Hill, Monica

Nast, Elsa Ruth
  Werner, Jane
WERTENBAKER, Lael Tucker
  Tucker, Lael
WEST, Betty Bowen
  Bowen, Betty
WEST, Gertrude
  West, Trudy
WEST, Morris
  East, Michael
  Morris, Julian
WEST-WATSON, Keith Campbell
  Campbell, Keith
WESTHEIMER, David
  Smith, Z. Z.
WESTLAKE, Donald Edwin
  Coe, Tucker
  Stark, Richard
WESTMARLAND, Ethel Louisa
  Courtney, Christine
  Elliott, Ellen
WESTMORELAND, Vera Gertrude
  Elysian, Anne
WHARMBY, Margot
  Winn, Alison
WHARTON, Michael
  Simple, Peter
WHEAR, Rachel
  Low, Rachel
WHEELER, Hugh Callingham *and*
  WEBB, Richard Wilson
  Patrick Q.
  Quentin, Patrick
  Stagge, Jonathan
WHELAN, Jerome Bernard
  Brien, R. N.
WHELPTON, Eric
  Lyte, Richard

WHEWAY, John
  Armitage, Hazel
WHISH, Violet E.
  Swift, Stella
WHITBY, Anthony Charles
  Lesser, Anthony
WHITE, Alan
  Fraser, James
WHITE, Celia
  Tustin, Elizabeth
WHITE, Frank James
  Stewart-Hargreaves, E. H. I.
WHITE, Herbert Oliver
  Martyn, Oliver
WHITE, Pauline Arnold
  Arnold, Pauline
WHITE, Stanhope
  Dan Bana
  Sabiad
WHITE, Stanley
  Krull, Felix
  White, James Dillon
WHITE, William Anthony P.
  Boucher, Anthony
  Holmes, H. H.
WHITE, William Hale
  Rutherford, Mark
WHITEHAND, James *and*
  SATHERLEY, David
  Whitehand, Satherley
WHITEHOUSE, Arthur George
  Joseph
  Whitehouse, Arch
WHITEING, Richard
  Thorn, Whyte
WHITEMAN, William Meredith
  Turner, C. John

111

WHITFIELD, John
  Pilio, Gerone
WHITFORD, Joan
  Ford, Barry
  Oldham, Hugh R.
WHITNEY, Julie
  Yulya
WHITSON, John Harvey
  Sims, *Lieut.* A. K.
WHITTEN, Wilfred
  John o'London
WHITTET, George Sorley
  Kerr, John O'Connell
  Monkland, George
WHITTINGTON, Harry
  Harrison, Whit
  Holland, Kel
  Myers, Harriet Kathryn
  Philips, Steve
  Stuart, Clay
  Wells, Hondo
  White, Harry
  Whitney, Hallam
WIBBERLEY, Leonard Patrick
 O'Connor
  Holton, Leonard
  O'Connor, Patrick
  Webb, Christopher
WICKER, Tom
  Connolly, Paul
WICKSTEED, Margaret Hope
  Hope, Margaret
WIEDENBECK, Emilie Agnes
  Mable, Peter
WIGGINS, David
  Priestley, Robert
WIGGLESWORTH, Martin
  Worth, Martin

WIGHT, J. A.
  Herriot, James
WILBY, Basil
  Knight, Gareth
WILCOX, Harry
  Derby, Mark
WILCOXEN, Harriett
  Harriett
WILD, Dora Mary
  Broome, Dora
WILD, Reginald
  Edwards, Leonard
WILDING, Philip
  Fraser, Jefferson
  Haynes, John Robert
  Marshall, Lloyd
  Russell, Erle
  Stanton, Borden
  Stewart, Logan
  Stuart, Logan
WILKES-HUNTER, Richard
  Douglas, D.
  Douglas, Shane
  Farr, C.
  Gray, Adrian
  Mitchell, Kerry
WILKINS, Mary Louise
  Calhoun, Mary
WILKINSON, Louis Umfreville
  Marlow, Louis
WILKINSON, Percy F. H
  Wilkinson, Tim
WILLANS, Angela
  Grant, Mary
WILLARD, Josiah Flynt
  Flynt, Josiah
WILLETT, Franciscus
  McKern, Pat

WILLIAMS, Carol Elizabeth
  Fenner, Carol
WILLIAMS, D. F. *and* PATRY, M.
  Williams, Patry
WILLIAMS, Edward John
  Farrer, E. Maxwell
WILLIAMS, Gordon Maclean *and*
  VENABLES, Terry
  Yuill, P. B.
WILLIAMS, Guy Richard Owen
  Guinness, Owen
  Wooland, Henry
WILLIAMS, Jay
  Delving, Michael
WILLIAMS, Kathryn
  Vinson, Kathryn
WILLIAMS, Margaret Wetherby
  Erskine, Margaret
  Williams, Wetherby
WILLIAMS, Meurig
  Carrington, Michael
WILLIAMS, Ned
  Harbin, Robert
WILLIAMS, Peggy Eileen Arabella
  Evans, Margiad
WILLIAMSON, Ellen Douglas
  Douglas, Ellen
WILLIAMSON, Ethel
  Veheyne, Cherry
WILLIAMSON, Jack
  Stewart, Will
WILLIAMSON, Leila Isobel
  Orme, Eve
WILLIAMSON, Thames Ross
  Dagonet, Edward
  Fleming, Waldo
  Morgan, De Wolfe
  Smith, S. S.

WILLIS, A. A.
  A. A.
WILLIS, Corinne
  Denning, Patricia
WILLIS, George Anthony
  Armstrong
  Armstrong, Anthony
WILLIS, Priscilla D.
  Adams, Mary Scott
WILLOUGHBY-HIGSON, Philip
  John
  Higson, P. J. W.
WILLSON, Mitchell A. *and*
  POLANSKY, Abraham
  Hogarth, Emmett
WILMOT, Frank Leslie Thompson
  Maurice, Furnley
WILMOT, James Reginald
  Trevor, Ralph
WILSON, Albert
  Wilson, Yates
WILSON, Christine
  Geach, Christine
  Lowing, Anne
  Neil, Frances
WILSON, Desemea
  Patrick, Diana
WILSON, Helen
  Wilson, Holly
WILSON, John Anthony Burgess
  Burgess, Anthony
  Kell, Joseph
  Wilson, John Burgess
WILSON, Robert McNair
  Wynne, Anthony
WILSON, William *and* GRANT,
  Donald
  Ness, K. T.

WIMHURST, Cecil Gordon Eugene
  Brent, Nigel
WINCHELL, Prentice
  Collans, Dev
  De Bekker, Jay
  Dean, Spencer
  St Clair, Dester
  Sterling, Stewart
WINDER, Mavis Areta
  Areta, Mavis
  Winder, Mavis
  Wynder, Mavis Areta
WINKWORTH, Derek W.
  5029
WINNINGTON, Richard
  Ross, John
WINTER, Bevis
  Bocca, Al
  Cagney, Peter
  Hill, Bennet
  Shayne, Gordon
WINTERFIELD, Henry
  Michael, Manfred
WINTERS, Bayla
  Winters, Bernice
WINTERTON, Paul
  Bax, Roger
  Garve, Andrew
  Somers, Paul
WINTRINGHAM, Tom
  Gracchus
WIRT, Mildred
  Bell, Frank
  Clark, Joan
  West, Dorothy
WISE, Arthur
  McArthur, John

WITCOMBE, Rick
  Marker, Clare
WOHL, Ludwig von
  De Wohl, Louis
WOLFF, William
  Martindale, Spencer
WOLFSON, Victor
  Dodge, Langdon
WOOD, Christopher
  Dixon, Rosie
  Grape, Oliver
  Lea, Timothy
WOOD, Grace, Ashley
  Ancilla
WOOD, James
  McLeod, Finlay
  Stuart, Gordon
WOOD, Lilian Catherine
  Cymry Bach
WOOD, Patricia E. W.
  Ross, Patricia
WOOD, Samuel Andrew
  Temple, Robin
WOOD, Violet
  Wood, Quality
WOODCOCK, E. Page
  Uncle Reg
WOODFORD, Irene-Cecile
  Barrie, Jane
  Goff, Madeleine
  Lee, Veronica
  Woodford, Cecile
WOODHAM-SMITH, Cecil
  Gordon, Janet
WOODRICH, Mary Neville
  Neville, Mary
WOODROFFE, *Sir* John G.
  Avalon, Arthur

WOODS, Olwen
  Woods, Jonah
WOOLFOLK, Josiah Pitts
  Britt, Sappho Henderson
  Kennedy, Howard
  Sayre, Gordon
  Woodford, Jack
WOOLLEY, Catherine
  Thayer, Jane
WOOLSEY, Sarah Chauncey
  Coolidge, Susan
WORBOYS, Anne Eyre
  Eyre, Annette
WORDINGHAM, James A.
  Dare, Michael
WORNER, Philip A. I.
  Incledon, Philip
  Sylvester, Philip
WORNUM, Miriam
  Dennis, Eve
WORTHINGTON-STUART, Brian
  Arthur
  Meredith, Peter
  Stuart, Brian
WORTHY, Brian Hohnson
  Johnson, Brian
WORTIS, Avi
  Avi
WORTS, George F.
  Brent, Loring
WRIGHT, Elinor
  Lyon, Elinor
WRIGHT, George T.
  Wright, Ted
WRIGHT, John
  Wright, Wade
WRIGHT, Marjory Beatrice
  Pilgrim

WRIGHT, Mary
  Bawn, Mary
WRIGHT, R. L. Gerard
  Bristowe, Edwin
WRIGHT, Ronald Selby
  Radio Padre
WRIGHT, Sydney Fowler
  Fowler, Sydney
WRIGHT, Willard Huntington
  Van Dine, S. S.
WURMBRAND, Richard
  Moses, Ruben
WYLER, Rose
  Thayer, Peter
WYLLIE, James McLeod
  Barras Seer
WYND, Oswald
  Black, Gavin
WYNDHAM LEWIS, D. B.
  Beachcomber
  Shy, Timothy
WYNNE-TYSON, Esme
  De Morny, Peter

YARDUMIAN, Miryam
  Miryam
YATES, Alan Geoffrey
  Brown, Carter
YATES, George Worthing *and*
  MARSHALL, Charles Hunt
  Hunt, Peter
YATES, Raymond Francis
  Hall, Borden
YAUKEY, Grace
  Spencer, Cornelia
YELLOT, Barbara Leslie
  Jordan, Barbara Leslie

Real names

YIN, Leslie Charles Bowyer
  Charteris, Leslie
YOCKEY, Francis Parker
  Varange, Ulick
YONGE, Charlotte Mary
  Aunt Charlotte
YORKE, Henry Vincent
  Green, Henry
YOSELOFF, Thomas
  Young, Thomas
YOUD, Samuel
  Christopher, John
  Ford, Hilary
  Godfrey, William
  Graaf, Peter
  Nichols, Peter
  Rye, Anthony
YOUNG, Agnes
  Young, Agatha
YOUNG, Eric Brett
  Leacroft, Eric
YOUNG, Ernest
  Gilcraft
YOUNG, Janet Randall
  Randall, Janet
  Young, Jan
YOUNG, Nedrick
  Douglas, Nathan
YOUNG, Phyllis Brett
  Young, Kendal
YOUNGER, Elizabeth
  Hely, Elizabeth
YOUNGER, William Anthony
  Mole, William

ZAFFO, George J.
  Stewart, Scott

ZALBERG, Daniel
  Daniel, S.
ZARCHY, Harry
  Lewis, Roger
ZILLIACUS, Konni
  Covenanter
  Diplomaticus
  Vigilantes
  Williams, Roth
ZIM, Sonia
  Bleeker, Sonia
ZIMMER, Maude Files
  Baird, Maude F.
  Fileman, Nan
ZIMMERMAN, Robert Allen
  Dylan, Bob
ZINBERG, Len
  Lacy, Ed
ZINSSER, Hans
  R. S.
ZUBER, Mary E. L.
  Rowlands, Lesley

Pseudonyms

'What's the use of their having names', the Gnat said, 'if they won't answer to them?'
—Lewis Carroll. Through the looking glass

A. A.
  Willis, A. A.
A. A. B.
  Baumann, Arthur A.
A. E.
  Russell, George William
A. H.
  Hawkins, *Sir* Anthony Hope
A. H. G.
  Girdleston, A. H.
A. P. H.
  Herbert, *Sir* Alan Patrick
ABBEY, Kieran
  Reilly, Helen K.
ABBEY, Ruth
  Pattison, Ruth
ABBEY, Staton
  Staton-Bevan, William Norman
ABBOT, Anthony
  Oursler, Fulton
ABBOTT, A. A.
  Spewack, Samuel
ABBOTT, A. C.
  Meinzer, Helen Abbott
ABBOTT, Alice
  Speicher, Helen Ross
ABBOTT, *Dr* John
  Trumbo, Dalton

ABDULLAH, Achmed
  Romanoff, Alexander
    Nicholayevitch
ABERCROMBIE, Patricia Barnes
  Barnes, Patricia
ABHAVANANDA
  Crowley, Edward Alexander
ACHARYA, Pundit
  Bhattacharya, Basudeb
ACLAND, Alice
  Marreco, Anne
ACRE, Stephen
  Gruber, Frank
ADAIR, Cecil
  Green, Evelyn Everett
ADAIR, Dennis
  Cronin, Bernard
ADAIR, Hazel
  Addis, Hazel Iris
ADAIR, Sally
  Mannock, Laura
ADAMS, Andy
  Harkins, Peter
ADAMS, Annette
  Rowland, Donald Sydney
ADAMS, Bart
  Bingley, David Ernest
ADAMS, Clayton
  Holmes, Charles Henry
ADAMS, Mary Scott
  Willis, Priscilla D.
ADDISCOMBE, John
  Hunter, Alfred John
ADDISON, Carol
  Clarke, J. Calvitt
ADELER, Max
  Clark, Charles Heber

117

ADKINS, M. D.
  Pound, Ezra
ADRIAN, Mary
  Venn, Mary Eleanor
AGARD, H. E.
  Evans, Hilary Agard
AGATE
  Reid, Whitelaw
AINSWORTH, Harriet
  Cadell, Elizabeth
AINSWORTH, Oliver
  Sharp, *Sir* Henry
AINSWORTH, Patricia
  Bigg, Patricia Nina
AINSWORTH, Ruth
  Gilbert, Ruth
AINSWORTHY, Roy
  Paine, Lauran Bosworth
AIRD, Catherine
  McIntosh, Kinn Hamilton
AIRLIE, Catherine
  Macleod, Jean Sutherland
AJAX
  Jackson, Ada Acraman
AKENS, Floyd
  Baum, Lyman Frank
ALAIN
  Brustlein, Daniel
ALAN, A. J.
  Lambert, Leslie Harrison
ALAN, Jane
  Chisholm, Lilian
ALAN, Marjorie
  Bumpus, Doris Marjorie
ALBAN, Antony
  Thompson, Antony Allert
ALBERT, Ned
  Braun, Wilbur

ALBION, Ken
  King, Albert
ALBRAND, Martha
  Loewengard, Heidi H. F.
ALCYONE
  Krishnamurti, Jiddu
ALDEN, Jack
  Barrows, Marjorie
ALDON, Adair
  Meigs, Cornelia Lynde
ALEXANDER, Dair
  Thomson, Christine Campbell
ALEXANDER, Jean
  Penner, Manola J.
ALEXANDER, Joan
  Pepper, Joan
ALEXANDER, John
  Vlasto, John Alexander
ALEXANDER, L. G.
  Ftyaras, Louis George
ALEXANDER, Martin
  Daventry, Leonard John
ALEXANDER, Ruth
  Rogers, Ruth
ALGOL
  Bretherton, C. H.
ALI-MAR
  Porn, Alice
ALIEN
  Baker, Louisa Alice
ALIKI
  Brandenberg, Alyce Christina
ALIUNAS
  Baronas, Aloyzas
ALLABEN, Anne E.
  Farrell, Anne Elisabeth
ALLAN, Dennis
  Denniston, Elinore

118

ALLAN, Luke
  Amy, William Lacey
ALLARDYCE, Paula
  Torday, Ursula
ALLCOT, Guy
  Pocock, Tom
ALLEN, Adam
  Epstein, Beryl *and* Epstein,
  Samuel
ALLEN, Allyn
  Eberle, Irmengarde
ALLEN, Barbara
  Mann, Violet Vivian
ALLEN, Betsy
  Headley, Elizabeth
ALLEN, Clay
  Paine, Lauran Bosworth
ALLEN, Dixie
  Kohls, Olive N. Allen
ALLEN, Eric
  Allen-Ballard, Eric
ALLEN, F. M.
  Downey, Edmund
ALLEN, John W. Jr
  Lesley, Peter
ALLEN, Ronald
  Ayckbourne, Alan
ALLEN, Steve
  Allen, Stephen Valentine
ALLENBY, Gordon
  Matusow, Harvey Mitchell
ALLERTON, Mark
  Cameron, William Ernest
ALLERTON, Mary
  Govan, Mary Christine
ALLISON, Clay
  Keevill, Henry John

ALLWORTHY, A. W.
  Milam, Lorenzo W.
ALLYSON, Alan
  Nuttall, Anthony
ALMONTE, Rosa
  Paine, Lauran Bosworth
ALPHA OF THE PLOUGH
  Gardiner, Alfred George
ALTHEA
  Braithwaite, Althea
ALVORD, Burt
  Keevill, Henry John
AMBERLEY, Richard
  Bourquin, Paul
AMBERLEY, Simon
  Hoar, Peter
AMES, Felicia
  Burden, Jean
AMES, Jennifer
  Greig, Maysie
AMES, Leslie
  Rigoni, Orlando Joseph
AMES, Leslie
  Ross, William Edward Daniel
AMICUS CURIAE
  Fuller, Edmund
AMID, John
  Stearns, Myron Morris
AMIS, Breton
  Best, Rayleigh Breton Amis
AMOR, Amos
  Harrell, Irene Burk
AMOS, Alan
  Knight, Kathleen Moore
AMPHIBIAN
  Aston, *Sir* George
AMPLEGIRTH, Anthony
  Dent, Anthony

119

Pseudonyms

ANAUTA
  Blackmore, Anauta
ANCILLA
  Wood, Grace Ashley
ANDERS, Rex
  Barrett, Geoffrey John
ANDERSON, Ella
  Macleod, Ellen
ANDERSON, Rachel
  Bradby, Rachel
ANDOM, R.
  Barrett, Alfred Walter
ANDREWS, A. A.
  Paine, Lauran Bosworth
ANDREWS, Lucilla
  Crichton, Lucilla Matthew
ANDRÉZEL, Pierre
  Blixen-Finecke, Karen
    Christence *Baroness*
ANGELL, Norman
  Lane, *Sir* Ralph Norman Angell
ANGUS, Ian
  Mackay, James Alexander
ANISE
  Strong, Anna Louise
ANMAR, Frank
  Nolan, William F.
ANNIXTER, Jane
  Sturtzel, Jane L.
ANNIXTER, Paul
  Sturtzel, Howard Allison
ANSTEY, F.
  Guthrie, Thomas Anstey
ANSTRUTHER, James
  Graham, James Maxtone
ANTHONY, C. L.
  Smith, Dorothy Gladys

ANTHONY, Charles
  Akerman, Anthony Charles
ANTHONY, Evelyn
  Stephens, Eve
ANTHONY, John
  Beckett, Ronald Brymer
ANTHONY, Peter
  Shaffer, Anthony *and* Shaffer,
    Peter
ANTHONY, Piers
  Jacob, Piers Anthony
AP EVANS, Humphrey
  Drummond, Humphrey
AR, Esjay
  Rubinstein, Stanley Jack
ARCHER, A. A.
  Joscelyn, Archie
ARCHER, Frank
  O'Connor, Richard
ARCHER, G. Scott
  Larbalestier, Phillip George
ARCHER, Owen
  Greenwood, Augustus George
ARCHER, S. E.
  Soderberg, Percy Measday
ARCHER-BATTEN, S.
  Walker, Stella Archer
ARCHESTRATUS
  Driver, Christopher
ARDEN, Clive
  Nutt, Lily Clive
ARDEN, Mary
  Murry, Violet
ARDEN, William
  Lynds, Dennis
ARESBYS, The
  Bamberger, Helen R. *and*
    Bamberger, Raymond

120

ARETA, Mavis
  Winder, Mavis Areta
ARGUS, M. K.
  Eisenstadt-Jeleznov, Mikhail
ARIEL
  Arden, Adrian
ARION
  Chesterton, G. K.
ARLEY, Catherine
  D'Arley, Catherine
ARMITAGE, Hazel
  Wheway, John
ARMOUR, John
  Paine, Lauran Bosworth
ARMSTRONG, Anthony
  Willis, George Anthony
    Armstrong
ARMSTRONG, George
  Tate, George
ARMSTRONG, Raymond
  Lee, Norman
ARMSTRONG, Sybil
  Edmondson, Sybil
ARMSTRONG, Warren
  Bennett, William E.
ARNOLD, Pauline
  White, Pauline Arnold
ARNOLD, Wilcox
  Aitken, Andrew
ARP, Bill
  Smith, Charles H.
ARRE, Helen
  Ross, Zola Helen
ARSDALE, Wirt Van
  Davis, Martha Wirt
ARTHUR, Burt
  Arthur, Herbert

ARTHUR, Elisabeth
  Irish, Betty M.
ARTHUR, Frank
  Ebert, Arthur Frank
ARTHUR, Gavin
  Arthur, Chester Alan
ARTHUR, Gladys
  Osborne, Dorothy Gladys
ARTHUR, Phyllis
  Shipman, Natalie
ARTHUR, William
  Baker, William Howard
ARTHUR, William
  Neubauer, William Arthur
ASCHE, Oscar
  Heiss, John Stanger
ASCOTT, Adelie
  Bobin, John W.
ASH, Fenton
  Atkins, Frank A.
ASH, Pauline
  Walker, Emily Kathleen
ASHDOWN, Clifford
  Freeman, R. Austin
ASHE, Elizabeth
  Hyde, Lavender Beryl
ASHE, Gordon
  Creasey, John
ASHE, Susan
  Best, Carol Anne
ASHFORD, Jeffrey
  Jeffries, Roderic Graeme
ASHLEY, Elizabeth
  Salmon, Annie Elizabeth
ASHLEY, Mary
  Townsend, Mary Ashley
ASHTON, A. B.
  Basch, Ernst

121

ASHTON, Ann
　Kimbro, John
ASHTON, E. B.
　Basch, Ernst
ASHTON, E. E.
　Basch, Ernst
ASHTON, Lucy
　Martin, Netta
ASKHAM, Francis
　Greenwood, Julia E. C.
ASQUITH, Nan
　Pattinson, Nancy
ASSIAC
　Fraenkel, Heinrich
ASTLEY, Juliet
　Lofts, Norah
ATHELING, William
　Pound, Ezra
ATHOS
　Walkerley, Rodney L. de Burgh
ATLEE, Philip
　Phillips, James Atlee
AUBREY, Frank
　Atkins, Frank A.
AUCHTERLONIE, Dorothy
　Green, Dorothy
AUDIART
　Wainhouse, Austryn
AUGUST, John
　De Voto, Bernard Augustine
AUGUSTUS
　Lynn, Elwyn
AULD, Philip
　Burns, Bernard
AUNT CHARLOTTE
　Yonge, Charlotte Mary
AUNT DAISY
　Basham, Daisy

AUNT KATE
　Souter, Helen Greig
AUNT MAYSIE
　Jeffrey-Smith, May
AUNTIE MARGARET
　Keddie, Margaret Manson
AUREN, Paul
　Uris, Auren
AUSTIN, Brett
　Floren, Lee
AUSTIN, Frank
　Faust, Frederick
AUSTIN, Hugh
　Evans, Hugh Austin
AUSTWICK, John
　Lee, Austin
AVALON, Arthur
　Woodroffe, *Sir* John G.
AVERILL, H. C.
　Snow, Charles Horace
AVERY, Al
　Montgomery, Rutherford
　George
AVERY, June
　Rees, Joan
AVERY, Richard
　Cooper, Edmund
AVI
　Wortis, Avi
AVON, Margaret
　Keatley, Sheila
AWDRY, R. C.
　Charles, Richard
AYE, John
　Atkinson, John
AYES, Anthony
　Sambrot, William Anthony

AYRES, Paul
   Aarons, Edward Sidney

*'The case of the prisoner Leon
Trotsky—which', he said, giving
Sippy the eye again, 'I am strongly
inclined to think an assumed and
fictitious name—is more serious.'
—P. G. Wodehouse. Carry on,
Jeeves*

B. B.
   Watkins-Pitchford, Denys
     James
B. L.
   Pound, Ezra
B. L. T.
   Taylor, Bert Leston
BAB
   Gilbert, William Schwenck
BACHELOR OF ARTS, A
   Bentley, Phyllis
BACK-BACK
   Brown, Kay
BACON, J. D.
   Dodge, Josephine Daskam
BACON, Jeremy
   Read, James
BAGBY, George
   Stein, Aaron Marc
BAGBY, George A.
   Stein, Aaron Marc
BAGNOLD, Enid
   Jones, *Lady* Roderick
BAILEY, Guy
   Simpson, Keith

BAILEY, Hilea
   Marting, Ruth Lenore
BAILEY, Matilda
   Radford, Ruby Lorraine
BAILEY, Thomas
   Partridge, Bellamy
BAIRD, Maude F.
   Zimmer, Maude Files
BAKER, Asa
   Dresser, Davis
BALAAM
   Lamb, Geoffrey Frederick
BALBUS
   Huxley, Julian Sorell
BALDRY, Enid
   Citovich, Enid
BALDWIN, Bates
   Jennings, John Edward
BALDWIN, Faith
   Cuthrell, Faith Baldwin
BALL, Zachary
   Masters, Kelly
BALLARD, K. G.
   Roth, Holly
BALLARD, P. D.
   Ballard, Willis Todhunter
BALLARD, Todhunter
   Ballard, Willis Todhunter
BALLENTINE, John
   Da Cruz, Daniel
BALLEW, Charles
   Snow, Charles Horace
BALLINGER, W. A.
   Baker, William Howard
BALLINGER, W. A.
   Baker, William Howard *and*
     McNeilley, Wilfred

BALLINGER, W. A.
  McNeilly, Wilfred
BAMFYLDE, Walter
  Bevan, Tom
BANA, Dan
  White, Stanhope
BANCROFT, John
  Jenkins, Alan Charles
BANKOFF, George
  Milkomane, George Alexis
  Milkomanovich
BANNATYNE, Jack
  Gaston, William J.
BANNER, Angela
  Maddison, Angela Mary
BANNERMAN, Mark
  Lewing, Anthony
BANNON, Mark
  King, Albert
BANNON, Peter
  Durst, Paul
BANTON, Coy
  Norwood, Victor George
  Charles
BARAK, Michael
  Bar-Zohar, Michael
BARAKA, Imamu Amiri
  Jones, Le Roi
BARBELLION, W. N. P.
  Cummings, Bruce Frederick
BARBER, Antonia
  Anthony, Barbara
BARBETTE, Jay
  Spicer, Bart *and* Spicer, Betty
  Coe
BARCLAY, Alan
  Tait, George B.

BARCLAY, Ann
  Greig, Maysie
BARCYNSKA, Hélène *Countess*
  Evans, Marguerite Florence
BARDSLEY, Michael
  Nuttall, Anthony
BARKER, Jack
  Barker, Michael
BARLAY, Bennett
  Crossen, Kendell Foster
BARLING, Charles
  Barling, Muriel Vere
BARNARD, Nancy
  Hale, Sylvia
BARNETT, Adam
  Fast, Julius
BARNWELL, J. O.
  Caruso, Joseph
BARON, Paul
  Landells, Richard
BARON, Peter
  Clyde, Leonard Worswick
BARON, Willie
  Bryant, Baird
BARR, Cecil
  Kahane, Jack
BARR, Elisabeth
  Edward, Irene
BARRAS SEER
  Wyllie, James McLeod
BARRATT, Robert
  Beeton, D. R.
BARRIE, Hester
  Hector, Barbara
BARRIE, Jane
  Savage, Mildred
BARRIE, Jane
  Woodford, Irene-Cecile

BARRINGTON, E.
  Beck, Lily Adams
BARRINGTON, Maurice
  Brogan, Denis
BARRINGTON, P. V.
  Barling, Muriel Vere
BARRINGTON, Pamela
  Barling, Muriel Vere
BARROW, George
  Ruchlis, Hyman
BARRY
  Humphries, Barry
BARRY, Ann
  Byers, Amy
BARRY, Charles
  Bryson, Charles
BARRY, Eileen
  Walker, Emily Kathleen
BARRY, Jocelyn
  Bowden, Jean
BARRY, Joe
  Lake, Joe Barry
BARTIMEUS
  Ricci, Lewis Anselm da Costa
BARTLETT, Kathleen
  Paine, Lauran Bosworth
BARTLETT, Laura
  Baum, Lyman Frank
BARTON, Jack
  Chadwick, Joseph
BASSETT, Jack
  Rowland, Donald Sydney
BASSETT, John Keith
  Keating, Lawrence Alfred
BASUDEB, Sree
  Bhattacharya, Basudeb
BATCHELOR, Reg
  Paine, Lauran Bosworth

BATTLE, Felix
  Levin, Bernard
BAWN, Mary
  Wright, Mary
BAX, Roger
  Winterton, Paul
BAXTER, George Owen
  Faust, Frederick
BAXTER, Gillian
  Hirst, Gillian
BAXTER, Gregory
  Ressich, John S. M. *and* De
  Banzie, Eric
BAXTER, Hazel
  Rowland, Donald Sydney
BAXTER, John
  Hunt, E. Howard
BAXTER, Olive
  Eastwood, Helen B.
BAXTER, Shane V.
  Norwood, Victor George
  Charles
BAXTER, Valerie
  Meynell, Laurence Walter
BAYARD, Fred
  Campbell, Margaret *and*
  Jansen, Johanna
BAYER, Oliver Weld
  Bayer, Eleanor *and* Bayer, Leo
BAYLISS, Timothy
  Baybars, Taner
BAZAGANOV, M. S.
  Stoe, M.
BEA, Empy
  Babcock, Maurice P.
BEACHCOMBER
  Morton, J. B.

BEACHCOMBER
  Wyndham Lewis, D. B.
BEAR, Bullen
  Donnelly, Augustine
BEAR, I. D.
  Douglass, Percival Ian
BEATON, George
  Brenan, Edward Fitzgerald
BEATON, Jane
  Long, Gladys
BEATTY, Baden
  Casson, Frederick
BECK, Christopher
  Bridges, Thomas Charles
BECK, Harry
  Paine, Lauran Bosworth
BECKET, Lavinia
  Course, Pamela
BECKETT, Mark
  Truman, Marcus George
BECKWITH, Lillian
  Comber, Lillian
BEDFORD, A. N.
  Werner, Elsa Jane
BEDFORD, Annie North
  Werner, Elsa Jane
BEDFORD, Donald F.
  Bedford-Jones, Henry; Friede,
    Donald *and* Fearing, Kenneth
BEDFORD, Kenneth
  Paine, Lauran Bosworth
BEE
  Boshell, Gordon
BEECH, Margaret
  Barclay, Vera C.

BEEDING, Francis
  Saunders, Hilary Aidan St
    George *and* Palmer, John
    Leslie
BEG, Callum
  Mack, J. C. O.
BEG, Toram
  McKillop, Norman
BELL, Catherine
  Weir, Rosemary
BELL, Frank
  Wirt, Mildred
BELL, John
  Johnson, Victor
BELL, Josephine
  Ball, Doris Bell
BELL, Nancy
  Irish, Betty M.
BELL, Neil
  Southwold, Stephen
BELLAIRS, George
  Blundell, Harold
BELLMAN, Walter
  Barrett, Hugh Gilchrist
BELVEDERE, Lee
  Grayland, Valerie M.
BENARY-ISBERT, Margot
  Benary, Margot
BENDER, Jay
  Deindorfer, Robert G.
BENDIT, Gladys
  Presland, John
BENEDICT, Billy
  Paul, Maury
BENNETT, Dwight
  Newton, Dwight Bennett
BENNETT, H. O.
  Hardison, O. B.

BENNETT, Margaret
  Toohey, Barbara *and* Biermann,
  June
BENNEY, Mark
  Degras, Henry Ernest
BENSON, Adam
  Bingley, David Ernest
BENSON, S. Vere
  Taylor, Stephana Vere
BENSON, Thérèse
  Knipe, Emilie
BENTINCK, Ray
  Best, Rayleigh Breton Amis
BENTLEY, James
  Hanley, James
BENTLEY, W. J.
  Ullyett, Kenneth
BENTON, Karla
  Rowland, Donald Sydney
BENTON, Will
  Paine, Lauran Bosworth
BERESFORD, Russell
  Roberts, Cecil
BERG, Ila
  Garber, Nellia B.
BERGER, Helen
  Bamberger, Helen R.
BERKELEY, Anthony
  Cox, A. B.
BERKLEY, Tom
  Geen, Clifford
BERNARD, Robert
  Martin, Robert Bernard
BERNE, Leo
  Davies, Leslie Purnell
BERRINGTON, John
  Brownjohn, Alan

BERRISFORD, Judith
  Lewis, Clifford *and* Lewis,
  Judith Mary
BERRISFORD, Mary
  Lewis, Mary Christianna
BERRY, Erick
  Best, Allena
BERRY, Helen
  Rowland, Donald Sydney
BERTON, Guy
  La Coste, Guy R. *and*
  Bingham, E. A.
BERTRAM, Arthur
  Ibbott, Arthur Pearson
BETHUNE, Mary
  Clopet, Liliane M. C.
BETTERIDGE, Anne
  Potter, Margaret
BETTERIDGE, Don
  Newman, Bernard
BETTINA
  Ehrlich, Bettina
BEVAN, Alistair
  Roberts, Keith J. K.
BEVANS, Torre
  Hood, Torrey
BEVERLY, Linda
  Quentin, Dorothy
BEXAR, Phil
  Borg, Philip Anthony John
BEYNON, John
  Harris, John Wyndham Parkes
  Lucas Beynon
BICKERDYKE, John
  Cooke, C. H.
BIELY, Andrey
  Bugaev, Boris Nikolaevich

BIJ-BIJCHENKO, B.
  Rudnyckyj, Jaroslav B.
BILL
  Strachan, Gladys Elizabeth
BILLINGS, Buck
  Rister, Claude
BIRD, Brandon
  Evans, George *and* Evans, Kay
BIRD, Lilian
  Barradell-Smith, Walter
BIRD, Richard
  Barradell-Smith, Walter
BIRKENHEAD, Edward
  Birkenhead, Elijah
BIRKLEY, Dolan
  Hitchens, Dolores
BIRMINGHAM, George A.
  Hannay, James Owen
BISHOP, Morchard
  Stonor, Oliver
BIZET, George
  Bisset-Smith, G. T.
BLACK, Gavin
  Wynd, Oswald
BLACK, Ivory
  Janvier, Thomas Allibone
BLACK, Jack
  Ames, R. F.
BLACK, Jett
  Black, Oliver
BLACK, Kitty
  Black, Dorothy
BLACK, Lionel
  Barker, Dudley
BLACK, Mansell
  Dudley-Smith, Trevor
BLACK, Veronica
  Black, Maureen

BLACKBURN, John
  Mott, J. Moldon
BLACKBURN, Martin
  Allfree, P. S.
BLACKER, Hereth
  Chalke, Herbert
BLACKLIN, Malcolm
  Chambers, Aidan
BLACKSNAKE, George
  Richardson, Gladwell
BLACKSTOCK, Charity
  Torday, Ursula
BLACKSTOCK, Lee
  Torday, Ursula
BLACKWELL, John
  Collings, Edwin
BLAIKE, Avona
  Macintosh, Joan
BLAINE, Jeff
  Barrett, Geoffrey John
BLAINE, John
  Goodwin, Harold Leland *and*
    Harkins, Peter J.
BLAINE, Sara
  Morgan, Diana
BLAIR
  Blair-Fish, Wallace Wilfred
BLAIRMAN, Jacqueline
  Pinto, Jacqueline
BLAISDELL, Anne
  Linington, Elizabeth
BLAKE
  Adam, Ronald
BLAKE, Andrea
  Weale, Anne
BLAKE, Cameron
  Mason, Michael

BLAKE, Eleanor
  Pratt, E. B. Atkinson
BLAKE, Katherine
  Walter, Dorothy Blake
BLAKE, Kay
  Walter, Dorothy Blake
BLAKE, Monica
  Muir, Marie
BLAKE, Nicholas
  Day Lewis, Cecil
BLAKE, Robert
  Davies, Leslie Purnell
BLAKE, Vanessa
  Brown, May
BLAKE, William
  Blech, William James
BLAKE, William James
  Blech, William James
BLAND, Jennifer
  Bowden, Jean
BLAUTH, Christopher
  Blauth-Muszkowski, Peter
BLEECK, Oliver
  Thomas, Ross
BLEEKER, Sonia
  Zim, Sonia
BLINDERS, Belinda
  Coke, Desmond
BLINKHOALIE
  Allison, William
BLISS, Adam
  Burkhardt, Eve *and* Burkhardt,
    Robert Ferdinand
BLISS, Reginald
  Wells, H. G.
BLIXEN, Karen
  Blixen-Finecke, Karen
    Christence *Baroness*

BLOOD, Joan Wilde
  Murray, Joan
BLOOMFIELD, Robert
  Edgley, Leslie
BLUNDELL, Peter
  Butterworth, Frank Nestle
BLUTIG, Eduard
  Gorey, Edward St John
BLY, Nellie
  Seaman, Elizabeth C.
BLYTH, John
  Hibbs, John
BOAKE, Capel
  Kerr, Doris Boake
BOAS, Marie
  Hall, Marie
BOCCA, A. L.
  Winter, Bevis
BODEN, Hilda
  Bodenham, Hilda
BOGLE, Charles
  Dukenfield, William Claude
BOILEAU, Marie
  Hardy, Jane
BOLD, Ralph
  Griffiths, Charles
BOLDREWOOD, Rolf
  Browne, Thomas Alexander
BOLITHO, Ray D.
  Blair, Dorothy
BOLITHO, William
  Ryall, William Bolitho
BOLSTER, Evelyn
  Bolster, *Sister* M. Angela
BOLT, Ben
  Binns, Ottwell
BOLT, Lee
  Faust, Frederick

BOLTON, Isabel
  Miller, Mary Britton
BON GAULTIER
  Martin, *Sir* Theodore
BON VIVEUR
  Cradock, Phyllis Nan Sortain
  and Cradock, John
BOND, Gillian
  McEvoy, Marjorie
BONEHILL, Ralph
  Stratemeyer, Edward
BONETT, Emery
  Carter, Felicity Winifred
BONETT, John
  Coulson, John
BONNAMY, Francis
  Walz, Audrey
BONNER, Michael
  Glasscock, Anne Bonner
BONNER, Parker
  Ballard, Willis Todhunter
BONNEY, Bill
  Keevill, Henry John
BOON, August
  Breton-Smith, Clare
BORDEN, Leo
  Borden, Deal
BORER, Mary Cathcart
  Myers, Mary Cathcart
BORG, Jack
  Borg, Philip Anthony John
BORLAND, Hal
  Borland, Harold Glen
BORNE, D.
  Rice, Dorothy
BORODIN, George
  Milkomane, George Alexis
  Milkomanovich

BORTH, Willan G.
  Bosworth, Willan George
BOSCAWEN, Linda
  Smithells, Doreen
BOSCO, Jack
  Holliday, Joseph
BOSTON, Charles K.
  Gruber, Frank
BOSWELL, James
  Kent, Arthur
BOSWELL, John
  King, John
BOSWORTH, Frank
  Paine, Lauran Bosworth
BOUCHER, Anthony
  White, William Anthony P.
BOURCHIER, Jules
  Posner, David Louis
BOURNE, George
  Sturt, George
BOURNE, John
  John, Owen
BOURNE, Peter
  Jeffries, Bruce Graham
  Montague
BOVEE, Ruth
  Paine, Lauran Bosworth
BOWDEN, Jim
  Spence, William
BOWEN, Betty
  West, Betty Bowen
BOWEN, Marjorie
  Campbell, Gabrielle Margaret
  Vere
BOWER, B. M.
  Sinclair, Bertha Muzzy
BOWERS, *Mrs* J. Milton
  Bierce, Ambrose

130

BOWIE, Jim
 Norwood, Victor George
  Charles
BOWIE, Sam
 Ballard, Willis Todhunter
BOWMAN, Jeanne
 O'More, Peggy
BOWOOD, Richard
 Daniell, Albert Scott
BOWYER, Nina
 Conarain, Alice Nina
BOX, Edgar
 Vidal, Gore
BOY
 Fowkes, Aubrey
BOYD, Edward
 Tunley, Roul
BOYD, Frank
 Kane, Frank
BOYD, John
 Upchurch, Boyd
BOYD, Nancy
 Millay, Edna St Vincent
BOYD, Prudence
 Gibbs, Norah
BOYER, Robert
 Lake, Kenneth Robert
BRACE, Timothy
 Pratt, Theodore
BRACKEN, Steve
 Farris, John Lee
BRACKETT, Leigh
 Hamilton, Leigh Brackett
BRADBURNE, E. S.
 Lawrence, Elizabeth
BRADDON, George
 Milkomane, George Alexis
  Milkomanovich

BRADEN, Walter
 Finney, Jack
BRADFIELD, Nancy
 Sayer, Nancy Margetts
BRADFORD, De Witt
 Blossom, D. Bradford
BRADFORD, Will
 Paine, Lauran Bosworth
BRADLEY, Concho
 Paine, Lauran Bosworth
BRADLEY, Shelland
 Birt, Francis Bradley
BRADWELL, James
 Kent, Arthur
BRAHMS, Caryl
 Abrahams, Doris Caroline
BRAIN, Leonard
 Peck, Leonard
BRAMAH, Ernest
 Smith, Ernest Bramah
BRAMWELL, Charlotte
 Kimbro, John
BRAND, Christianna
 Lewis, Mary Christianna
BRAND, Clay
 Norwood, Victor George
  Charles
BRAND, David
 Nutt, David
BRAND, Max
 Faust, Frederick
BRAND, Mona
 Fox, Mona Alexis
BRANDANE, John
 Macintyre, John
BRANDON, Bruce
 Braun, Wilbur

BRANDON, Curt
  Bishop, Curtis Kent
BRANDON, Joe
  Davis, Robert Prunier
BRANDON, Sheila
  Rayner, Claire
BRANDT, Tom
  Dewey, Thomas Blanchard
BRANT, Lewis
  Rowland, Donald Sydney
BRAY, Alison
  Rowland, Donald Sydney
BRAYCE, William
  Rowland, Donald Sydney
BRECK, Vivian
  Breckenfeld, Vivian Gurney
BRENAN, Gerald
  Brenan, Edward Fitzgerald
BRENDA
  Castle Smith, *Mrs* G.
BRENNAN, Walt
  King, Albert
BRENNAN, Will
  Paine, Lauran Bosworth
BRENNING, L. H.
  Hunter, Alfred John
BRENT, *of Bin Bin*
  Franklin, Stella Maria Sarah
  Miles
BRENT, Calvin
  Hornby, John W.
BRENT, Catherine
  King, Albert
BRENT, Loring
  Worts, George F.
BRENT, Nigel
  Wimhurst, Cecil Gordon
  Eugene

BRENT, Romney
  Larralde, Romulo
BREOLA, Tjalmar
  De Jong, David Cornel
BRETT, John Michael
  Tripp, Miles Barton
BRETT, Martin
  Sanderson, Douglas
BRETT, Michael
  Brett, Leslie Frederick
BRETT, Rosalind
  Blair, Kathryn
BREWER, Mike
  Guinness, Maurice
BREWSTER, Benjamin
  Elting, Mary
BREWSTER, Franklin
  Folsom, Franklin Brewster
BREWSTER, Robin
  Staples, Reginald Thomas
BRIDE, Jack
  Marteau, F. A.
BRIDGE, Ann
  O'Malley, *Lady*
BRIDGE, John
  Peters, Robert Louis
BRIDGEMAN, Richard
  Davies, Leslie Purnell
BRIDGER, Adam
  Bingley, David Ernest
BRIDGES, Tom
  Bridges, Thomas Charles
BRIDGES, Victor
  De Freyne, George
BRIDGWATER, Donald
  Henderson, Donald Landels
BRIDIE, James
  Mavor, Osborne Henry

BRIEN, R. N.
  Whelan, Jerome Bernard
BRIEN, Raley
  McCulley, Johnston
BRIGGS, Philip
  Briggs, Phyllis
BRINSMEAD, H. F.
  Brinsmead, Hesba
BRIONY, Henry
  Ellis, Oliver
BRISTOWE, Edwin
  Wright, R. L. Gerrard
BRITT, Sappho Henderson
  Woolfolk, Josiah Pitts
BROCK, Gavin
  Lindsay, Maurice
BROCK, Lynn
  Macallister, Alister
BROCK, Stuart
  Trimble, Louis
BROCKLEY, Fenton
  Rowland, Donald Sydney
BRODIE, Gordon
  Smith, Sidney Wallace
BROGAN, James
  Hodder-Williams, Christopher
BRONSON, Lynn
  Lampman, Evelyn
BRONSON, Oliver
  Rowland, Donald Sydney
BRONSON, Wade
  King, Albert
BROOK, Barnaby
  Brooks, Collin
BROOK, Esther
  Huggett, Berthe
BROOK, Peter
  Chovil, Alfred Harold

BROOKE, Carol
  Ramskill, Valerie
BROOKER, Clark
  Fowler, Kenneth A.
BROOKS, Jonathan
  Mellett, John Calvin
BROOKS, W. A.
  Fryefield, Maurice P.
BROOKS, William Allan
  Fryefield, Maurice P.
BROOME, Adam
  James, Godfrey Warden
BROOME, Dora
  Wild, Dora Mary
BROTHER ANTONINUS
  Everson, William Oliver
BROTHER CHOLERIC
  Van Zeller, Claud H.
BROTHER FLAVIUS
  Ellison, James
BROTHER GRAHAM
  Jeffery, Graham
BROUILLETTE, Emil
  Rydberg, Ernie
BROUN, Emily
  Sterne, E. G.
BROWN, Carter
  Yates, Alan Geoffrey
BROWN, Douglas
  Gibson, Walter Brown
BROWN, Eve
  Nichols, Mary Eudora
BROWN, Jones
  Munby, Arthur Joseph
BROWN, Mandy
  Brown, May

BROWN, Marel
  Brown, Margaret Elizabeth
  Snow
BROWNE, Barum
  Dennis, Geoffrey Pomeroy
BROWNE, Courtney
  Courtney-Browne, Reginald
  D. S.
BROWNING, John
  Brown, John
BRUCE, Charles
  Francis, Arthur Bruce Charles
BRUCE, Leo
  Croft-Cooke, Rupert
BRUNSWICK, James
  Stitt, James M.
BRYAN, John
  Delves-Broughton, Josephine
BRYANS, Robin
  Bryans, Robert
BRYHER
  Ellerman, Annie Winifred
BRYHER, Winifred
  Ellerman, Annie Winifred
BRYSON, Leigh
  Rutledge, Nancy
BUCHANAN, Chuck
  Rowland, Donald Sydney
BUCHANAN, Patrick
  Corley, Edwin *and* Murphy,
  John
BUCKINGHAM, Bruce
  Lilley, Peter *and* Stansfield,
  Anthony
BUCKINGHAM, David
  Villiers, David Hugh
BUCKLEY, Eunice
  Scott, Rose Laure

BUCKMASTER, Henrietta
  Henkle, Henrietta
BUCKROSE, J. E.
  Jameson, Annie Edith
BUDD, Jackson
  Budd, William John
BULLEN BEAR
  Donnelly, Augustine
BULLINGHAM, Ann
  Jones, A. Miles
BURCHELL, Mary
  Cook, Ida
BURFIELD, Eva
  Ebbett, Eve
BURFORD, Eleanor
  Hibbert, Eleanor Alice
  Burford
BURGEON, G. A. L.
  Barfield, Arthur Owen
BURGER, John
  Marquand, Leopold
BURGESS, Anthony
  Wilson, John Anthony
  Burgess
BURGESS, Gelett
  Sturgis, Justin
BURGESS, Trevor
  Dudley-Smith, Trevor
BURKE, Edmund
  Boggs, Winifred
BURKE, Fielding
  Dargan, Olive
BURKE, Jonathan
  Burke, John Frederick
BURKE, Leda
  Garnett, David
BURKE, Noel
  Hitchens, Dolores

BURKE, Shifty
  Benton, Peggie
BURNABY, Nigel
  Ellett, Harold Pincton
BURNS, Bobby
  Burns, Vincent
BURNS, Elizabeth
  Behanna, Gertrude Florence
BURNS, Mary
  Hare, Walter B.
BURNS, Sheila
  Bloom, Ursula
BURNS, Tex
  L'Amour, Louis
BURR, Elsie
  Milligan, Elsie
BURROUGHS, Margaret
  Feldman, Eugene P. R.
BURROWAY, Janet
  Eysselinck, Janet Gay
BURTON, Conrad
  Edmundson, Joseph
BURTON, Thomas
  Longstreet, Stephen
BUTLER, Ivan
  Beuttler, Edward I. O.
BUTLER, Joan
  Alexander, Robert William
BUTLER, Richard
  Allbeury, Theo Edward le
    Bouthillier
BUTLER, Richard
  Butler, Arthur Ronald
BUTLER, Walter C.
  Faust, Frederick
BUTTLE, Myra
  Purcell, Victor W. W. S.

BYRNE, Donn
  Donn-Byrne, Brian Oswald
BYROM, James
  Bramwell, James Guy
BYSTANDER, A
  Smith, Goldwin

C. D.
  Lawrence, T. E.
C. J. G.
  Lawrence, T. E.
C. O.
  Collinson Owen, H.
CABBY WITH CAMERA
  Green, Maxwell
CABLE, Boyd
  Ewart, Ernest Andrew
CABOCHON, Francis
  Allan, Philip Bertram Murray

*A self-made man may prefer a
self-made name.
—Judge Learned Hand*

CADE, Alexander
  Methold, Kenneth
CADE, Robin
  Nicole, Christopher
CADWALLADER
  Clemens, Paul
CAGNEY, Peter
  Winter, Bevis
CAHILL, Mike
  Nolan, William F.
CAILLOU, Alan
  Lyle-Smythe, Alan

CAILLOUX, Pousse
  Bethell, Leonard Arthur
CAINE, Mark
  Maschler, Tom *and* Raphael,
    Frederic
CAL, Dakota
  Waldron, Corbin A.
CALDECOTT, Veronica
  Cohen, Victor
CALDWELL, Elinor
  Breton-Smith, Clare
CALEHAS
  Garvin, J. L.
CALEY, Rod
  Rowland, Donald Sydney
CALHOUN, Mary
  Wilkins, Mary Louise
CALIBAN
  Phillips, Hubert
CALIBAN
  Reid, John
CALLAHAN, John
  Chadwick, Joseph
CALLAS, Theo
  McCarthy, Shaun
CALLAWAY, Hugh
  Nisbet, Ulric
CALLENDER, Julian
  Lee, Austin
CALLISTHENES
  Costa, Gabriel
CALLUM, Michael
  Greaves, Michael
CALLUM BEG
  Mack, J. C. O.
CALVERT, John
  Leaf, Munro

CALVIN, Henry
  Hanley, Clifford
CALVIN, Kenneth
  Hogben, Lancelot Thomas
CAM
  Campbell, Barbara Mary
CAMBRIDGE, Elizabeth
  Hodges, Barbara K.
CAMDEN, Richard
  Beeston, L. J.
CAMERON, Brett
  Martin, Reginald Alec
CAMERON, D. Y.
  Cook, Dorothy Mary
CAMERON, Hector
  Macquarrie, Hector
CAMERON, Ian
  Payne, Donald Gordon
CAMERON, John
  Macdonell, A. G.
CAMERON, Margaret
  Lindsay, Kathleen
CAMPBELL, Berkeley
  Duddington, Charles Lionel
CAMPBELL, Bruce
  Epstein, Samuel
CAMPBELL, Colin
  Christie, Douglas
CAMPBELL, Duncan
  Thorpe, John
CAMPBELL, Hope
  Wallis, Geraldine
CAMPBELL, Judith
  Pares, Marion
CAMPBELL, Keith
  West-Watson, Keith Campbell
CAMPBELL, R. T.
  Todd, Ruthven Campbell

CAMPBELL, Scott
  Davis, Frederick William
CAMPBELL, Stuart
  Campbell, Sydney George
CAMPION, Sarah
  Alpers, Mary Rose
CANAWAY, Bill
  Canaway, W. H.
CANDIDUS
  Brogan, Colm
CANDY, Edward
  Neville, Alison
CANFIELD, Cleve
  Mitchell, Clare May
CANFIELD, Dorothy
  Fisher, Dorothea F. C.
CANIS
  Hubbard, Clifford Lionel Barry
CANNAN, Denis
  Pullein-Thompson, Dennis
CANNAN, Joanna
  Pullein-Thompson, Josephine
CANNELL, Charles
  Vivian, Evelyn C. H.
CANNON, Brenda
  Moore, Bertha B.
CANNON, Curt
  Hunter, Evan
CANNON, Elliott
  Elliott-Cannon, Arthur Elliott
CANTRELL, Wade B.
  Hogan, Robert Jasper
CANUCK, Abe
  Bingley, David Ernest
CANUSI, Jose
  Barker, S. Omar
CANYON, Claudia
  Anderson, Betty

CAPE, Judith
  Page, P. K.
CAPON, Peter
  Oakley, Eric Gilbert
CAPP, Al
  Caplin, Alfred Gerald
CAPSTAN
  Hardinge, Rex
CARDER, Michael
  Fluharty, Vernon L.
CAREW, Jean
  Corby, Jane
CAREW, Tim
  Carew, John Mohun
CAREY, Charles
  Waddel, Charles Carey
CAREY, James
  Carew-Slater, Harold James
CARFAX, Catherine
  Fairburn, Eleanor
CARGOE, Richard
  Payne, Pierre Stephen Robert
CARLETON, Janet
  Adam Smith, Janet Buchanan
CARLETON, S.
  Jones, Susan Carleton
CARLOTA
  Oppenheimer, Carlota
CARLTON, Ann
  Trent, Ann
CARLTON, Roger
  Rowland, Donald Sydney
CARLYLE, Anthony
  Milton, Gladys Alexandra
CARMAN, Dulce
  Drummond, Edith
CARMEN, Felix
  Sherman, Frank Dempster

CARMICHAEL, Harry
  Ognall, Leopold Horace
CARMICHAEL, Philip
  Harrison, Philip
CARNAC, Carol
  Rivett, Edith Caroline
CARNEGIE, Sacha
  Carnegie, Raymond Alexander
CAROL, Bill J.
  Knott, William Cecil
CARP, Augustus
  Bashford, *Sir* Henry Howarth
CARR, Basil
  Kahane, Jack
CARR, Catherine
  Wade, Rosalind
CARR, Charles
  Mason, Sydney Charles
CARR, Elaine
  Mason, Sydney Charles
CARR, Glyn
  Styles, Showell
CARR, H. D.
  Crowley, Edward Alexander
CARR, Philippa
  Hibbert, Eleanor Alice Burford
CARR, Roberta
  Roberts, Irene
CARREL, Mark
  Paine, Lauran Bosworth
CARRICK, Edward
  Craig, Edward Anthony
CARRICK, John
  Crosbie, Hugh Provan
CARRINGTON, Michael
  Williams, Meurig
CARRINGTON, V.
  Hughes, Valerie Anne

CARROLL, Martin
  Carr, Margaret
CARRUTH, Agnes K.
  Tucker, Agnes
CARSON, Anthony
  Brooke, Peter
CARSON, Lance
  Kelly, Harold Ernest
CARSTAIRS, Kathleen
  Jacobs, Thomas Curtis Hicks
CARSTAIRS, Rod
  Dalton, Gilbert
CARSTENS, Netta
  Laffeaty, Christina
CARTER, Ann
  Brooks, Ann
CARTER, Anne
  Brooks, Ann
CARTER, Bruce
  Hough, Richard Alexander
CARTER, Diana
  Copper, Dorothy
CARTER, John L.
  Carter, Compton Irving
CARTER, Nevada
  Paine, Lauran Bosworth
CARTER, Nick
  Avallone, Michael Angelo Jr
CARTER, Nick
  Carter, Bryan
CARTER, Phyllis Ann
  Eberle, Irmengarde
CARTLAND, Barbara
  McCorquodale, Barbara
    Hamilton
CARVER, Dave
  Bingley, David Ernest

CARY, Arthur
  Cary, Joyce
CARY, D. M.
  Macmillan, Douglas
CARYL, Jean
  Kaplan, Jean Caryl
CASAVINI, Pieralessandro
  Wainhouse, Austry
CASE, Justin
  Gleadow, Rupert
CASEY, Mart
  Casey, Michael T. *and* Casey,
    Rosemary
CASEY, T.
  Cordes, Theodor K.
CASSADY, Claude
  Paine, Lauran Bosworth
CASSANDRA
  Connor, *Sir* William
CASSELLS, John
  Duncan, William Murdoch
CASSILS, Peter
  Keele, Kenneth David
CASSIUS
  Foot, Michael
CASTLE, Douglas
  Brown, John Ridley
CASTLE, John
  Payne, Ronald Charles *and*
    Garrod, John William
CASTLEMON, Harry
  Fosdick, Charles Austin
CATALAN, Henri
  Dupuy-Mazuel, Henri
CATHODE RAY
  Scroggie, Marcus Graham
CATLIN, Ralph
  Lavender, David Sievert

CATO
  Foot, Michael; Howard, Peter
    and Owen, Frank
CATTO, Max
  Catto, Maxwell Jeffrey
CAUDWELL, Christopher
  Sprigg, Christopher St John
CAULDWELL, Frank
  King, Francis
CAUSEWAY, Jane
  Cork, Barry
CAVANNA, Betty
  Harrison, Elizabeth C.
CAVENDISH, Peter
  Horler, Sydney
CECIL, Edward
  Maiden, Cecil
CECIL, Henry
  Leon, Henry Cecil
CELTICUS
  Bevan, Aneurin
CENSOR
  Bunce, Oliver Bell
CENTAUR
  Thorpe, John
CERAM, C. W.
  Marek, Kurt W.
CHABER, M. E.
  Crossen, Kendell Foster
CHACE, Isobel
  Hunter, Elizabeth
CHAITANYA, Krishna
  Nair, K. K.
CHALLIS, George
  Faust, Frederick
CHALLIS, Simon
  Phillips, Dennis John Andrew

CHALMERS, Allen
  Upward, Edward Falaise
CHALLONER, H. K.
  Mills, Janet Melanie Ailsa
CHALON, Jon
  Chaloner, John Seymour
CHAMBERS, Dana
  Leffingwell, Albert
CHAMBERS, Peter
  Phillips, Dennis John Andrew
CHANAIDH, Fear
  Campbell, John Lorne
CHANCE, Jonathan
  Chance, John Newton
CHANCE, Stephen
  Turner, Philip
CHANCELLOR, John
  Rideaux, Charles
CHANDOS, Fay
  Swatridge, Irene M. M.
CHANEY
  Leeming, Jill
CHANNEL, A. R.
  Catherall, Arthur
CHAPMAN, Marison
  Chapman, Mary I. *and*
    Chapman, John Stanton
CHAPMAN, Walker
  Silverberg, Robert
CHARLES, Franklin
  Adams, Cleve Franklin
CHARLES, Frederick
  Ashford, F. C.
CHARLES, Nicholas
  Kuskin, Karla Seidman
CHARLES, Robert
  Smith, Robert Charles

CHARQUES, Dorothy
  Emms, Dorothy
CHARTERIS, Leslie
  Yin, Leslie Charles Bowyer
CHASE, Alice
  McHargue, Georgess
CHASE, Beatrice
  Parr, Olive Katherine
CHASE, James Hadley
  Raymond, Rene
CHASE, Lesley
  Verner, Christopher Stuart
CHATHAM, Larry
  Bingley, David Ernest
CHATTAN, Robert
  Smith, Robert
CHEETHAM, Hal
  Cheetham, James
CHEIRO
  Hamon, Louis *Count*
CHELTON, John
  Durst, Paul
CHERNICHEWSKI, Vladimir
  Duff, Charles
CHERRYHOLMES, Anne
  Price, Olive
CHERRYMAN, A. E.
  Levin, Bernard
CHESHAM, Henry
  Bingley, David Ernest
CHESHIRE, Giff
  Cheshire, Gifford Paul
CHESTER, Elizabeth
  Ransome, L. E.
CHESTER, Peter
  Phillips, Dennis John Andrew
CHESTOR, Rui
  Courtier, Sidney Hobson

CHILD, Alan
  Langner, Laurence
CHIPPERFIELD, Robert Orr
  Ostrander, Isabel Egerton
CHISHOLM, Matt
  Watts, Peter Christopher
CHRISTIAN, Frederick H.
  Nolan, Frederick
CHRISTIAN, Jill
  Dilcock, Noreen
CHRISTOPHER, John
  Youd, Samuel
CHRONIQUEUSE
  Logan, Olive
CHRYSTIE, Edward M.
  Watson, Jack Charles
  Wauchope
CHU FENG
  Blofeld, John
CHUB, Sergeant
  Abrahamson, Maurice Noel
CHURCH, Granville
  People, Granville Church
CHURCH, Jeffrey
  Kirk, Richard Edmund
CHURCHILL, Luanna
  Dughman, John Karl *and*
  Dughman, Frieda Mae
CIRCUMLIBRA
  Lockwood, Frank
CLADPOLE, Jim
  Richards, James
CLAIRE, Keith
  Andrews, Claire *and* Andrews,
  Keith
CLANDON, Henrietta
  Vahey, John George Haslette

CLAPP, Patricia
  Cone, P. C. L.
CLARE, Elizabeth
  Cook, Dorothy Mary
CLARE, Helen
  Blair, Pauline Hunter
CLARE, Marguerite
  Heppell, Mary
CLARK, Dale
  Kayser, Ronal
CLARK, Joan
  Wirt, Mildred
CLARK, Margery
  Clark, Mary Elizabeth *and*
  Quigley, M. C.
CLARK, Mary Lou
  Clark, Maria
CLARKE, John
  Laughlin, Virginia Carli
CLARKE, Merle
  Gessner, Lynne
CLARKE, Pauline
  Blair, Pauline Hunter
CLARKE, Richard
  Paine, Lauran Bosworth
CLARKE, Robert
  Paine, Lauran Bosworth
CLAUDE
  Forde, Claude Marie
CLAUGHTON-JAMES, James
  Bentley, James W. B.
CLAY, Bertha M.
  Braeme, Charlotte Monica
CLAY, Weston
  Ford, T. W.
CLAYMORE, Tod
  Clevely, Hugh Desmond
  Claymore

CLEAR, Claudius
  Nicoll, *Sir* William Robertson
CLEAVER, Denis
  Leyland, Eric
CLEMENT, Hal
  Stubbs, Harry Clement
CLEMENTIA
  Feehan, *Sister* Mary Edward
CLEMENTS, E. H.
  Hunter, Eileen
CLEMONS, Elizabeth
  Nowell, Elizabeth Cameron
CLEO ET ANTHONY
  Anthony, Edward
CLERGYMAN, A
  Morison, John
CLERIHEW, E.
  Bentley, Edmund Clerihew
CLEVE, Janita
  Rowland, Donald Sydney
CLEVEDON, John
  Plumley, Ernest F.
CLEVELAND, Jim
  King, Albert
CLEVELAND, John
  McElfresh, Adeline
CLIFFORD, Eth
  Rosenberg, Ethel
CLIFFORD, Francis
  Thompson, Arthur Leonard
  Bell
CLIFFORD, John
  Bayliss, John Clifford
CLIFFORD, Martin
  Hamilton, Charles Harold St
  John
CLINTON, Jeff
  Bickham, Jack Miles

CLIVE, Clifford
  Home-Gall, Edward Reginald
CLIVE, William
  Bassett, Ronald
CLOSE, Upton
  Hall, Josef Washington
CLOUD, Yvonne
  Kapp, Yvonne
CLYDE, Craig
  Gossman, Oliver
COBBLEIGH, Tom
  Raymond, Walter
COCHRAN, Jeff
  Durst, Paul
COCHRANE, Corinna
  Peterson, Corinna
COCKIN, Joan
  Burbridge, Edith Joan
CODY, A. R.
  Joscelyn, Archie Lynn
CODY, Al
  Joscelyn, Archie Lynn
CODY, C. S.
  Waller, Leslie
CODY, Stetson
  Gribble, Leonard Reginald
CODY, Stone
  Mount, Thomas Ernest
CODY, Walt
  Norwood, Victor George
  Charles
COE, Douglas
  Epstein, Beryl *and* Epstein,
  Samuel
COE, Tucker
  Westlake, Donald Edwin
COFFEY, Brian
  Koontz, Dean R.

COFFIN, Geoffrey
  Mason, F. Van Wyck
COIGNARD, John
  Barach, Alvan Leroy
COLAM, Lance
  Cooper, Gordon
COLBERE, Hope
  Coolbear, Marian H.
COLE, Ann Kilborn
  Callahan, Claire
COLE, Davis
  Elting, Mary
COLE, Jackson
  Scott, Leslie
COLE, Richard
  Barrett, Geoffrey John
COLE, Stephen
  Webbe, Gale Dudley
COLEMAN, Lonnie
  Coleman, William Lawrence
COLES, Manning
  Manning, Adelaide Frances Oke
  and Coles, Cyril Henry
COLLANS, Dev
  Winchell, Prentice
COLLIER, Douglas
  Fellowes-Gordon, Ian
COLLIER, Joy
  Millar, Minna
COLLIN, Rodney
  Collin Smith, Rodney
COLLINGS, Jillie
  Collings, I. J.
COLLINGSWOOD, Frederick
  Lakritz, Esther
COLLINS, D.
  Bulleid, H. A. V.

COLLINS, Geoffrey
  Jeffries, Greg
COLLINS, Hunt
  Hunter, Evan
COLLINS, Joan
  Collins, Mildred
COLLINS, Michael
  Lynds, Dennis
COLLINSON, Peter
  Hammett, Dashiell
COLLYER, Doric
  Fellows, Dorothy Alice
COLMAN, George
  Glassco, John
COLSON, Thora
  Orton, Thora
COLT, Clem
  Nye, Nelson Coral
COLT, Russ
  Kerr, D.
COLTMAN, Will
  Bingley, David Ernest
COLTON, A. J.
  Hook, Alfred Samuel
COLTON, Mel
  Braham, Hal
COLUMBINE
  Ferguson, Rachel
COLVER, Anne
  Harris, Polly Anne Colver
COMPERE, Mickie
  Davidson, Margaret
COMPTON, Frances Snow
  Adams, Henry
COMPTON, Guy
  Compton, D. G.
COMRADE, Robert W.
  Brooks, Edwy Searles

COMYNS, Barbara
  Carr, Barbara Irene Veronica
    Comyns
CONARAIN, Nina
  Conarain, Alice Nina
CONDON, Patricia
  Gooden, P. E.
CONDRAY, Bruno
  Humphrys, Leslie George
CONISTON, Ed
  Bingley, David Ernest
CONNELL, John
  Robertson, James Robin
CONNELL, Norreys
  O'Riordan, Conal O'Connell
CONNEY, Barbara
  Porter, Barbara Conney
CONNINGTON, J. J.
  Stewart, Alfred Walter
CONNOLLY, Paul
  Wicker, Tom
CONNOR, Ralph
  Gordon, Charles William
CONQUEST, Owen
  Hamilton, Charles Harold
    St John
CONRAD, Clive
  King, Frank
CONRAD, Jack
  Conrad, Isaac
CONRAD, Jessie
  Korzeniowski, Jessie
CONRAD, Joseph
  Korzeniowski, Teodor Józef
    Konrad
CONRAD, Kenneth
  Lottich, Kenneth

CONRAD, Paul
  King, Albert
CONROY, Jim
  Chadwick, Joseph
CONROY, Robert
  Goldston, Robert
CONSTANT READER
  Parker, Dorothy
CONTE, Charles
  Mackinnon, Charles Roy
CONWAY, Celine
  Blair, Kathryn
CONWAY, Hugh
  Fargus, Frederick John
CONWAY, Keith
  Hetherington, Keith James
CONWAY, Laura
  Ansle, Dorothy Phoebe
CONWAY, Olive
  Walton, John *and* Brighouse,
    Harold
CONWAY, Peter
  Gautier-Smith, Peter Claudius
CONWAY, Peter
  Milkomane, George Alexis
    Milkomanovich
CONWAY, Troy
  Avallone, Michael Angelo Jr
COO-EE
  Walker, W. Sylvester
COOK, John Estes
  Baum, Lyman Frank
COOK, Vera
  Ryder, Vera
COOK, Will
  Cook, William Everett
COOKE, M. E.
  Creasey, John

144

COOKE, Margaret
  Creasey, John
COOKRIDGE, E. H.
  Spiro, Edward H.
COOKRIDGE, John Michael
  Holroyd, Ethel Mary
COOLIDGE, Susan
  Woolsey, Sarah Chauncey
COOMBS, Murdo
  Davis, Frederick Clyde
COOPER, Charles
  Lock, Arnold Charles Cooper
COOPER, Craig
  King, Albert
COOPER, Henry St John
  Creasey, John
COOPER, William
  Hoff, Harry Summerfield
COPPLESTONE, Bennet
  Kitchin, F. H.
COQUINA
  Shields, George Oliver
CORAM, Christopher
  Walker, Peter Norman
CORBY, Dan
  Catherall, Arthur
CORD, Barry
  Germano, Peter
CORDELL, Alexander
  Graber, George Alexander
CORELLI, Marie
  Mackay, Minnie
CORENANDA, A. L. A.
  Numano, Allen
CORIOLANUS
  McMillan, James
CORLETT, Joyce I.
  Kirkwood, Joyce

CORNERS, George F.
  Viereck, George Sylvester
CORNO DI BASSETTO
  Shaw, George Bernard
CORNWALL, Nellie
  Sloggett, Nellie
CORONET
  James, Charles
CORREY, Lee
  Stine, George Harry
CORRIGAN, Mark
  Lee, Norman
CORSON, Geoffrey
  Sholl, Anna McClure
CORTEEN, Craig
  Norwood, Victor George
    Charles
CORTEEN, Wes
  Norwood, Victor George
    Charles
CORVO, *Baron*
  Rolfe, Frederick
CORY, Caroline
  Freeman, Kathleen
CORY, Desmond
  McCarthy, Shaun
COST, March
  Morrison, Margaret Mackie
COSTLER, *Dr* A.
  Koestler, Arthur
COSTS
  Booth, John Bennion
COTTERELL, Brian
  Dingle, Aylward Edward
COULSDON, John
  Hincks, Cyril Malcolm
COURAGE, John
  Goyne, Richard

COURT, Sharon
  Rowland, Donald Sydney
COURTLAND, Roberta
  Dern, Erolie Pearl
COURTNEY, Christine
  Westmarland, Ethel Louisa
COURTNEY, John
  Cournos, John
COUSIN VIRGINIA
  Johnson, Virginia Wales
COVENANTER
  Zilliacus, Konni
COVENTRY, John
  Palmer, John Williamson
COVERACK, Gilbert
  Warren, John Russell
COWAN, Alan
  Gilchrist, Alan
COWEN, Frances
  Minto, Frances
COWPER, Richard
  Murray, John Middleton Jr
COX, Edith
  Goaman, Muriel
COX, Jack
  Cox, John
COX, Lewis
  Cox, Euphrasia Emeline
COXE, Kathleen Buddington
  Long, Amelia R. *and* McHugh,
  Edna
COX-JOHNSON, Ann
  Saunders, Ann Loreille
COYSH, Edward
  Stuart-Jervis, Charles Edward
CRAD, Joseph
  Ansell, Edward Clarence
  Trelawney

CRADDOCK, Charles Egbert
  Murfee, Mary Noailles
CRADOCK, Fanny
  Cradock, Phyllis Nan Sortain
CRAIG, A. A.
  Anderson, Poul
CRAIG, Alison
  Nicholson, Joan
CRAIG, David
  Tucker, James
CRAIG, Denys
  Stoll, Dennis Gray
CRAIG, Georgia
  Gaddis, Peggy
CRAIG, Jennifer
  Brambleby, Ailsa
CRAIG, Jonathan
  Smith, Frank E.
CRAIG, John Eland
  Chipperfield, Joseph E
CRAIG, Lee
  Sands, Leo G.
CRAIG, Peter
  MacClure, Victor
CRAIG, Vera
  Rowland, Donald Sydney
CRAIGIE, David
  Craigie, Dorothy M.
CRAILE, Wesley
  Rowland, Donald Sydney
CRANE, Henry
  Douglass, Percival Ian
CRANE, Robert
  Robertson, Frank Chester
CRANSTON, Edward
  Fairchild, William
CRAVEN HILL
  Parsons, Charles P.

CRAWFORD, Anthony
  Hugill, John Anthony Crawford
CRAWFORD, Robert
  Rae, Hugh Cranford
CRECY, Jeanne
  Creasey, Jeanne
CREEDI, Joel
  King, Albert
CREEK, Nathan
  Sheppard, John Hamilton
  George
CRESCENDO
  Kalisch, A.
CRESSY, Edward
  Creasey, Clarence Hamilton
CRESTON, Dormer
  Baynes, Dorothy Julia
CREYTON, Paul
  Trowbridge, John Townsend
CRIBLECOBLIS, Otis
  Dukenfield, William Claude
CRISPIE
  Crisp, S. E.
CRISPIN, Edmund
  Montgomery, Robert Bruce
CRISTY, R. J.
  De Cristoforo, R. J.
CRITIC
  Martin, Kingsley
CROFT, Sutton
  Lunn, *Sir* Arnold
— CROFT, Taylor
  Croft-Cooke, Rupert
CROMARTY, Deas
  Watson, R. A.
CROMIE, Stanley
  Simmons, J. S. A.

CROMPTON, John
  Lamburn, John Battersby
  Crompton
CROMPTON, Richmal
  Lamburn, Richmal Crompton
CROMWELL, Elsie
  Sheridan, Elsie Lee
CRONHEIM, F. G.
  Godfrey, Frederick M.
CRONIN, Michael
  Cronin, Brendan Leo
CROSBIE, Elizabeth
  Ewer, Monica
CROSBIE, Provan
  Crosbie, Hugh Provan
CROSBY, Lee
  Torrey, Ware
CROSS, Amanda
  Heilbrun, Carolyn
CROSS, Brenda
  Colloms, Brenda
CROSS, James
  Parry, Hugh J.
CROSS, Mark
  Pechey, Archibald Thomas
CROSS, Nancy
  Baker, Anne
CROSS, T. T.
  Da Cruz, Daniel
CROSSE, Elaine
  Trent, Ann
CROSSE, Victoria
  Griffin, Vivian Cory
CROWE, John
  Lynds, Dennis
CROWLEY, Aleister
  Crowley, Edward Alexander

CRUMPET, Peter
  Buckley, Fergus Reid
CRUNDEN, Reginald
  Cleaver, Hylton Reginald
CULEX
  Stanier, Maida
CULLINGFORD, Guy
  Taylor, Constance Lindsay
CULLNER, Lenard
  Mazure, Alfred Leonardus
CULOTTA, Nino
  O'Grady, John P.
CULPEPER, Martin
  Pullen, George
CUMBERLAND, Gerald
  Kenyon, Fred
CUMBERLAND, Roy
  Mégroz, R. L.
CUNNINGHAM, E. V.
  Fast, Howard
CUNNINGHAM, Mary
  Pierce, Mary Cunningham
CUNNINGHAM, Ray
  Arthur, Frances Browne
CURLING, Audrey
  Clark, Marie Catherine Audrey
CURRIER, Jay L
  Henderson, James Leal
CURRY, Avon
  Bowden, Jean
CURTAYNE, Alice
  Rynne, Alice
CURTIN, Philip
  Lowndes, Marie Adelaide
    Belloc
CURTIS, Peter
  Lofts, Norah

CURTIS, Spencer
  Nuttall, Anthony
CURTIS, Tom
  Jacobs, Thomas Curtis Hicks
CURZON, Sam
  Krasney, Samuel A.
CURZON, Virginia
  Hawton, Hector
CUSTER, Clint
  Paine, Lauran Bosworth
CYMRY BACH
  Wood, Lilian Catherine
CYNICUS
  Anderson, Martin

D. M. S.
  Stuart, Dorothy Margaret
DAEDALUS
  Cordes, Theodor K.
DAGONET
  Sims, George Robert
DAGONET, Edward
  Williamson, Thames Ross
DAIMLER, Harriet
  Owens, Iris
DAINTON, Courtney
  Dainton, William
DALE, Edwin
  Home-Gall, Edward Reginald
DALE, Frances
  Cradock, Phyllis Nan Sortain
DALE, Jack
  Holliday, Joseph
DALE, Maxine
  Covert, Alice Lent
DALE, Norman
  Denny, Norman George

DALEY, Bill
  Appleman, John Alan
DALHEATH
  Magrill, David S.
DALL, Ian
  Higgins, Charles
DALLAS, John
  Duncan, William Murdoch
DALLAS, Steve
  King, Albert
D'ALLENGER, Hugh
  Kershaw, John H. D.
DALTON, Clive
  Clark, Frederick Stephen
DALTON, Priscilla
  Avallone, Michael Angelo Jr
D'AMBROSIO, Raymond
  Brosia, D. M.
DAMIANO, Laila
  Rosenkrantz, Linda
DAN BANA
  White, Stanhope
DANA, Amber
  Paine, Lauran Bosworth
DANA, Richard
  Paine, Lauran Bosworth
DANA, Rose
  Ross, William Edward Daniel
DANBY, Frank
  Frankau, Julia Davis
DANE, Clemence
  Ashton, Winifred
DANE, Joel Y.
  Delany, Joseph Francis
DANE, Mark
  Avallone, Michael Angelo Jr
DANE, Mary
  Morland, Nigel

DANFORTH, Paul M.
  Allen, John E.
DANGERFIELD, Clint
  Norwood, Victor George
  Charles
DANGERFIELD, Harlan
  Padgett, Ron
DANGLE
  Thompson, A. M.
DANIEL, S.
  Zalberg, Daniel
DANIELL, David Scott
  Daniell, Albert Scott
DANIELS, John S.
  Overholser, Wayne D.
DANNING, Melrod
  Gluck, Sinclair
DANVERS, Jack
  Casseleyr, Camille
DANVERS, Peter
  Henderson, James Maddock
DARBY, Catherine
  Black, Maureen
DARBY, Emma
  Stubbs, Jean
DARBY, J. N.
  Govan, Mary Christine
DARBYSHIRE, Shirley
  Meynell, Shirley Ruth
DARDI
  Singh, Gopal
DARE, Alan
  Goodchild, George
DARE, Michael
  Wordingham, James A.
DARE, Simon
  Huxtable, Marjorie

D'ARFEY, William
  Plomer, William
DARLING, V. H.
  Dryhurst, Michael John
DARLINGTON, Con
  Best, Carol Anne
DATALLER, Roger
  Eaglestone, Arthur Archibald
DAVEY, Jocelyn
  Raphael, Chaim
DAVID, Jay
  Adler, Bill
DAVIDSON, Mickie
  Davidson, Margaret
DAVIES, Louise
  Golding, Louise
DAVIES, Lucian
  Beeston, L. J.
DAVIOT, Gordon
  Mackintosh, Elizabeth
DAVIS, Audrey
  Paine, Lauran Bosworth
DAVIS, Don
  Dresser, Davis
DAVIS, Foxcroft
  Seawell, Molly Elliot
DAVIS, Gordon
  Hunt, E. Howard
DAVIS, Julia
  Marsh, John
DAVIS, Rosemary L.
  Davis, Lily May *and* Davis,
    Rosemary
DAVIS, Stratford
  Bolton, Miriam
DAVISON, Lawrence H.
  Lawrence, D. H.

DAWLISH, Peter
  Kerr, James Lennox
DAWSON, Jane
  Critchlow, Dorothy
DAWSON, Michael
  Boyle, John Howard Jackson
DAWSON, Oliver
  Coxall, Jack Arthur
DAWSON, Peter
  Faust, Frederick
DAWSON, Peter
  Glidden, Jonathan H.
DAX, Anthony
  Hunter, Alfred John
DAY, Adrian
  Harvey, Peter Noel
DAY, Harvey
  Cleary, C. V. H.
DAY, Irene
  Orme, Eve
DAY, Lionel
  Black, Ladbroke Lionel Day
DAYLE, Malcolm
  Hincks, Cyril Malcolm
DE BEKKER, Jay
  Winchell, Prentice
DE CASTRO, Lyne
  Lyne, Charles
DE COSQUEVILLE, Pierre
  Stacey, P. M. de Cosqueville
DE CULWEN, Dorothea
  Hines, Dorothea
DE FACCI, Liane
  De Bellet, Liane
DE HART, Robert
  Hanzelon, Robert M.
DE LA TORRE, Lillian
  McCue, Lillian Bueno

DE LACY, Louise
Hickey, Madelyn E.
DE LAS LUNAS, Carmencita
Trocchi, Alexander
DE LAUBE
Cardena, Clement
DE LIMA, Sigrid
Greene, Sigrid
DE MORNY, Peter
Wynne-Tyson, Esme
DE PRE, Jean-Anne
Avallone, Michael Angelo Jr
DE SALIGNAC, Charles
Hasson, James
DE VERE, Jane
Watson, Julia
DE WITT, James
Lewis, Mildred
DE WOHL, Louis
Wohl, Ludwig von
DEACON, Richard
McCormick, George
DEAN, Dudley
McGaughy, Dudley Dean
DEAN, Gregory
Posner, Jacob D.
DEAN, Lyn
Garret, Winifred Selina
DEAN, Spencer
Winchell, Prentice
DEANE, Norman
Creasey, John
DEBRETT, Hal
Dresser, Davis *and* Rollins,
Kathleen
DEE, John
Tullett, Denis John

DEHAN, Richard
Graves, Clotilda Inez Mary
DEKKER, Carl
Laffin, John
DELAFIELD, E. M.
De la Pasture, Edmée E. M.
DELANEY, Denis
Green, Peter
DELANO, Al
Livingston, A. D.
DELL, Belinda
Bowden, Jane
DELMONICO, Andrea
Morrison, Eula A.
DELTA
Hazlewood, Rex
DELVING, Michael
Williams, Jay
DEMAINE, C. F.
Trumbo, Dalton
DEMAREST, Anne
Bond, Florence D. F.
DEMAREST, Doug
Barker, Will
DEMARIS, Ovid
Desmarais, Ovide E.
DEMBRY, R. Emmet
Murfree, Mary Noailles
DEMIJOHN, Thom
Disch, Thomas M. *and* Sladek,
John Thomas
DEMPSTER, Guy
Heming, Dempster E.
DENBIE, Roger
Brodie, Julian Paul *and* Green,
Alan Baer
DENDER, Jay
Deindorfer, Robert G.

151

DENHAM, Peter
  Jones, P. D.
DENNING, Patricia
  Willis, Corinne
DENNIS, Eve
  Wornum, Miriam
DENNIS, Patrick
  Tanner, Edward Everett
DENNISON, Dorothy
  Golden, Dorothy
DENOVAN, Saunders
  Harvey, William
DENVER, Boone
  Rennie, James Alan
DENVER, Drake C.
  Nye, Nelson Coral
DENVER, Lee
  Gribble, Leonard Reginald
DERBY, Mark
  Wilcox, Harry
DERMOTT, Stephen
  Bradbury, Parnell
DERN, Peggy
  Dern, Erolie Pearl
DERVENTIO
  Hughes, Walter Dudley
DESANA, Dorothy
  Trent, Ann
DESPARD, Leslie
  Howitt, John Leslie Despard
DESTRY, Vince
  Norwood, Victor George
    Charles
DEVEREUX, Roy
  Pember-Devereux, Margaret
    R. R.
DEVON, Sara
  Walker, Emily Kathleen

DEWDNEY, Peter
  Brock, Alan St Hill
DEWES, Simon
  Muriel, John
DEXTER, John
  Coleman, John
DEXTER, Martin
  Faust, Frederick
DEXTER, Ross
  Reynolds, John E.
DEXTER, William
  Pritchard, William Thomas
DICANT, V. L.
  Hewetson, Sara
DICK, Alexandra
  Dick-Erikson, Cicely Sibyl
    Alexandra
DICK, R. A.
  Leslie, Josephine A. C.
DICK, T.
  Osler, Eric Richard
DICKENS, Irene
  Copper, Dorothy
DICKINSON, Margaret
  Muggeson, Margaret
DICKSON, Carr
  Carr, John Dickson
DICKSON, Carter
  Carr, John Dickson
DICKSON, Frank C.
  Danson, Frank Corse
DIETRICH, Robert
  Hunt, E. Howard
DIGGES, Jeremiah
  Berger, Josef
DILL, Walter
  Thomas, Walter Dill Jr

DIMSDALE, C. D.
  Mégroz, R. L.
DINESEN, Isak
  Blixen-Finecke, Karen
  Christence *Baroness*
DINGWALL, Peter
  Forsythe, Robin
DIPLOMAT
  Carter, John Franklin
DIPLOMATICUS
  Zilliacus, Konni
DITTON,James
  Clark, Douglas
DIVINE, David
  Divine, Arthur Durham
D'IVRY, Ursula
  Russell, Ursula d'Ivry
DIX, Dorothy
  Gilmer, Elizabeth Meriwether
DIXON, Lesley
  Vernon, Kathleen Rose
DIXON, Rex
  Martin, Reginald Alec
DIXON, Rosie
  Wood, Christopher
DIXON, Ruth
  Barrows, Marjorie
DOAN, Reece
  King, Albert
DOCHERTY, James L.
  Raymond, Rene
DR A.
  Asimov, Isaac
DR SEUSS
  Geisel, Theodor Seuss
DR SOFT
  Sward, Robert S.

DODGE, Langdon
  Wolfson, Victor
DODGE, Steve
  Becker, Stephen David
DOE, John
  Thayer, Tiffany Ellsworth
DOGBERRY
  Phillips, Hubert
DOGBOLD, Barnaby
  Silvette, Herbert
DOLBERG, Alexander
  Burg, David
DOLLEY, Marcus J.
  Watney, Bernard
DOMINI, Rey
  Lorde, Andre Geraldin
DOMINIC, *Sister* Mary
  Parker, Marion
DOMINIC, R. B.
  Latis, Mary J. *and* Hennissart,
    Martha
DOMPO, Kwesi
  Parkes, Frank
DONALD, Vivian
  Mackinnon, Charles Roy
DONALDS, Gordon
  Shirreffs, Gordon D.
DONAVAN, John
  Morland, Nigel
DONNE, Jack
  Bloom, Jack Don
DONNE, Maxim
  Duke, Madelaine
DONOVAN, Dick
  Muddock, Joyce Emerson
DOOLEY, Martin
  Dunne, Finley Peter

DORMAN, Luke
  Bingley, David Ernest
DOUBLEDAY, Roman
  Long, Lily Augusta
DOUGLAS, Albert
  Armstrong, Douglas
DOUGLAS, D.
  Wilkes-Hunter, Richard
DOUGLAS, Ellen
  Williamson, Ellen Douglas
DOUGLAS, George
  Brown, George Douglas
DOUGLAS, George
  Fisher, Douglas George
DOUGLAS, Malcolm
  Sanderson, Douglas
DOUGLAS, Nathan
  Young, Nedrick
DOUGLAS, Noel
  Chetham-Strode, Warren
DOUGLAS, O.
  Buchan, Anna
DOUGLAS, Shane
  Wilkes-Hunter, Richard
DOWER, Penn
  Jacobs, Thomas Curtis Hicks
DOWLEY, D. M.
  Marrison, Leslie William
DOWNES, Quentin
  Harrison, Michael
DOWNING, Century
  Palmer, Paul
DOWNMAN, Francis
  Oldmeadow, Ernest James
DOYLE, Emmett
  Trumbo, Dalton
DOYLE, John
  Graves, Robert

DOYLE, Lynn
  Montgomery, Leslie Alexander
DRACO, F.
  David, Julia
DRAKE, Hamilton
  Hoffenberg, Mason
DRAKE, Joan
  Davies, Joan Howard
DRAX, Peter
  Addis, E. E.
DREWERY, Mary
  Smith, Mary
DREXLER, J. F.
  Paine, Lauran Bosworth
DRINAN, Adam
  Macleod, Joseph Todd Gordon
DRISCOLL, Eli
  King, Albert
DRUG, Victor
  Moretti, Ugo
DRUMMOND, Anthony
  Hunter, Alfred John
DRUMMOND, Ivor
  Longrigg, Roger Erskine
DRUMMOND, John
  Chance, John Newton
DRUMMOND, Violet Hilda
  Swetenham, Violet Hilda
DRUMMOND, Walter
  Silverberg, Robert
DRURY, C. M.
  Abrahall, Clare Hoskyns
DRURY, Clare
  Abrahall, Clare Hoskyns
DRYDEN, John
  Rowland, Donald Sydney
DRYDEN, Keith
  Landells, Richard

DU BOIS, M.
Kent, Arthur
DU VAUL, Virginia
Coffman, Virginia
DUCHESNE, Antoinette
Paine, Lauran Bosworth
DUDLEY, Frank
Greene, Ward
DUDLEY, Nancy
Cole, Lois Dwight
DUELL, Eileen-Marie
Petrie, Rhona
DUFFER, Allan
May, John
DUFFIELD, Anne
Duffield, Dorothy Dean
DUKE, Margaret
Dunk, Margaret
DUNCAN, A. H.
Cleary, C. V. H.
DUNCAN, Alex
Duke, Madelaine
DUNCAN, Gregory
McClintock, Marshall
DUNCAN, Jane
Cameron, Elizabeth Jane
DUNNE, Desmond
Lee-Richardson, James
DUPLEX
Bradley, Ian *and* Hollows,
Norman F.
DUPONT, Paul
Frewin, Leslie Ronald
DURACK, Mary
Miller, Mary
DURHAM, John
Paine, Lauran Bosworth

DURIE, Lynn
Christie, Douglas
DURRANT, Theo
Mystery Writers of America
Inc; California Chapter
DYKES, Jack
Owen, Jack
DYLAN, Bob
Zimmerman, Robert Allen
DYMOKE, Juliet
De Schanschieff, Juliet
Dymoke

E. H.
Hiscock, Eric
E. H. A.
Aitken, E. H.
E. V. L.
Lucas, E. V.
EAGLE, Solomon
Squire, *Sir* John Collings
EAGLESFIELD, Francis
Guirdham, Arthur
EARLE, Olive L.
Daughtrey, Olive Lydia
EARP, Virgil
Keevill, Henry John
EAST, Michael
West, Morris
EAST, Roger
Burford, Roger d'Este
EASTAWAY, Edward
Thomas, Edward
EASTERTIDE
Blagbrough, Harriet
EASTLUND, Madelyn
Hickey, Madelyn E.

155

EDEN, Matthew
  Newnham, Don
EDEN, Bob
  Burkhardt, Eve *and* Burkhardt,
  Robert Ferdinand
EDGAR, Icarus Walter
  Bishop, Stanley
EDGAR, Josephine
  Mussi, Mary
EDMONDS, Charles
  Carrington, Charles
EDWARD, Stephen
  Palestrant, Simon
EDWARDS, Charman
  Edwards, Frederick Anthony
EDWARDS, Ellen
  Horkan, Nelle Irwin
EDWARDS, F. E.
  Nolan, William F.
EDWARDS, James G.
  Macqueen, James William
EDWARDS, June
  Bhatia, June
EDWARDS, Laurence
  Edwards, Florence
EDWARDS, Leonard
  Wild, Reginald
EDWARDS, Olwen
  Owen, Dilys
EDWARDS, Samuel
  Gerson, Noel Bertram
EFF, B.
  Carney, Jack
EGAN, Lesley
  Linington, Elizabeth
EGERTON, Denise
  Duggan, Denise Valerie

EGERTON, George
  Bright, Mary C.
EGLINTON, John
  Magee, William Kirkpatrick
EGOMET
  Fowler, Henry Watson
ELAND, Charles
  Rimanoczy, A.
ELDERSHAW, M. Barnard
  Barnard, Marjorie Faith *and*
  Eldershaw, Flora Sydney
ELGIN, Mary
  Stewart, Dorothy Mary
ELIOT, Alice C.
  Jewett, Sarah Orne
ELIOT, Anne
  Cole, Lois Dwight
ELIOTT, E. C.
  Martin, Reginald Alec
ELISABETH
  Quigley, Elizabeth Pauline
ELIZABETH
  Rose, Elizabeth Jane
ELIZABETH
  Russell, Elizabeth Mary
  Countess
ELIZABETH, Anne
  Fleur, Anne Elizabeth
ELLIOTT, Charles
  Ewart-Biggs, Christopher
ELLIOTT, Ellen
  Westmarland, Ethel Louisa
ELLISON, Marjorie
  Norton, Marjorie
ELLSWORTH, Elmer
  Thayer, Tiffany Ellsworth
ELLSWORTH, Paul
  Triem, Paul Ellsworth

ELPHINSTONE, Francis
  Powell-Smith, Vincent
ELRON
  Hubbard, L. Ron
ELSEY, J. J.
  Herron, Elsie Ellerington
ELSNA, Hebe
  Ansle, Dorothy Phoebe
ELTON, John
  Marsh, John
ELWART, Joan Potter
  Elwart, Joan Frances
ELY, David
  Lilienthal, David Jr
ELYSIAN, Anne
  Westmoreland, Vera Gertrude
EMSLEY, Clare
  Plummer, Clare
ENGLAND, Edith M.
  Anders, Edith Mary
ENGLAND, Jane
  Jervis, Vera Murdock Stuart
ENGLAND, Norman
  Webb, Godfrey E. C.
ENGLISH, Brenda H.
  Riddolls, Brenda H.
ENQUIRING LAYMAN
  Grierson, Walter
ENRIGHT, Elizabeth
  Gillham, Elizabeth Wright
    Enright
EPHESIAN
  Bechoffer Roberts, C. E.
ERIC, Kenneth
  Henley, Art
ERICSON, Sybil
  Dick-Erikson, Cicely Sybil
    Alexandra

ERICSON, Walter
  Fast, Howard
ERIKSON, Charlotte
  Dick-Erikson, Cicely Sybil
    Alexandra
ERIMUS
  Fall, William E.
ERMINE, Will
  Drago, Harry Sinclair

*'My own Ernest! I felt from the
start that you could have no other
name.'*
*—Oscar Wilde. The Importance
of being Ernest*

ERNEST, Paul
  Focke, E. P. W.
ERSKINE, John T.
  Tuck, John Erskine
ERSKINE, Margaret
  Williams, Margaret Wetherby
ERSKINE, Rosalind
  Longrigg, Roger Erskine
ERSKINE-GRAY
  Cordes, Theodor K.
ESDAILE, David
  Walker, David Esdaile
ESMOND, Harriet
  Burk, John Frederick
ESSE, James
  Stephens, James
ESSEX, Frank
  Simmonds, Michael Charles
ESSEX, Jon
  Watford, Joel

157

ESSEX, Mary
  Bloom, Ursula
ESSEX, Richard
  Starr, Richard
ESTERBROOK, Tom
  Hubbard, L. Ron
ESTEVEN, John
  Shellabarger, Samuel
ESTORIL, Jean
  Allan, Mabel Esther
ETIENNE
  King-Hall, Stephen
ETON, Robert
  Meynell, Laurence Walter
EUPHAN
  Todd, Barbara Euphan
EUSTACE, Robert
  Rawlins, Eustace
EVAN, Evin
  Faust, Frederick
EVAN, Paul
  Lehman, Paul Evan
EVANS, Alan
  Stoker, Alan
EVANS, Cherry
  Drummond, Cherry
EVANS, Evan
  Faust, Frederick
EVANS, Harris
  Evans, George *and* Evans, Kay
EVANS, John
  Brown, Howard
EVANS, Margiad
  Williams, Peggy Eileen
    Arabella
EVANS, Morgan
  Davies, Leslie Purnell

EVERARD, Henry
  Smith, H. Everard
EVERETT, Wade
  Cook, William Everett
EVERMAY, March
  Eiker, Mathilde
EVERTON, Francis
  Stokes, Francis William
EVOE
  Knox, E. V.
EYRE, Annette
  Worboys, Anne Eyre

F. P. A.
  Adams, Franklin Pierce
FABIAN, Ruth
  Quigley, Aileen
FABIAN, Warner
  Adams, Samuel Hopkins
FABRIZIUS, Peter
  Fabry, Joseph B.
FAGYAS, Maria
  Bush-Fekete, Marie Ilona
FAID, Mary
  Dunn, Mary
FAIR, A. A.
  Gardner, Erle Stanley
FAIRBURN, Ann
  Tait, Dorothy
FAIRLESS, Michael
  Barber, Margaret Fairless
FAIRWAY, Sidney
  Daukes, Sidney Herbert
FALK, Elsa
  Escherlich, Elsa Antonie
FALL, Thomas
  Snow, Donald Clifford

FALLON, George
  Bingley, David Ernest
FALLON, Martin
  Patterson, Henry
FANE, Violet
  Currie, *Lady*
FANSHAWE, Caroline
  Cust, Barbara Kate
FARELY, Alison
  Poland, Dorothy E. H.
FAREWELL, Nina
  Klein, Grace *and* Cooper, Mae
    Klein
FARGO, Doone
  Norwood, Victor George
    Charles
FARLEY, Ralph Milne
  Hoar, Roger Sherman
FARMER, Wendell
  Davis, Lavinia
FARQUHARSON, Martha
  Finley, Martha
FARR, C.
  Wilkes-Hunter, Richard
FARR, John
  Webb, Jack
FARRELL, David
  Smith, Frederick E.
FARRELL, M. J.
  Keane, Mary Nesta
FARRER, E. Maxwell
  Williams, Edward John
FAULKNER, Mary
  Seuffert, Muriel
FAWCETT, Catherine
  Cookson, Catherine
FAWKES, Guy
  Benchley, Robert

FAY, Dorothy
  Lindholm, Anna Chandler
FEARN, Elena
  Smith, Marjorie Seymour
FEARN, Roberta
  Hutchinson, Barbara Beatrice
FECAMPS, Elise
  Creasey, John
FECHER, Constance
  Heaven, Constance
FEIKEMA, Keike
  Manfred, Frederick Feikema
FELLOWES, Anne
  Mantle, Winifred Langford
FELMERSHAM, Michael
  Leyland, Eric
FEMORA
  Brodey, Jim
FENIX, *Comte de*
  Crowley, Edward Alexander
FENNER, Carol
  Williams, Carol Elizabeth
FENNIMORE, Stephen
  Collins, Dale
FENTON, Freda
  Rowland, Donald Sydney
FENWICK, Elizabeth
  Way, Elizabeth Fenwick
FENWICK, Peter
  Holmes, Peter
FERGUSON, Anthony
  Read, Anthony
FERGUSON, Helen
  Edmonds, Helen
FERN, Edwin
  Cryer, Neville
FERNWAY, Peggy
  Braun, Wilbur

FERRAND, Georgina
  Castle, Brenda
FERRARS, E. X.
  Brown, Morna D.
FERRARS, Elizabeth
  Brown, Morna D.
FERRIS, Tom
  Walker, Peter Norman
FESENMEYER
  Luxmore, Robert
FETHERSTON, Patrick
  Fetherstonhaugh, Patrick
    William Edward
FETTSMAN, Ann
  Hoffman, Anita
FEW, Betty
  Few, Eunice Beatty
FIACC, Padraic
  O'Connor, Patrick Joseph
FICKLING, G. G.
  Fickling, Forrest E. *and*
  Fickling, Gloria
FIDLER, Kathleen
  Goldie, Kathleen Annie
FIELD, Charles
  Rowland, Donald Sydney
FIELD, Frank Chester
  Robertson, Frank Chester
FIELD, Hill
  Fielding, Molly Hill
FIELD, Joanna
  Milner, Marion
FIELD, Michael
  Bradley, Katherine H. *and*
  Cooper, Edith E.
FIELDING, A. E.
  Feilding, Dorothy

FIELDING, Ann Mary
  Mostyn, Anita Mary
FIELDING, Anthony
  Leyland, Eric
FIELDING, Dorothy
  Fielding, Archibald
FIELDING, Gabriel
  Barnsley, Alan G.
FIELDING, Howard
  Hooke, Charles W.
FIELDING, Xan
  Fielding, Alexander
FIELDS, W. C.
  Dukenfield, William Claude
FILEMAN, Nan
  Zimmer, Maude Files
FINCH, John
  Cooper, John
FINCH, Matthew
  Fink, Merton
FINCH, Merton
  Fink, Merton
FINCHER, Beth
  Trumbo, Dalton
FINDLATER, Richard
  Bain, Kenneth Bruce
    Findlater
FINDLEY, Ferguson
  Frey, Charles Weiser
FINKELL, Max
  Catto, Maxwell Jeffrey
FINLEY, Scott
  Clark, Winifred
FINNEGAN, Robert
  Ryan, Paul William
FINNEGAN, Ruth
  Murray, Ruth Hilary

FINNIGAN, Joan
  Mackenzie, Joan
FISHER, Clay
  Allen, Henry
FISHER, Cyrus T.
  Teilhet, Darwin le Ora
FISHER, Laine
  Howard, James Arch
FISHER, Margot
  Paine, Lauran Bosworth
FITT, Mary
  Freeman, Kathleen
FITZALAN, Roger
  Dudley-Smith, Trevor
FITZGERALD, Barbara
  Newman, Mona A. J.
FITZGERALD, Errol
  Clarke, *Lady*
FITZGERALD, *Capt* Hugh
  Baum, Lyman Frank
FITZWILLIAM, Michael
  Lyons, John Benignus
5029
  Winkworth, Derek W.
FLACCUS
  Levy, Newman
FLAMANK, E.
  Harper, Edith
FLECK, Betty
  Paine, Lauran Bosworth
FLEMING, George
  Fletcher, Constance
FLEMING, Harry
  Bird, William Henry Fleming
FLEMING, Oliver
  MacDonald, Philip
FLEMING, Rhoda
  Fleming, Ronald

FLEMING, Waldo
  Williamson, Thames Ross
FLEMMING, Cardine
  Grieveson, Mildred
FLEMMING, Sarah
  Gilderdale, Michael
FLETCHER, Adam
  Flexner, Stuart
FLETCHER, David
  Barber, Dulan Friar
FLETCHER, George U.
  Pratt, Fletcher
FLETCHER, John
  Fletcher, Harry L. Verne
FLEXMAN, Theodore
  Trumbo, Dalton
FLIGHT, Francies
  Birch, Jack Ernest Lionel *and*
  Murray, Venetia Pauline
FLYING OFFICER X
  Bates, H. E.
FLYNT, Josiah
  Willard, Josiah Flynt
FOLEY, Helen
  Fowler, Helen
FOLEY, Rae
  Denniston, Elinore
FOLEY, Scott
  Dareff, Hal
FORBES, Colin
  Sawkins, Raymond Harold
FORBES, Kathryn
  McLean, Kathryn
FORBES, Stanton
  Forbes, Deloris Stanton
FORD, Barry
  Whitford, Joan

FORD, Elbur
  Hibbert, Eleanor Alice Burford
FORD, Ford Madox
  Hueffer, Ford Madox
FORD, Hilary
  Youd, Samuel
FORD, Kirk
  Spence, William
FORD, Langridge
  Coleman-Cooke, John C.
FORD, Leslie
  Brown, Zenith
FORD, Marcia
  Radford, Ruby Lorraine
FORD, Norrey
  Dilcock, Noreen
FORD, Wallace
  King, Albert
FORDE, Nicholas
  Elliott-Cannon, Arthur Elliott
FORDEN, James
  Barlow, James
FOREMAN, Lee
  King, Albert
FORREST, Carol
  Tennyson, Margaret
FORREST, *Colonel* Cris
  Stoddard, William Osborn
FORREST, David
  Denholm, David
FORREST, David
  Eliades, David *and* Webb,
    Robert Forrest
FORREST, Julian
  Wagenknecht, Edward
FORREST, Norman
  Morland, Nigel

FORRESTER, Mary
  Humphries, Elsie Mary
FORSTER, Christine
  Forte, Christine
FORSYTH, Jean
  M'Ilwraith, Jean N.
FORSYTH, R. A.
  Johnston, Robert Thomson
FORSYTHE, Robert
  Crichton, Kyle
FORTINA, Martha
  Laffeaty, Christina
FORTUNE, Dion
  Firth, Violet Mary
FOSSE, Alfred
  Jelly, Oliver
FOSTER, Delia
  Walker, Emily Kathleen
FOSTER, Evan
  King, Albert
FOSTER, George
  Haswell, C. J. D.
FOSTER, Richard
  Crossen, Kendell Foster
FOUGASSE
  Bird, Cyril Kenneth
FOWLER, Sydney
  Wright, Sydney Fowler
FOX, David
  Ostrander, Isabel Egerton
FOX, Eleanor
  St John, Wylly Folk
FOX, James M.
  Knipscheer, James M. W.
FOX, John
  Todd, John Murray
FOX, Petronella
  Balogh, Penelope

FOX, Sebastian
  Bullett, Gerald
FRA ELBERTUS
  Hubbard, Elbert
FRANCE, Claire
  Morin, Claire
FRANCE, Evangeline
  France-Hayhurst, Evangeline
FRANCHON, Lisa
  Floren, Lee
FRANCIS, C. D. E.
  Howarth, Patrick John Fielding
FRANCIS, Victor
  Hammond, Lawrence
FRANCIS, William
  Urell, William Francis
FRANK, R. Jr
  Ross, Frank Xavier
FRANK, Theodore
  Gardiner, Dorothea Frances
FRANKLIN, Charles
  Usher, Frank Hugh
FRANKLIN, E.
  Hurt, Edwin Franklin
FRANKLIN, Eugene
  Bandy, Eugene Franklin Jr
FRANKLIN, Jay
  Carter, John Franklin
FRANKLIN, Max
  Deming, Richard
FRASER, Alex
  Brinton, Henry
FRASER, James
  White, Alan
FRASER, Jane
  Pilcher, Rosamunde
FRASER, Jefferson
  Wilding, Philip

FRASER, Peter
  Coles, Phoebe Catherine
FRASER, Peter
  Watt, Alexander Peter
  Fordham
FRATER PERDURABO
  Crowley, Edward Alexander
FRAZER, Martin
  Clarke, Percy A.
FRAZER, Renee
  Fleming, Ronald
FRAZER, Robert Caine
  Creasey, John
FRAZER, Shamus
  Fraser, James Ian Arbuthnot
FRECKLES
  Dietz, Howard
FREDERICK, John
  Faust, Frederick
FREDERICKS, Arnold
  Kummer, Frederick Arnold
FREDERICKS, Frank
  Franck, Frederick S.
FREDERICKS, Vic
  Fell, Frederick Victor
FREDERICS, Jocko
  Frede, Richard
FREMLIN, Celia
  Goller, Celia Margaret
FRENCH, Ashley
  Robins, Denise
FRENCH, Ellen Jean
  English, Jean Ellen
FRENCH, Fergus
  Friedlander, Peter
FRENCH, Paul
  Asimov, Isaac

FRENKEN-MELONEY
Meloney, William
FRESHFIELD, Mark
Field, M. J.
FREYER, Frederic
Ballinger, William Sanborn
FRICK, C. H.
Irwin, Constance
FRIEND, Oscar Jerome
Jerome, Owen Fox
FROEST, Frank
Dilnot, George
FROME, David
Brown, Zenith
FROST, Frederick
Faust, Frederick
FROST, Joni
Paine, Lauran Bosworth
FROY, Herald
Deghy, Guy *and* Waterhouse,
Keith
FRY, Jane
Drew, Jane B.
FRY, Pete
King, James Clifford
FUCHS, Sonia
Seedo, Sonia
FULLER, Ed
Fuller, Harold Edgar
FULLER, Lester
Rolfe, Edwin
FULLER, Roger
Tracy, Donald Fiske
FULMAN, Al
Fuller, Harold Edgar
FURBER, Douglas
Lewin, Michael Sultan

FYVEL, T. R.
Feiwel, Raphael Joseph

G. B. S.
Shaw, George Bernard
G. K. C.
Chesterton, G. K.
GADDES, Peter
Sheldon, Peter
GADDIS, Peggy
Dern, Erolie Pearl
GAGE, Gervais
Rentoul, T. Laurence
GAGE, Wilson
Steele, Mary Quintard Govan
GAITE, Francis
Manning, Adelaide Frances
Oke *and* Coles, Cyril Henry
GALE, John
Gase, Richard
GALE, Newton
Guinness, Maurice
GALLAGHER, Gale
Oursler, William Charles
GALWAY, Robert Conington
McCutchan, Philip D.
GAME COCK
Looker, Samuel Joseph
GAMBIER, Kenyon
Lathrop, Lorin Andrews
GANNOLD, John
Langdon, John
GANPAT
Gompertz, Martin Louis Alan
GARDEN, John
Fletcher, Harry L. Verne
GARDNER, Nancy Bruff
Bruff, Nancy

GARDONS, S. S.
 Snodgrass, W. D.
GARFORD, James
 Blackburn, James Garford
GARLAND, George
 Roark, Garland
GARLAND, Lisette
 Gibbs, Norah
GARLAND, Madge
 Ashton, *Lady*
GARNETT, David S.
 Rush, Noel
GARNETT, Roger
 Morland, Nigel
GARRATT, Teddie
 Garratt, Alfred
GARRETT, Truman
 Judd, Harrison
GARRISON, Joan
 Neubauer, William Arthur
GARRITY
 Garrity, David James
GARRY, Stephen
 Stevens, Henry Charles
GARTH, Cecil
 Carlton, Grace
GARTH, Will
 Kuttner, Henry
GARTNER, Chloe
 Trimble, Chloe Maria
GARVE, Andrew
 Winterton, Paul
GASKELL, Jane
 Denvil, Jane Gaskell
GATE, A. G.
 Anthony, Edward
GATH
 Townsend, George Alfred

GAULT, Mark
 Cournos, John
GAUNT, Jeffrey
 Rochester, George Ernest
GAUNT, Michael
 Robertshaw, James Denis
GAUNT, Richard
 Landells, Richard
GAVIN, Amanda
 Fry, Clodagh Micaela Gibson
GAWAIN
 Newton, H. Chance
GAWSWORTH, John
 Fytton Armstrong, T. I.
GAY, Amelia
 Hogarth, Grace
GAYE, Carol
 Shann, Renée
GAYLE, Newton
 Guinness, Maurice
GEACH, Christine
 Wilson, Christine
GEARON, John
 Flagg, John
GEE, Kenneth F.
 Kay, Frederick George
GEE, Osman
 Hincks, Cyril Malcolm
GEERLINK, Will
 Hofdorp, Pim
GEISEL, Eva
 Bornemann, Eva
GELLERT, Roger
 Holmstrom, John Eric
GEMINI
 Goodwin, Geoffrey
GENE, Marta
 Powley, *Mrs* A. A.

GENET
  Flanner, Janet
GENTLEMAN OF THE
  UNIVERSITY OF CAMBRIDGE
  Crowley, Edward Alexander
GENTLEWOMAN, A
  Moore, Doris Langley
GEORGE, Daniel
  Bunting, D. G.
GEORGE, Eugene
  Chevalier, Paul Eugene George
GEORGE, G. S.
  Levin, Abraham
GEORGE, Jonathan
  Burke, John Frederick
GEORGE, Vicky
  Collings, I. J.
GERAINT, George
  Evans, George
GERARD, Gaston
  Ostergaard, Geoffrey
GERARD, Morice
  Teague, John Jessop
GERRARE, Wirt
  Greener, William Oliver
GIBB, Lee
  Deghy, Guy *and* Waterhouse,
  Keith
GIBBON, Lewis Grassic
  Mitchell, James Leslie
GIBBS, Henry
  Rumbold-Gibbs, Henry St
  John C.
GIBBS, Lewis
  Cove, Joseph Walter
GIBBS, Mary Ann
  Bidwell, Marjory Elizabeth
  Sarah

GIBSON, Floyd
  King, Albert
GIFFARD, Ann
  Greenhill, Elizabeth Ann
GIFFIN, Frank
  Carter, Ernest
GIFFORD, Matt
  King, Albert
GILBERT, Anthony
  Malleson, Lucy
GILBERT, John
  Harrison, John Gilbert
GILBERT, Nan
  Gilbertson, Mildred
GILCHRIST, John
  Gardner, Jerome
GILCRAFT
  Young, Ernest
GILDEN, K. B.
  Gilden, Katya *and* Gilden,
  Bert
GILES, Kris
  Nielson, Helen Berniece
GILES, Norman
  Mackeown, N. R.
GILL, Hugh
  Hugill, Robert
GILL, Patrick
  Creasey, John
GILLESPIE, Jane
  Shaw, Jane
GILLESPIE, Susan
  Turton-Jones, Edith C.
GILMAN, George G.
  Harknett, Terry
GILMAN, Robert Cham
  Coppel, Alfred

GILMER, Ann
  Ross, William Edward Daniel
GILMOUR, Ann
  McNaught, Ann Boyce
GIRTY, Simon
  King, Albert
GLANVILLE, Alec
  Grieve, Alexander Haig
    Glanville
GLASHAN, John
  MacGlashan, John
GLASS, Justine
  Corrall, Alice Enid
GLENDENNING, Donn
  Paine, Lauran Bosworth
GLENN, James
  Paine, Lauran Bosworth
GLINTO, Darcy
  Kelly, Harold Ernest
GLUTZ, Ambrose
  Knapp, Clarence
GLYN, Megan
  Parry, Margaret G.
GLYN-FOREST, D.
  Lynes, Daisy Elfreda
GOAMAN, Muriel
  Cox, Edith Muriel
GODDEN, Rumer
  Haynes Dixon, Margaret Rumer
GODEY, John
  Freedgood, Morton
GODFREY, Charles
  Webb, Godfrey E. C.
GODFREY, William
  Youd, Samuel
GOFF, Madeleine
  Woodford, Irene-Cecile

GOFFSTEIN, M. B.
  Schaaf, M. B.
GOLDEN GORSE
  Wace, M. A.
GOLDSMITH, Peter
  Priestley, John Boynton
GOODE, Bill
  Goodykoontz, William F.
GOODMAN, Winthrop
  Goodman, George Jerome
    and Knowlton, Winthrop
GOODSON, Bill
  Lucas, Edgar Ernest
GOODWIN, John
  Gowing, Sidney Floyd
GOODYEAR, Susan
  Matthews, Margaret Bryan
GORDON, Angela
  Paine, Lauran Bosworth
GORDON, Donald
  Payne, Donald Gordon
GORDON, Glenda
  Beadle, Gwyneth Gordon
GORDON, Ian
  Fellowes-Gordon, Ian
GORDON, Jane
  Sheridan, Elsie Lee
GORDON, Janet
  Woodham-Smith, Cecil
GORDON, Keith
  Bailey, Gordon
GORDON, Lew
  Baldwin, Gordon C.
GORDON, Mary
  Ostlere, Mary
GORDON, Neil
  Macdonell, A. G.

GORDON, Ray
  Wainwright, Gordon Ray
GORDON, Rex
  Hough, Stanley Bennett
GORDON, Richard
  Ostlere, Gordon Stanley
GORDON, Selma
  Lanes, Selma G.
GORDON, Stewart
  Shirreffs, Gordon D.
GORDON, William Murray
  Graydon, William Murray
GORE, William
  Gordon, Jan
GORHAM, Michael
  Folsom, Franklin Brewster
GORMAN, Beth
  Paine, Lauran Bosworth
GORMAN, Ginny
  Coleman, John
GOTTESMAN, S. D.
  Kornbluth, Cyril M. *and* Pohl,
    Frederik
GOUGH, Irene
  Hall, Irene
GOULD, Alan
  Canning, Victor
GOULD, Stephen
  Fisher, Stephen Gould
GOUTTIER, Maurice
  Moretti, Ugo
GOYNE, Richard
  Courage, John
GRAAF, Peter
  Youd, Samuel
GRACCHUS
  Wintringham, Tom

GRACE, Joseph
  Hornby, John W.
GRADY, Tex
  Webb, Jack
GRAEME, Bruce
  Jeffries, Bruce Graham
    Montague
GRAEME, David
  Jeffries, Bruce Graham
    Montague
GRAEME, Linda
  Jeffries, Gay
GRAEME, Roderic
  Jeffries, Roderic Graeme
GRAHAM, *Brother*
  Jeffery, Graham
GRAHAM, Ennis
  Molesworth, *Mrs* Mary Louisa
    Stewart
GRAHAM, Harvey
  Flack, Isaac Harvey
GRAHAM, James
  Patterson, Henry
GRAHAM, Jean
  Scott, Mary E.
GRAHAM, John
  Phillips, David Graham
GRAHAM, John
  Rose, Graham
GRAHAM, Neill
  Duncan, William Murdoch
GRAHAM, Peter
  Abraham, Peter L.
GRAHAM, Peter
  Langmaid, Kenneth Joseph
    Robb
GRAHAM, Ramona
  Cook, Ramona Graham

168

GRAHAM, Robin
  Raleigh-King, Robin Victor
    Lethbridge
GRAHAM, Scott
  Black, Hazleton
GRAHAM, Susan
  Graham, Maud Fitzgerald
GRAHAM, Viva
  Somerville, Edith Oenone
GRAMMATICUS
  Blaiklock, Edward
GRANADOS, Paul
  Kent, Arthur
GRAND, Sarah
  McFaul, Frances Elizabeth
GRANDMA
  Mulhearn, Winifred
GRANGE, Ellerton
  Fraser-Harris, D.
GRANGE, Peter
  Nicole, Christopher
GRANT, Alan
  Kennington, Gilbert Alan
GRANT, Ambrose
  Raymond, Rene
GRANT, Carol
  Copper, Dorothy
GRANT, Douglas
  Ostrander, Isabel Egerton
GRANT, Eve
  Gray, K. E.
GRANT, Jane
  Blackburn, Barbara
GRANT, Kay
  Grant, Hilda Kay
GRANT, Landon
  Gribble, Leonard Reginald

GRANT, Margaret
  Meloney, William
GRANT, Mary
  Willans, Angela
GRANT, Maxwell
  Gibson, Walter Brown
GRANT, Neill
  Mountfield, David
GRANT, Nesta
  Leyland, Eric
GRANT, Richard
  Clarke, J. Calvitt
GRAPE, Oliver
  Wood, Christopher
GRAVELEY, George
  Edwards, George Graveley
GRAY, Adrian
  Wilkes-Hunter, Richard
GRAY, Berkeley
  Brooks, Edwy Searles
GRAY, Christopher
  Usher, John Gray
GRAY, Elizabeth Janet
  Vining, Elizabeth
GRAY, Ellington
  Jacob, Naomi
GRAY, Harriet
  Pearson, Denise Naomi
GRAY, Harriet
  Robins, Denise
GRAY, Jane
  Evans, Constance May
GRAY, Jonathan
  Adams, Herbert
GRAYSON, Daphne
  Graveley, G. C.
GRAYSON, David
  Baker, Ray Stannard

GRAYSON, Richard
  Grindal, Richard
GREAVES, Gillian
  Macvean, Phyllis
GREEN, Charles M.
  Gardner, Erle Stanley
GREEN, Glint
  Peterson, Margaret
GREEN, Henry
  Yorke, Henry Vincent
GREEN, Linda
  Copper, Dorothy
GREEN, O. O.
  Durgnat, Raymond
GREEN, R.
  Weir, Rosemary
GREENE, Adam
  Scott, Peter Dale
GREENE, Robert
  Deindorfer, Robert G.
GREENHALGH, Katherine
  Bobin, John W.
GREENHILL, Jack
  Greenberg, Jack
GREENWOOD, Grace
  Lippincott, Sara Jane
GREER, Patrick
  Macrory, Patrick
GREGSON, Paul
  Oakley, Eric Gilbert
GRENDON, Stephen
  Derleth, August William
GRENVIL, William
  Martyn, Wyndham
GREW, William
  O'Farrell, William
GREX, Leo
  Gribble, Leonard Reginald

GREY, A. F.
  Neal, Adeline Phyllis
GREY, Brenda
  Mackinlay, Lelia A. S.
GREY, Donald
  Thomas, Eugene
GREY, Elizabeth
  Hogg, Beth
GREY, Harry
  Golberg, Harry
GREY, Louis
  Gribble, Leonard Reginald
GREY, Robin
  Gresham, Elizabeth F.
GREY, Rowland
  Brown, L. Rowland
GREY OWL
  Belaney, Archie
GREYSTONE, Alexander A.
  Goodavage, Joseph F.
GRIER, Sydney C.
  Gregg, Hilda
GRIFF, Alan
  Suddaby, William Donald
GRIFFITH, Jack
  Griffiths, Jack
GRIFFITH, Jeannette
  Eyerly, Jeannette *and*
  Griffith, Valeria W.
GRINGHUIS, Dirk
  Gringhuis, Richard H.
GRISWOLD, George
  Dean, Robert George
GROUPE, Darryl R.
  Bunch, David R.
GROVER, Marshall
  Meares, Leonard F.

170

GROVES, Georgina
  Symons, Dorothy G.
GUBBINS, Nathaniel
  Mott, Edward Spencer
GUILDFORD, John
  Hunter, Bluebell Matilda
GUINNESS, Owen
  Williams, Guy Richard
GULICK, Bill
  Gulick, Grover C.
GUN BUSTER
  Austin, John *and* Austin,
    Richard
GUNN, Victor
  Brooks, Edwy Searles
GURNEY, David
  Bair, Patrick
GUTHRIE, John
  Brodie, John
GWYNNE, Arthur
  Evans, Gwynfil Arthur
GWYNNE, Paul
  Slater, Ernest
GYE, Hal
  Gye, Harold Frederick Neville

Caro nome che il mio cor
Festi primo palpitar.
—G. Verdi; F. Piave. Rigoletto

H. A. K.
  Kennedy, H. A.
HAAS, Carola
  Catalani, Victoria
HACKSTON, James
  Gye, Harold Frederick Neville

HADDO, Oliver
  Puechner, Ray
HADDOCK, Albert
  Herbert, *Sir* Alan Patrick
HADDON, Christopher
  Palmer, John Leslie
HADDOW, Leigh
  Best, Rayleigh Breton Amis
HADHAM, John
  Parkes, James W.
HADLEY, Leila
  Smitter, Eliott-Burton
HAEFER, Hanna
  Condon, Madeline
HAGAR, Judith
  Polley, Judith Anne
HAGEN, Brett
  Hunter, William R.
HAGGARD, Paul
  Longstreet, Stephen
HAGGARD, William
  Clayton, Richard H. M.
HAGON, Priscilla
  Allan, Mabel Esther
HALE, Christopher
  Stevens, Frances Moyer
HALE, Hope
  Davis, Hope Hale
HALES, Joyce
  Coombs, Joyce
HALIBURTON, Hugh
  Robertson, James Logie
HALL, Adam
  Dudley-Smith, Trevor
HALL, B.
  Gunn, John Angus Lancaster
HALL, Bennett
  Hall, Bennie Caroline

171

HALL, Borden
Yates, Raymond Francis
HALL, Claudia
Floren, Lee
HALL, Eliza Calvert
Obenchain, Eliza Caroline
HALL, Holworthy
Porter, Harold Everett
HALL, John
Pound, Ezra
HALL, Martyn T.
Morris, David
HALL, Patrick
Hall, Frederick
HALL, Rupert
Home-Gall, Edward Reginald
HALL, Whyte
Rayner, Augustus Alfred
HALLAM, Jay
Rice, Joan
HALLARD, Peter
Catherall, Arthur
HALLAS, Richard
Knight, Eric
HALLIDAY, Brett
Dresser, Davis
HALLIDAY, Dorothy
Dunnett, Dorothy
HALLIDAY, James
Symington, David
HALLIDAY, Michael
Creasey, John
HAMBLEDON, Phyllis
Macvean, Phyllis
HAMILL, Ethel
Webb, Jean Frances
HAMILTON, Clive
Lewis, Clive Staples

HAMILTON, Ernest
Grossman, Judith
HAMILTON, Judith
Lawrence, Dulcie
HAMILTON, Julia
Watson, Julia
HAMILTON, Kay
De Leeuw, Cateau W.
HAMILTON, Max
Hamilton, Cecily
HAMILTON, Michael
Chetham-Strode, Warren
HAMILTON, Mollie
Kaye, Mary Margaret
HAMILTON, Paul
Dennis-Jones, Harold
HAMILTON, Roger
Rogerson, James
HAMILTON, Wade
Floren, Lee
HAMILTON, William
Canaway, W. H.
HAMILTON-WILKES, Monty
Hamilton-Wilkes, Edwin
HAMMOND, Brad
King, Albert
HAMMOND, Jane
Poland, Dorothy E. H.
HAMMOND, Ralph
Hammond-Innes, Ralph
HAMPSON, John
Simpson, John Frederick
Norman Hampson
HAN SUYIN
Comber, Elizabeth
HANCOCK, Frances Deane
Judson, Jeanne

HANCOCK, Robert
  Howell, Douglas Nayler
HANNAFORD, Justin
  Fitz-Gerald, S. J. A.
HARBIN, Robert
  Williams, Ned
HARBINSON, Robert
  Harbinson-Bryans, Robert
HARDIN, Dave
  Holmes, Llewellyn Perry
HARDIN, Peter
  Vaczek, Louis C.
HARDING, Bertita
  Radetzby von Radetz, *Countess*
HARDING, George
  Raubenheimer, George H.
HARDING, Matt
  Floren, Lee
HARDING, Richard
  Boulton, A. Harding
HARDING, Wes
  Keevill, Henry John
HARDWICK, Sylvia
  Doherty, Ivy Ruby
HARDY, Adam
  Harknett, Terry
HARDY, Arthur S.
  Steffens, Arthur Joseph
HARDY, Bobbie
  Hardy, Marjorie
HARDY, Russ
  Snow, Charles Horace
HARDY, Stuart
  Schisgall, Oscar
HARE, Cyril
  Clark, Alfred Alexander
    Gordon

HARE, Robert
  Hutchinson, Robert Hare
HARFORD, Henry
  Hudson, William Henry
HARGIS, Pauline
  Dillard, Polly Hargis
HARGIS, Polly
  Dillard, Polly Hargis
HARLAN, Ross
  King, Albert
HARLAND, Marion
  Terhune, Mary Virginia
HARLE, Elizabeth
  Roberts, Irene
HARLEQUIN
  Reed, Alexander Wyclif
HARLEY, John
  Marsh, John
HARMON, Gill
  King, Albert
HARMSTON, Donald
  Matheson, Donald H.
HARPOLE, James
  Abraham, James Johnston
HARRIETT
  Wilcoxen, Harriett
HARRIS, Colver
  Harris, Polly Anne Colver
HARRIS, John Beynon
  Harris, John Wyndham Parkes
    Lucas Beynon
HARRIS, Kathleen
  Humphries, Adelaide
HARRIS, Larry M.
  Janifer, Laurence M.
HARRIS, Macdonald
  Heiney, Donald William

HARRIS, Peter
  Harris, William
HARRISON, Whit
  Whittington, Harry
HART, Francis
  Paine, Lauran Bosworth
HART, Max
  Urquhart, Macgregor
HART, R. W.
  Ferneyhough, Roger Edmund
HART, Susanne
  Harthoorn, Susanne
HARTE, Marjorie
  McEvoy, Marjorie
HARTFORD, Via
  Donson, Cyril
HARTMAN, Roger
  Mehta, Rustam
HARTWELL, Nancy
  Callahan, Claire Wallis
HARVESTER, Simon
  Rumbold-Gibbs, Henry St
    John C.
HARVEY, Rachel
  Bloom, Ursula
HARVEY, Ross
  Hook, H. Clarke
HASLETTE, John
  Vahey, John George Haslette
HASSAN i SABBAH
  Butler, Bill
HASTINGS, Brook
  Edgley, Leslie *and* Edgley,
    Mary
HASWELL, Jock
  Haswell, C. J. D.
HATCH, Robert
  Lee, Manning de Villeneuve

HATRED, Peter
  Douglas, Keith
HATTON, Cliff
  Mason, Sydney Charles
HAWK, Affable
  MacCarthy, *Sir* Desmond
HAWKES, John
  Burne, Clendennin Talbot
HAWKEYE
  Carlisle, R. H.
HAWKINS, John
  Hagan, Stelia F.
HAWTHORNE, E. M. D.
  Dolbey, Ethel M.
HAY, Catherine
  Hughes, Ivy
HAY, Frances
  Dick-Erikson, Cicely Sibyl
    Alexandra
HAY, Ian
  Beith, John Hay
HAY, John
  Dalrymple-Hay, Barbara *and*
    Dalrymple-Hay, John
HAYDEN, Jay
  Paine, Lauran Bosworth
HAYES, Clanton
  Mason, Sydney Charles
HAYES, Henry
  Olney, Ellen Warner
HAYES, Timothy
  Rubel, James Lyon
HAYMAN, Hazel
  Peel, Hazel
HAYNES, Dorothy K.
  Gray, Dorothy K.
HAYNES, John Robert
  Wilding, Philip

HAZARD, Laurence
  Barr, Patricia
HEAD, Ann
  Morse, Anne Christenson
HEAD, Matthew
  Canaday, John
HEADLEY, Elizabeth
  Harrison, Elizabeth C.
HEALD, Edith
  Shackleton, Edith
HEARD, Gerald
  Heard, Henry Fitzgerald
HEARNDEN, Balfour
  Balfour, Eve *and* Hernden,
    Beryl
HEATH, Veronica
  Blackett, Veronica
HEATHCOTT, Mary
  Keegan, Mary Constance
HEATON, Peter
  Stuart-Heaton, Peter
HEBDEN, Mark
  Harris, John
HEBER, Austin
  Poole, Reginald Heber
HEBER, Reginald
  Poole, Reginald Heber
HEDLEY, Frank
  Barker, Clarence Hedley
HEGESIPPUS
  Schonfield, Hugh Joseph
HELLER, Frank
  Sernar, Gunnar
HELLERLAMB, Toni
  Lamb, Antonia
HELMHOLTZ, Bastien von
  Pound, Ezra

HELMI, Jack
  Sands, Leo G.
HELVICK, James
  Cockburn, Claud
HELY, Elizabeth
  Younger, Elizabeth
HEMINGWAY, Taylor
  Rywell, Martin
HENDERSON, Colt
  Mason, Sydney Charles
HENDERSON, Sylvia
  Ashton-Warner, Sylvia
HENRIQUES, Veronica
  Gosling, Veronica
HENRY, B. A.
  Abrahams, Henry B.
HENRY, Daniel Jr
  Holmes, Daniel Henry
HENRY, Lewis C.
  Copeland, Lewis
HENRY, O.
  Porter, William Sydney
HENRY, Will
  Allen, Henry
HEPPELL, Blanche
  Heppell, Mary
HEPPLE, Anne
  Dickinson, Anne Hepple
HEPTAGON
  Charlton, Joan; Falk,
    Katherine; Falk, Millicent;
    Fox, Winifred; Gill,
    Winifred; Jennings, Hilda
    and Stocks, Mary
HEREFORD, John
  Fletcher, Harry L. Verne
HERITAGE, A. J.
  Addis, Hazel Iris

HERITAGE, Martin
  Horler, Sydney
HERMAN, Jack
  Sands, Leo G.
HERMAN, William
  Bierce, Ambrose
HERMES
  Canaway, W. H.
HERNE, Eric
  Garvey, Eric William
HERRING, Geilles
  Somerville, Edith Oenone
HERRIOT, James
  Wight, J. A.
HESSING, Dennis
  Dennis-Jones, Harold
HEWES, Cady
  De Voto, Bernard Augustine
HEWETT, Anita
  Duke, Anita
HEWITT, Martin
  Morrison, Arthur
HEXT, Harrington
  Phillpotts, Eden
HICKEY, Lyn
  Hickey, Madelyn E.
HICKOK, Will
  Harrison, Chester William
HICKS, Eleanor
  Coerr, Eleanor Beatrice
HIGGINBOTHAM, Anne T.
  Higginbotham, Anne D.
HIGGINS, Jack
  Patterson, Henry
HIGSON, P. J. W.
  Willoughby-Higson, Philip John
HILL, Anne
  Muskett, Netta Rachel

HILL, Bennet
  Winter, Bevis
HILL, Craven
  Parsons, Charles P.
HILL, H. Haverstock
  Walsh, James Morgan
HILL, Headon
  Grainger, Francis Edward
HILL, Joe
  Hillstrom, Joseph
HILL, King
  Robertson, Frank Chester
HILL, Monica
  Werner, Elsa Jane
HILL, Murray
  Holliday, Robert Cortes
HILL, Prudence
  Maxfield, Prudence
HILLIARD, Jan
  Grant, Hilda Kay
HILLMAN, Martin
  Hill, Douglas
HINDE, Thomas
  Chitty, *Sir* Thomas Willes
HIPPOPOTAMUS, Eugene H.
  Kraus, Robert
HISTORICUS
  Nock, Albert Jay
HOBART, Robertson
  Lee, Norman
HOBBES, John Oliver
  Craigie, Pearl Mary Teresa
HOBSON, Polly
  Evans, Julia
HOCKABY, Stephen
  Mitchell, Gladys
HODGE, Merton
  Hodge, Horace Emerton

HODSON, Arthur
  Nickson, Arthur
HOFFMAN, Art
  King, Albert
HOFFMAN, Louise
  Fitzgerald, Beryl
HOFFNER, Dorothy
  Doane, Pelagie
HOFMEYER, Hans
  Fleischer, Anthony
HOGAN, David
  Gallagher, Frank
HOGARTH, Charles
  Creasey, John
HOGARTH, Emmett
  Willson, Mitchell *and* Polansky,
    Abraham
HOGARTH, John
  Finnin, Mary
HOGBIN, Ian
  Hogbin, Herbert
HOLCOMBE, Arnold
  Golsworthy, Arnold
HOLDEN, Genevieve
  Pou, Genevieve
HOLDEN, Joanne
  Corby, Jane
HOLDEN, Larry
  Lorenz, Frederic
HOLLAND, Clive
  Hankinson, Charles J.
HOLLAND, Elizabeth
  Baxter, Elizabeth
HOLLAND, Katrin
  Loewengard, Heidi H. F.
HOLLAND, Kel
  Whittington, Harry

HOLLAND, Rosemary
  Pattinson, Lee
HOLLAND, Tom
  King, Albert
HOLLIS, Jim
  Summers, Hollis
HOLMES, Arnold W.
  Fryefield, Maurice P.
HOLMES, *Captain* Howard
  Harbaugh, Thomas Chalmers
HOLMES, Caroline
  Mason, Sydney Charles
HOLMES, Gordon
  Shiel, M. P. *and* Tracy, Louis
HOLMES, Grant
  Fox, James
HOLMES, Grant
  Knipscheer, James M. W.
HOLMES, H. H.
  White, William Anthony P.
HOLMES, Rick
  Hardwick, Richard
HOLT, E. Carleton
  Guigo, Ernest Philip
HOLT, Elizabeth
  King, Kay
HOLT, Gavin
  Rodda, Charles
HOLT, Helen
  Paine, Lauran Bosworth
HOLT, Rackham
  Holt, Margaret Van Vechten
HOLT, Stephen
  Thompson, Harlan
HOLT, Tex
  Rister, Claude
HOLT, Victoria
  Hibbert, Eleanor Alice Burford

HOLTON, Leonard
  Wibberley, Leonard Patrick
    O'Connor
HOME, Michael
  Bush, Christopher
HOME-GALL, Reginald
  Home-Gall, Edward Reginald
HOME GUARD
  Ingamells, F. G.
HOMES, Geoffrey
  Mainwaring, Daniel
HON MEMBER FOR X
  De Chair, Somerset
HONEYCUTT, Richard
  Hardwick, Richard
HONEYMAN, Brenda
  Clarke, Brenda
HOOLEY, Teresa
  Butler, Teresa Mary
HOPE, Andrew
  Hern, Anthony
HOPE, Anthony
  Hawkins, *Sir* Anthony Hope
HOPE, Brian
  Creasey, John
HOPE, Edward
  Coffey, Edward Hope
HOPE, Lawrence
  Nicholson, Violet
HOPE, Margaret
  Wicksteed, Margaret Hope
HOPE, Noel
  Morewood, Sarah L.
HOPE, Stanton
  Stanton-Hope, W. E.
HOPF, Alice
  Lightner, A. M.

HOPKINS, A. T.
  Turngreen, Annette
HOPKINS, Stanley
  Holt, Henry
HOPLEY, George
  Hopley-Woolrich, Cornell
    George
HORN, Chester
  Mason, Sydney Charles
HORN, Trader
  Smith, Alfred Aloysius
HORNE, Howard
  Payne, Pierre Stephen Robert
HORSLEY, David
  Bingley, David Ernest
HORTON, Robert J.
  Roberts, James
HOUGH, Don
  Huff, Darrell
HOUGHTON, Claude
  Oldfield, Claude Houghton
HOUGHTON, Elizabeth
  Gilzean, Elizabeth Houghton
HOUSTON, R. B.
  Rae, Hugh Cranford
HOUSTON, Will
  Paine, Lauran Bosworth
HOWARD, Colin
  Shaw, Howard
HOWARD, Don
  Menzel, Donald H.
HOWARD, Elizabeth
  Mizner, Elizabeth Howard
HOWARD, Elizabeth
  Paine, Lauran Bosworth
HOWARD, George
  Kay, Frederic George

HOWARD, Hartley
Ognall, Leopold Horace
HOWARD, Helen
Jacobs, Thomas Curtis Hicks
HOWARD, John M.
Hincks, Cyril Malcolm
HOWARD, Keble
Bell, John Keble
HOWARD, Leigh
Lee Howard, L. A.
HOWARD, Mary
Mussi, Mary
HOWARD, Troy
Paine, Lauran Bosworth
HOWARD, Vechel
Rigsby, Howard
HOWE, Muriel
Smithies, Muriel
HOWELL, Scott
King, Albert
HOY, Elizabeth
Conarain, Alice Nina
HOYT, Nelson
King, Albert
HUBBARD, Joan
Jackson, Kathryn
HUBBARD, Kin
Hubbard, Frank McKinney
HUDSON, Jeffrey
Crichton, Michael
HUDSON, Stephen
Schiff, Sydney
HUGGINS, Ruth Mabel
Arthur, Ruth M.
HUGHES, Alison
Oliver, Doris M.
HUGHES, Brenda
Colloms, Brenda

HUGHES, Colin
Creasey, John
HUGHES, Matilda
Macleod, Charlotte
HUGHES, Philip
Phillips, Hugh
HUGHES, Terence
Best, Rayleigh Breton Amis
HUGHES, Valerina
Coleman, John
HUGHES, Zach
Coleman, John
HULL, H. Braxton
Jacobs, Helen Hull
HULL, Richard
Sampson, Richard Henry
HUMANA, Charles
Jacobs, Charles
HUME, David
Turner, John Victor
HUME, Frances
Buckland-Wright, Mary
HUMPHRYS, Geoffrey
Humphrys, Leslie George
HUNT, Charlotte
Hodges, Doris Marjorie
HUNT, Diana
Hunt-Bode, Gisele
HUNT, Dorothy
Fellows, Dorothy Alice
HUNT, Harrison
Ballard, Willis Todhunter
HUNT, John
Paine, Lauran Bosworth
HUNT, Kyle
Creasey, John

HUNT, Peter
  Yates, George Worthing *and*
  Marshall, Charles Hunt
HUNTER, Alison
  Blair, Norma Hunter
HUNTER, George
  Ballard, Willis Todhunter
HUNTER, Hall
  Marshall, Edison
HUNTER, Jean
  Hunter, Alfred John
HUNTER, John
  Ballard, Willis Todhunter
HUNTER, John
  Hunter, Alfred John
HUNTER, John
  Hunter, Christine
HUNTER, Mollie
  McIlwraith, Maureen Mollie
  Hunter
HUNTER, Pat
  Kempf, Pat
HUNTINGDON, John
  Phillips, Gerald William
HUNTLY, Frances E.
  Mayne, Ethel Colborn
HUNTON, Mary
  Gilzean, Elizabeth Houghton
HUNGERFORD, Pixie
  Brinsmead, Hesba
HUSSEY, Leonard
  Pearce, Brian
HUSSINGTREE, Martin
  Baldwin, Oliver
HUTCHINS, Anthony
  Morley, Leslie Reginald William
HUTCHINSON, Anne
  Burnett, Hallie

HUTCHINSON, Patricia
  Fullbrook, Gladys
HYDE, Eleanor
  Minto, Frances

I. B.
  Brown, Ivor
ICONOCLAST
  Hamilton, Mary A. A.
IDRIS
  Mee, Arthur
IGNOTUS
  Fuller, James Franklin
ILES, Bert
  Ross, Zola Helen
ILES, Francis
  Cox, A. B.
INCLEDON, Philip
  Worner, Philip A. I.
INGERSOL, Jared
  Paine, Lauran Bosworth
INGHAM, Daniel
  Lambot, Isobel Mary
INGRAM, Martin
  Campbell, Alice Ormond
INNES, Hammond
  Hammond-Innes, Ralph
INNES, Jean
  Saunders, Jean
INNES, Michael
  Stewart, John Innes
  Mackintosh
IRELAND, Baron
  Salsbury, Nate
IRELAND, Doreen
  Lord, Doreen Mildred Douglas
IRELAND, Noelle
  Gibbs, Norah

IRISH, William
  Hopley-Woolrich, Cornell
  George
IRONQUILL
  Ware, Eugene Fitch
IRONSIDE, John
  Tait, Euphemia Margaret
IRVINE, Lyn
  Newman, Lyn Lloyd
IRVING, Robert
  Adler, Irving
ISLAY, Nicholas
  Murray, Andrew Nicholas

J. A. H.
  Hammerton, J. A.
J. C.
  Lawrence, T. E.
J. C. T.
  Trewin, J. C.
J. L.
  Pound, Ezra
JABEZ
  Nicol, Eric Patrick
JACKS, Oliver
  Gandley, Kenneth Royce
JACKSON, Everatt
  Muggeson, Margaret
JACKSON, Giles
  Leffingwell, Albert
JACKSON, Joyce
  Crounse, Helene Louise
JACKSON, Neville
  Glaskin, G. M.
JACKSON, Sam
  Trumbo, Dalton
JACKSON, Wallace
  Budd, William John

JACKSTAFF
  Bennett, J. J.
JACOB, Herbert Mathias
  Davies, D. Jacob
JACOT, Bernard
  Jacot de Bolnod, B. L.
JAMES, Andrew
  Kirkup, James
JAMES, Brian
  Tierney, John
JAMES, Cy
  Watts, Peter Christopher
JAMES, Dan
  Sayers, James D.
JAMES, Dynely
  Mayne, William J. C. *and*
  Caesar, Richard Dynely
JAMES, Franklin
  Godley, Robert
JAMES, John
  Langdon-Davies, John
JAMES, Josephine
  Lindsay, Barbara *and*
  Sterne, E. G.
JAMES, Matthew
  Lucey, James D.
JAMES, Robert
  Heitner, Iris
JAMES, Vincent
  Gribben, James
JAMESON, Eric
  Trimmer, Eric
JAMIESON, Thomas
  Molloy, Edward
JAN
  Read, John
JANES, Kathleen
  Jamieson, Kathleen Florence

181

JANES, Kathleen F.
  Jamieson, Kathleen Florence
JANICE
  Brustlein, Janice
JANUS, Hiram
  Pound, Ezra
JAPONICA
  Holdaway, Marjorie F.
JARDIN, Rex
  Burkhardt, Eve *and* Burkhardt,
    Robert Ferdinand
JARRETT, Kay
  Saxon, Sophia
JASON, Craine John
  Craine, John
JASON
  Munro, Hugh
JASON, William
  Machlin, Milton
JASPER, Bob
  Hogan, Robert Jasper
JAY
  Jennings, E. C.
JAY, Charlotte
  Jay, Geraldine
JAY, Joan
  Davies, Edith
JAY, Simon
  Alexander, Colin James
JAYNES, Clare
  Spiegel, Clara E. *and* Mayer,
    Jane
JEANS, Angela
  Watt, Esme
JEEVES, Mahatma Kane
  Dukenfield, William Claude
JEFFERIES, Ian
  Hays, Peter

JEFFERIS, Jeff
  Curry, Thomas Albert
JEFFERSON, Ian
  Davies, Leslie Purnell
JEFFERSON, Sarah
  Farjeon, Eve
JEFFERY, E. Jeffery
  Marston, J. E.
JEFFORD, Bat
  Bingley, David Ernest
JEFFRIES, Jeff
  Boatfield, Jeffrey
JEFFS, Rae
  Sebley, Frances Rae
JEMONTE
  Mohan, Josephine Elizabeth
JEMYMA
  Holley, Marietta
JENNER, Heather
  Potter, Heather
JENNIFER
  Kenward, Betty
JENNINGS, D.
  Frazee, Steve
JENNINGS, S. M.
  Meyer, Jerome Sydney
JEREMY, Richard
  Fox, Charles
JEROME, Owen Fox
  Friend, Oscar Jerome
JESKINS, Richard
  Story, Rosamond Mary
JESSEL, John
  Weinbaum, Stanley Grauman
JINGLE
  Golsworthy, Arnold
JOB, Modern
  Taber, Clarence Wilbur

JOCELYN, Richard
  Clutterbuck, Richard
JODY, J. M.
  Edmundson, Joseph
JOHANSON, Elizabeth
  Verwer, Johanne
JOHN, Evan
  Simpson, Evan John
JOHN O'LONDON
  Whitten, Wilfred
JOHN O'THE NORTH
  Browne, Harry T.
JOHNS, Avery
  Cousins, Margaret
JOHNS, Foster
  Seldes, Gilbert Vivian
JOHNS, Hilary
  Barraud, E. M.
JOHNS, June
  Smith, June Johns
JOHNS, Richard
  Slater, Montagu
JOHNSON, A. E.
  Johnson, Annabel J. *and*
  Johnson, Edgar R.
JOHNSON, Benjamin F.
  Riley, James Whitcomb
JOHNSON, Brian
  Worthy, Brian Johnson
JOHNSON, Crockett
  Leisk, David Johnson
JOHNSON, Lee
  Johnson, Lilian Beatrice
JOHNSON, Marigold
  Gilles, Daniel
JOHNSON, W. Bolingbroke
  Bishop, Morris Gilbert

JOLLY, Susan
  Edwards, Florence
JONES, Bobi
  Jones, Robert Maynard
JONES, Bradshaw
  Bradshaw-Jones, Malcolm
  Henry
JONES, Calico
  Richardson, Gladwell
JONES, Clara
  Baldwin, Dorothy
JONES, Joanna
  Burke, John Frederick
JONES, H. S.
  Molloy, Edward
JONES, Nard
  Jones, Maynard Benedict
JONES, Webb
  Henley, Art
JONS, Hal
  Jones, Harry Austin
JORDAN, Barbara Leslie
  Yellot, Barbara Leslie
JORDAN, Bryn
  Henderson, James Maddock
JORDAN, Nell
  Barker, E. M.
JORGENSON, Ivar
  Silverberg, Robert
JOSE, Ellen J.
  Waye, Ellen
JOSIAH ALLEN'S WIFE
  Holley, Marietta
JOUDRY, Patricia
  Steele, Patricia M. V.
JOURNEYMAN
  Nock, Albert Jay

JOYCE, Thomas
  Cary, Joyce
JOYSTICK
  Holden, J. R.
JUDD, Cyril
  Grossman, Judith *and*
  Kornbluth, Cyril M.
JULIAN, Peter
  Körmendi, Ferens
JULIE
  Nettz, Julie
JUNE, Jenny
  Croly, Jane Cunningham
JUNIOR SUB
  Beith, John Hay
JUSTICIAR
  Powell-Smith, Vincent

KAIN, Saul
  Sassoon, Siegfried
KAJAR
  Bowen, Reuben
KANE, Jim
  Germano, Peter
KANE, Julia
  Robins, Denise
KANE, Mark
  King, Albert
KANTO, Peter
  Coleman, John
KARAGEORGE, Michael
  Anderson, Poul
KARIG, Walter
  Patrick, Keats
KARLOFF, Boris
  Pratt, William Henry
KAVAN, Anna
  Edmonds, Helen

KAY, Helen
  Goldfrank, *Mrs* Herbert
KAY, Wallace
  Arter, Wallace E.
KAYE, Barbara
  Muir, Marie
KAYE, Evelyn
  Evans, Kathleen
KAYE, Harold Bertram
  Kampf, Harold
KAYE, Mary Margaret
  Hamilton, Mary Margaret
  Kaye
KAYE, Tom
  Kaye, Barrington
KEATING, Walter S.
  Rosenberg, Henrietta
KEENE, Faraday
  Jarrett, Cora
KEENE, Frances W.
  Casman, Frances White
KEENE, James
  Cook, William Everett
KEESING, Nancy
  Hertzberg, Nancy
KEIR, Christine
  Pullein-Thompson, Christine
KEITH, Carlton
  Robertson, Keith
KEITH, David
  Steegmuller, Francis
KEITH, Donald
  Monroe, Donald *and* Monroe,
  Keith
KEITH, James
  Hetherington, Keith James
KELL, Joseph
  Wilson, John Anthony Burgess

KELLER, Dan
  Kaufman, Louis
KELLEY, Ray
  Paine, Lauran Bosworth
KELLIER, Elizabeth
  Kelly, Elizabeth
KELLOW, Kathleen
  Hibbert, Eleanor Alice Burford
KELLWAY, Mary D.
  Hillyard, Mary Dorothea
KELSEY, Janice
  King, Albert
KELWAY, Christine
  Gwinn, Christine M.
KENDALL, Jane
  Martens, Anne Louise
KENDALL, Lace
  Stoutenburg, Adrien
KENDRAKE, Carleton
  Gardner, Erle Stanley
KENEU
  Hazlewood, Rex
KENNEDY, Diana
  Duggleby, Jean Colbeck
KENNEDY, Elliott
  Godfrey, Lionel Robert
    Holcombe
KENNEDY, Howard
  Woolfolk, Josiah Pitts
KENNEDY, Milward
  Burge, Milward Rodon
    Kennedy
KENNEDY, R. C.
  Cortez-Columbus, Robert
    Cimabue
KENNEDY, X. J.
  Kennedy, Joseph Charles

KENNEGGY, Richard
  Nettell, Richard
KENNIE, Jessie
  Macpherson, Jessie
KENNINGTON, Alan
  Kennington, Gilbert Alan
KENNY, Charles J.
  Gardner, Erle Stanley
KENT, Alexander
  Reeman, Douglas
KENT, David
  Birney, Hoffman
KENT, Pete
  Richardson, Gladwell
KENT, Simon
  Catto, Maxwell Jeffrey
KENTIGERN, John
  Veitch, Thomas
KENTON, Maxwell
  Southern, Terry *and*
    Hoffenberg, Mason
KENWORTHY, Hugh
  Walker, Rowland
KENYON, Larry
  Engel, Lyle Kenyon
KENYON, Paul
  Engel, Lyle Kenyon
KEPPEL, Charlotte
  Torday, Ursula
KEPPS, Gerald E.
  Speck, Gerald Eugene
KERBY, Susan Alice
  Burton, Alice Elizabeth
KERR, Ben
  Ard, William
KERR, Carole
  Carr, Margaret

KERR, John O'Connell
  Whittet, George Sorley
KERR, Lennox
  Kerr, James Lennox
KERR, M. E.
  Meaker, Marijane
KERR, Orpheus C.
  Newell, Robert Henry
KERSEY, John
  Warriner, Thurman
KETCHUM, Jack
  Paine, Lauran Bosworth
KETTLE, Pamela
  Kettle, Jocelyn
KEVERNE, Richard
  Hosken, Clifford James
    Wheeler
KEW, Andrew
  Morton, A. Q.
KEYES, Gordon
  Bedford-Jones, Henry
KEYSTONE, Oliver
  Mantiband, James
KHAN, Khaled
  Crowley, Edward Alexander
KIDD, Russell
  Donson, Cyril
KIEFER, Middleton
  Middleton, Harry *and* Kiefer,
    Warren
KILBOURN, Matt
  Barrett, Geoffrey John
KILDARE, John
  King, John
KILDARE, Maurice
  Richardson, Gladwell
KILGORE, John
  Paine, Lauran Bosworth

KILPATRICK, Sarah
  Underwood, Mavis Eileen
KIM
  Sweet, John
KIMBER, Lee
  King, Albert
KIMBRO, Jean
  Kimbro, John
KIMBROUGH, Katheryn
  Kimbro, John
KINDLER, Asta
  Hicken, Una
KING, Ames
  King, Albert
KING, Arthur
  Cain, Arthur Homer
KING, Arthur
  Lake, Kenneth Robert
KING, Berta
  King, Albert
KING, Charles
  Avenell, Donne
KING, Christopher
  King, Albert
KING, Clifford
  King, James Clifford
KING, Evan
  Ward, Robert Spencer
KING, Kennedy
  Brown, George Douglas
KING, Oliver
  Mount, Thomas Ernest
KING, Paul
  Drackett, Phil
KING, Reefe
  Barker, Albert H.
KING, Richard
  Huskinson, Richard King

KING, Robin
  Raleigh-King, Robin Victor
  Lethbridge
KING, Sampson
  Bennett, Arnold
KING, Stella
  Glenton, Stella Lennox
KING, Stephanie
  Russell, Shirley
KING, W. Scott
  Greenland, W. K.
KINGSLEY, Laura
  Bennett, Dorothy
KINGSMILL, Hugh
  Lunn, Hugh Kingsmill
KINGSTON, Charles
  O'Mahony, Charles Kingston
KINGSTON, Syd
  Bingley, David Ernest
KINNOCH, R. G. B.
  Barclay, George
KINSEY-JONES, Brian
  Ball, Brian N.
KIRBY, Kate
  Elgin, Betty
KIRK, Laurence
  Simson, Eric Andrew
KISH
  Le Riche, P. J.
KLAXON
  Bower, John Graham
KLOSE, Norma Cline
  Cline, Norma
KNICKERBOCKER, Cholly
  Paul, Maury
KNIGHT, Adam
  Lariar, Lawrence

KNIGHT, Brigid
  Sinclair, Kathleen Henrietta
KNIGHT, David
  Prather, Richard
KNIGHT, Gareth
  Wilby, Basil
KNIGHT, Isobel
  Lockie, Isobel
KNIGHT, Mallory T.
  Hurwood, Bernhardt J.
KNOTT, Bill
  Knott, William Cecil
KNOTT, Hermann
  Smith, Walter Chalmers
KNOTTS, Raymond
  Volk, Gordon
KNOWALL, George
  O'Nolan, Brian
KNOX, Bill
  Macleod, Robert
KNOX, Calvin
  Silverberg, Robert
KNUDSEN, Greta
  Knudsen, Margrethe
KONING, Hans
  Koningsberger, Hans
KRAMER, George
  Heuman, William
KREUZENAU, Michael
  Law, Michael
KRISLOV, Alexander
  Lee Howard, L. A.
KROLL, Burt
  Rowland, Donald Sydney
KRUGER, Paul
  Sebenthall, Roberta
KRULL, Felix
  White, Stanley

KUTHUMI
  Fleishmann, Helle
KYD, Thomas
  Harbage, Alfred
KYLE, Elisabeth
  Dunlop, Agnes M. R.

*What good can it do an ass to be
called a lion?*
—Thomas Fuller. Gnomologia

LA FAYETTE, Rene
  Hubbard, L. Ron
LACY, Ed
  Zinberg, Len
LADY OF QUALITY
  Jones, *Lady* Roderick
LAFARGUE, Philip
  Philpot, Joseph H.
LAING, Kenneth
  Langmaid, Kenneth Joseph
  Robb
LAING, Patrick
  Long, Amelia R.
LAKE, Sarah
  Weiner, Margery
LAKER, Rosalind
  Øvstedal, Barbara
LAKLAN, Carli
  Laughlin, Virginia Carli
LAMBERT, Christine
  Loewengard, Heidi H. F.
LAMONT, Frances
  Jourdain, Eleanor F.
LAMONT, Marianne
  Rundle, Anne

LAMONT, N. B.
  Barnitt, Nedda Lemmon
LAMPLAUGH, Lois
  Davis, Lois Carlile
LAMPTON, Austen
  Dent, Anthony
LAN
  Landon, Melville de Lancey
LANCASTER, A. F.
  Fleur, Anne Elizabeth
LANCASTER, G. B.
  Lyttleton, Edith Joan
LANCASTER, Vicky
  Ansle, Dorothy Phoebe
LANCE, Leslie
  Swatridge, Irene M. M.
LANCER, Jack
  Lawrence, James Duncan
LANDELS, D. H.
  Henderson, Donald Landels
LANDELS, Stephanie
  Henderson, Donald Landels
LANDER, Dane
  Clarke, Percy A.
LANDERS, Ann
  Lederer, Esther Pauline
LANDGRAVE OF HESSE
  Rosen, Michael
LANDIS, John
  Bell, Gerard
LANDON, Louise
  Hauck, Louise Platt
LANE, Elizabeth
  Farmers, Eileen Elizabeth
LANE, Grant
  Fisher, Stephen Gould
LANE, Jane
  Dakers, Elaine

LANE, Marvyn
Price, Jeremie
LANE, Mary D.
Delaney, Mary Murray
LANG, Anthony
Vahey, John George
Haslette
LANG, Frances
Mantle, Winifred Langford
LANG, Grace
Floren, Lee
LANG, Theo
Langbehn, Theo
LANGDALE, Stanley
Moorhouse, Sydney
LANGDON, Mary
Pike, Mary Hayden
LANGE, John
Crichton, Michael
LANGFORD, Jane
Mantle, Winifred Langford
LANGLEY, Helen
Rowland, Donald Sydney
LANGLEY, John
Mason, Sydney Charles
LANGLEY, Lee
Langley, Sarah
LANGLEY, Peter
Fleming, Ronald
LANGSTAFF, Tristram
Lord, William Wilberforce
LANIN, E. B.
Dillon, E. J.
LANSING, Henry
Rowland, Donald Sydney
LANT, Harvey
Rowland, Donald Sydney

LANZOL, Cesare
Landells, Richard
LAREDO, Johnny
Caesar, Gene
LARRIMORE, Lida
Turner, Lida Larrimore
LARRY
Parkes, Terence
LARSEN, Egon
Lehrburger, Egon
LARSON, Eve
St John, Wylly Folk
LASCELLES, Alison
Parris, John
LATHAM, Mavis
Thorpe-Clark, Mavis
LATHAM, Murray
Latham, Alison *and* Latham,
Esther
LATHAM, O'Neill
O'Neill, Rose Cecil
LATHEN, Emma
Latis, Mary J. *and* Hennissart,
Martha
LATHROP, Francis
Leiber, Fritz
LATIMER, Rupert
Mills, Algernon Victor
LAUDER, George Dick
Dick-Lauder, *Sir* George
LAUGHLIN, P. S.
Shea, Patrick
LAUNAY, André
De Launay, André Joseph
LAUNAY, Droo
De Launay, André Joseph
LAURA
Hunter, Eileen

189

LAURENCE, Robert
  Fischer, Matthias Joseph
LAVINGTON, Hubert
  Carrington, Hereward
LAW, Marjorie J.
  Liddelow, Marjorie Joan
LAWLESS, Anthony
  MacDonald, Philip
LAWRENCE, Hilda
  Kronmiller, Hildegarde
LAWRENCE, Irene
  March, John
LAWRENCE, James
  Tames, Richard Lawrence
LAWRENCE, Steven C.
  Murphy, Lawrence D.
LAWSON, Christine
  Walker, Emily Kathleen
LAWSON, Michael
  Ryder, M. L.
LAWTON, Dennis
  Faust, Frederick
LE BRETON, Thomas
  Ford, T. Murray
LE CARRÉ, John
  Cornwell, David John Moore
LE GRAND
  Henderson, Le Grand
LE GRYS, Walter
  Norgate, Walter
LEA, Timothy
  Wood, Christopher
LEACROFT, Eric
  Young, Eric Brett
LEADER, Charles
  Smith, Robert Charles
LEADERMAN, George
  Robinson, Richard Blundell

LEDGARD, Jake
  Mason, Sydney Charles
LEE, Andrew
  Auchincloss, Louis
LEE, Babs
  Lee, Marion Van Der Veer
LEE, Charles H.
  Story, Rosamond Mary
LEE, David
  Rush, Noel
LEE, Edward
  Foutts, Edward Lee
LEE, Elsie
  Sheridan, Elsie Lee
LEE, Gypsy Rose
  Hovick, Rose Louise
LEE, Jesse
  Mason, Sydney Charles
LEE, Ranger
  Snow, Charles Horace
LEE, Rowena
  Bartlett, Marie
LEE, Vernon
  Paget, Violet
LEE, Veronica
  Woodford, Irene-Cecile
LEE, William
  Burroughs, William
LEES, Hannah
  Fetter, Elizabeth
LEES, Marguerite
  Baumann, Margaret
LEIGH, Johanna
  Sayers, Dorothy L.
LEIGH, Olivia
  Clamp, Helen M. E.
LEIGH, Ursula
  Gwynn, Ursula Grace

LEIGHTON, Lee
  Overholser, Wayne D.
LEINSTER, Murray
  Jenkins, William Fitzgerald
LEJEUNE, Anthony
  Thompson, Edward Anthony
LEMON, Grey
  Gray, Lindsay Russell Nixon
LENANTON, C.
  Lananton, *Lady*
LENGEL, Frances
  Trocchi, Alexander
LENTON, Anthony
  Nuttall, Anthony
LEO, Alan
  Allan, Frederick William
LEODHAS, Sorche Nic
  Alger, Leclaire Gowans
LEONA
  Button, Margaret
LEONARD, Charles L.
  Heberden, Mary Violet
LEONID
  Bosworth, Willan George
LESIEG, Theo
  Geisel, Theodor Seuss
LESLIE, A.
  Scott, Leslie
LESLIE, A. Scott
  Scott, Leslie
LESLIE, Colin
  Roome, Gerald Antony
LESLIE, Doris
  Fergusson-Hannay, *Lady*
LESLIE, Henrietta
  Schütze, Gladys Henrietta
LESLIE, J. P.
  Leslie, Peter

LESLIE, O. H.
  Slesar, Henry
LESLIE, Val
  Knights, Leslie
LESS, Milton
  Marlowe, Stephen
LESSER, Anthony
  Whitby, Anthony Charles
LESTER, Frank
  Usher, Frank Hugh
LESTER, Jane
  Walker, Emily Kathleen
LESTER-RANDS, A.
  Judd, Frederick
LETHBRIDGE, Olive
  Banbury, Olive Lethbridge
LETHBRIDGE, Rex
  Meyers, Roy
LEVINREW, Will
  Levine, William
LEWIS, Ernest
  Vesey, Ernest Blakeman
LEWIS, Francine
  Wells, Helen
LEWIS, J. B.
  Lewis, Roy
LEWIS, Lange
  Beynon, Jane
LEWIS, Mervyn
  Frewer, Glyn
LEWIS, Paul
  Gerson, Noel Bertram
LEWIS, Roger
  Zarchy, Harry
LIGGETT, Hunter
  Paine, Lauran Bosworth
LIMNELIUS, George
  Robinson, Lewis George

LINCOLN, Geoffrey
  Mortimer, John
LINCOLN, John
  Cardif, Maurice
LIND, Jakov
  Landwirth, Heinz
LINDALL, Edward
  Smith, Edward Ernest
LINDLEY, Erica
  Quigley, Aileen
LINDLEY, Gerard
  Pilley, Phil
LINDSAY, H.
  Hudson, H. Lindsay
LINDSAY, Josephine
  Story, Rosamond Mary
LINDSAY, Lee
  Barre, Jean
LINDSEY, John
  Muriel, John
LINESMAN
  Grant, M. H.
LINKLATER, Lane
  Watkins, Alex
LINSON
  Tomlinson, Joshua Leonard
LIPSTICK
  Long, Lois
LISLE, Mary
  Cornish, Doris Mary
LITTLE, Conyth
  Little, Gwenyth *and* Little,
  Constance
LITTLE, Sylvia
  Leyland, Eric
LITTLEJOHN, Jon R.
  Kleinhaus, Theodore John

LIVINGSTON, Kenneth
  Stewart, Kenneth Livingston
LIVINGSTONE, Margaret
  Flynn, Mary
LLEWELLYN
  Lucas, Beryl Llewellyn
LLEWELLYN, Richard
  Lloyd, Richard Dafydd Vivian
  Llewellyn
LLEWMYS, Weston
  Pound, Ezra
LLOYD, John
  Cooper, John
LLOYD, Joseph M.
  Purves, Frederick
LLOYD, Willson
  Dennison, Enid
LOCHIONS, Colin
  Jackson, Caary Paul
LOCKE, Martin
  Duncan, William Murdoch
LODER, Vernon
  Vahey, John George Haslette
LODGE, John
  Leyland, Eric
LOEWENTHAL, Karen
  Tripp, Kathleen
LOGAN, Agnes
  Adams, Agnes
LOGAN, Mark
  Nicole, Christopher
LOGROLLER
  Le Gallienne, Richard
LOMAX, Bliss
  Drago, Harry Sinclair
LOMAX, Jeff
  Mason, Sydney Charles

LOMBARD, Nap
  Johnson, Pamela Hansford *and*
  Stewart, Neil
LONDON, Anne
  Gordon, Robert I.
LONDON, Robert
  Gordon, Robert I.
LONG, Gerry
  Larkins, William
LONG, Shirley
  Long, Leonard
LONGBAUGH, Harry
  Goldman, William
LONGFIELD, Jo
  Howard, Felicity
LONGLEY, John
  Denton, John
LONSDALE, Frederick
  Leonard, Lionel Frederick
LORAC, E. C. R.
  Rivett, Edith Caroline
LORAINE, Philip
  Estridge, Robin
LORD, Douglas
  Lord, Doreen Mildred Douglas
LORD, Jeremy
  Redman, Ben Ray
LORD, Nancy
  Titus, Eve
LORING, Peter
  Shellabarger, Samuel
LORNA
  Stoddart, Jane T.
LORNE, Charles
  Brand, Charles Neville
LORRAINE, Anne
  Chisholm, Lilian

LOVE, Arthur
  Liebers, Arthur
LOVE, David
  Lasky, Jesse L.
LOVEGOOD, John
  Watson, Elliot Grant
LOVELL, Ingraham
  Bacon, Josephine Dodge
LOW, Dorothy Mackie
  Paxton, Lois
LOW, Rachel
  Whear, Rachel
LOWE, Edith
  Kovar, Edith May
LOWE, Kenneth
  Lobaugh, Elma K.
LOWELL, Elaine
  Covert, Alice Lent
LOWELL, J. R.
  Lowell, Jan *and* Lowell,
  Robert
LOWING, Anne
  Wilson, Christine
LOWNDES, Susan
  Marques, Susan Lowndes
LUARD, L.
  Luard, William Blaine
LUCAS, J. K.
  Paine, Lauran Bosworth
LUCAS, Victoria
  Plath, Sylvia
LUDLOW, George
  Kay, Ernest
LUDLOW, Geoffrey
  Meynell, Laurence Walter
LUDLOW, John
  Palmer, Cecil

LUDWELL, Bernice
  Stokes, Manning Lee
LUELLEN, Valentina
  Polley, Judith Anne
LUIMARDEL
  Martinez-Delgado, Luis
LUK, Charles
  Lu Kuan Yu
LUM, Peter
  Lum, Bettina Peter
LUMMINS
  Melling, Leonard
LUNCHBASKET, Roger
  Reeve-Jones, Alan
LUNN, Peter
  Crowe, *Lady*
LUSKA, Sidney
  Harland, Henry
LYALL, David
  Swan, Annie S.
LYDECKER, J. J.
  Dudley, Ernest
LYMINGTON, John
  Chance, John Newton
LYNCH, Eric
  Bingley, David Ernest
LYNCH, Frances
  Compton, D. G.
LYNCH, Lawrence
  Van Deventer, Emma M.
LYNDALE, Sydney M.
  Moorhouse, Sydney
LYNDE, H. H.
  Huntington, Helen
LYNDON, Barrie
  Edgar, Alfred
LYNN, Carol
  Goetcheus, Carolyn

LYNN, Irene
  Rowland, Donald Sydney
LYNN, Margaret
  Battye, Gladys
LYNN, Stephen
  Bradbury, Parnell
LYNTON, Ann
  Rayner, Claire
LYON, Buck
  Paine, Lauran Bosworth
LYON, Elinor
  Wright, Elinor
LYON, Jessica
  De Leeuw, Cateau W.
LYRE, Pinchbeck
  Sassoon, Siegfried
LYTE, Richard
  Whelpton, Eric
LYTTON, Jane
  Clarke, Percy A.

M. B.
  Faust, Frederick
MABLE, Peter
  Wiedenbeck, Emilie Agnes
MACADAM, Eve
  Leslie, Cecilie
McALPIN, Grant
  McCulley, Johnston
MACALPIN, Rory
  Mackinnon, Charles Roy
MACANDREW, Rennie
  Elliot, Andrew George
McARTHUR, John
  Wise, Arthur
McBAIN, Ed
  Hunter, Evan

MACBRIDE, Aeneas
    MacKay, Fulton
McCABE, Cameron
    Borneman, Ernest
McCABE, Rory
    Greenwood, T. E.
McCALL, Anthony
    Kane, Henry
McCALL, Isabel
    Boyd, Elizabeth Orr
McCALL, Vincent
    Morland, Nigel
McCANN, Edson
    Pohl, Frederik
McCARY, Reed
    Rydberg, Ernie
McCLEAN, Kathleen
    Hale, Kathleen
McCONNELL, Will
    Snodgrass, W. D.
McCORD, Whip
    Norwood, Victor George
      Charles
McCORMACK, Charlotte
    Ross, William Edward Daniel
McCORMICK, Theodora
    Du Bois, Theodora
McCOY, Hank
    Martin, Reginald Alec
McCOY, Malachy
    Caulfield, Max
McCOY, Marshall
    Meares, Leonard F.
McCREADY, Jack
    Powell, Talmage
MACCREIGH, James
    Pohl, Frederik

MACDIARMID, Hugh
    Grieve, Christopher Murray
MACDONALD, Anson
    Heinlein, Robert A.
MACDONALD, Jo
    Macdonald, Margaret
      Josephine
MACDONALD, John
    Millar, Kenneth
MACDONALD, John Ross
    Millar, Kenneth
MACDONALD, Marcia
    Hill, Grace
MACDONALD, Ross
    Millar, Kenneth
MACDOUALL, Robertson
    Mair, George Brown
MACDOWELL, Frederics
    Frede, Richard
MACDUFF, Ilka
    List, Ilka Katherine
MACE, Margaret
    Lawrence, Dulcie
MACEY, Carn
    Barrett, Geofrey John
MACFARLAND, Anne
    MacDonald, Susanne
MACFARLANE, Kenneth
    Walker, Kenneth Macfarlane
MACFARLANE, Stephen
    Cross, John Keir
McGAVIN, Moyra
    Crichton, Eleanor
McGAW, J. M.
    Morris, John
McGILL, Ian
    Allegro, John Marco

McGREW. Fenn
   McGrew, Julia *and* Fenn,
     Caroline K.
McGUINNESS, Brian
   McGuinness, Bernard
MACGUIRE, Nicolas
   Melides, Nicholas
McGURK, Slater
   Roth, Arthur
MACHLIS, Joseph
   Selcamm, George
McHUGH, Stuart
   Rowland, Donald Sydney
McINTOSH, Ann T.
   Higginbotham, Anne D.
McINTOSH, J. T.
   Macgregor, James Murdoch
MACK, Evalina
   McNamara, Lena
McKENZIE, Paige
   Blood, Marje
McKENNA, Evelyn
   Joscelyn, Archie Lynn
McKERN, Pat
   Willett, Franciscus
MACKIN, Anita
   Donson, Cyril
McKINLEY, Karen
   Runbeck, Margaret Lee
MACLAREN, Ian
   Watson, John
MACLEAN, Art
   Shirreffs, Gordon D.
MACLEAN, Barry
   Chosack, Cyril
MACLEAN, Christina
   Casement, Christina

MACLEOD, Finlay
   Wood, James
MACLEOD, Fiona
   Sharp, William
MACLEODHAS, Sorche
   Alger, Leclaire Gowans
McLOWERY, Frank
   Keevill, Henry John
McMASTER, Alison
   Baker, Marjorie
McMEEKIN, Clark
   Clark, Dorothy *and*
     McMeekin, Isabel
McMUD, Dok
   McLachlan, Dan
MACNAMARA, Brinsley
   Weldon, A. E.
MACNEIL, Duncan
   McCutchan, Philip D.
MACNEIL, Neil
   Ballard, Willis Todhunter
McNEILL, Janet
   Alexander, Janet
MACNELL, James
   MacDonnell, James Edmond
MACNIB
   Mackie, Albert David
MACOMBER, Daria
   Stevenson, Ferdinan *and*
     Robinson, Patricia
MACQUEEN, Jay
   Minto, Mary
MACRAE, Hawk
   Barker, Albert H.
MACRAE, Mason
   Rubel, James Lyon
MACRAE, Travis
   Feagles, Anita MacRae

MACTYRE, Paul
  Adam, Robin
MACUMBER, Mari
  Sandoz, Mari
MADDERN, Stan
  Mason, Sydney Charles
MADEOC
  Robinson, H.
MADGETT, Naomi Long
  Andrews, Naomi Cornelia
MADISON, Dolly
  Paul, Maury
MADISON, Hank
  Rowland, Donald Sydney
MAGILL, Marcus
  Hill, Brian
MAGNUS, Gerald
  Bowman, Gerald
MAGRISKA, Hélène *Countess*
  Brockies, Enid Florence
MAINE, Charles Eric
  McIlwain, David
MAINE, Stirling
  Mason, Sydney Charles
MAINSAIL
  Duff, Douglas Valder
MAIZEL, Leah
  Maizel, Clarice Louise
MAIZIE
  Rose, Mary H.
MALCOLM, Charles
  Hincks, Cyril Malcolm
MALCOLM, John
  Batt, Malcolm John
MALCOLM, John
  Uren, Malcolm
MALCOLM, Ronald
  Hincks, Cyril Malcolm

MALCOLM X
  Little, Malcolm
MALET, Lucas
  Kingsley, Mary
MALET, Oriel
  Vaughan, *Lady* Auriel
MALLERY, Amos
  Gelb, Norman
MALLOCH, Peter
  Duncan, William Murdoch
MALLORY, Jay
  Carey, Joyce
MALLOWEN, Agatha Christie
  Christie, *Dame* Agatha
MALONE, Louis
  MacNeice, Louis
MANDEVILLE, D. E.
  Coates, Anthony
MANN, Abel
  Creasey, John
MANN, Deborah
  Bloom, Ursula
MANN, John
  Stevens, Henry Charles
MANN, Patricia
  Earnshaw, Patricia
MANN, Patrick
  Waller, Leslie
MANN, Stanley
  Mason, Sydney Charles
MANNERS, Julia
  Greenaway, Gladys
MANNGIAN, Peter
  Monger, Ifor
MANNING, David
  Faust, Frederick
MANNING, Lee
  Stokes, Manning Lee
MANNING, Marsha
  Grimstead, Hettie

197

MANNING, Roy
  Reach, James
MANNINGHAM, Basil
  Homersham, Basil Henry
MANNOCK, Jennifer
  Mannock, Laura
MANNON, M. M.
  Mannon, Martha *and* Mannon,
  Mary Ellen
MANOR, Jason
  Hall, Oakley Maxwell
MANSBRIDGE, Pamela
  Course, Pamela
MANSELL, C. R.
  Payne, Eileen Mary
MANSFIELD, Katherine
  Beauchamp, Kathleen Mansfield
MANTON, Jo
  Gittings, Jo
MANTON, Paul
  Walker, Peter Norman
MANTON, Peter
  Creasey, John
MANVILLE, George
  Fenn, George Manville
MAO
  Addis, Hazel Iris
MAPLESDEN, Ray
  Pearce, Raymond
MARA, Thalia
  Mahoney, Elizabeth
MARCH, Emma
  Stubbs, Jean
MARCH, Hilary
  Green, Lalage Isobel
MARCH, Jermyn
  Webb, Dorothy Anna

MARCH, Stella
  Marshall, Marjorie
MARCH, William
  Campbell, William Edward
  March
MARCHANT, Catherine
  Cookson, Catherine
MARCHBANKS, Samuel
  Davies, Robertson
MARCO
  Mountbatten, *Lord* Louis
MARCUS AURELIUS
  Padley, Walter
MARDLE, Jonathan
  Fowler, Eric
MARGERISON, David
  Davies, David Margerison
MARIA, Hermann Karl Georg
  Jesus
  Pound, Ezra
MARIANA
  Foster, Marian Curtis
MARIN, A. C.
  Coppel, Alfred
MARIN, Alfred
  Coppel, Alfred
MARINER, David
  Macleod-Smith, D.
MARION, S. T.
  Lakritz, Esther
MARJORAM, J.
  Mottram, Ralph Hale
MARK, David
  Buitenkant, Nathan
MARK, Edwina
  Fadiman, Edwin J.
MARK, Matthew
  Babcock, Frederic

MARKANDAYA, Kamala
Taylor, Kamala
MARKER, Clare
Witcombe, Rick
MARKHAM, Robert
Amis, Kingsley
MARLE, T. B.
Lambert, Hubert Steel
MARLIN, Roy
Ashmore, Basil
MARLOW, Joyce
Connor, Joyce Mary
MARLOW, Louis
Wilkinson, Louis Umfreville
MARLOW, Phyllis
Mason, Sydney Charles
MARLOWE, Hugh
Patterson, Henry
MARLOWE, Piers
Gribble, Leonard Reginald
MARLOWE, Stephen
Lesser, Milton
MARO, Judith
Jones, Judith Anastasia
MARQUIS, Don
Perry, Robert
MARR, Nancy J.
Johnson, Nancy Marr
MARRIC, J. J.
Creasey, John
MARSDEN, Anthony
Sutton, Graham
MARSDEN, James
Creasey, John
MARSDEN, June
Ingram-Moore, Erica
MARSH, Henry
Saklatvala, Beram

MARSH, Jean
Marshall, Evelyn
MARSH, Joan
Marsh, John
MARSH, Patrick
Hiscock, Leslie
MARSH, Rebecca
Neubauer, William Arthur
MARSHALL, Archibald
Marshall, Arthur Hammond
MARSHALL, Beverley
Holroyd, Ethel Mary
MARSHALL, Douglas
McClintock, Marshall
MARSHALL, Gary
Snow, Charles Horace
MARSHALL, James Vance
Payne, Donald Gordon
MARSHALL, Joanne
Rundle, Anne
MARSHALL, Joseph
Krechniak, Joseph Marshall
MARSHALL, Lloyd
Wilding, Philip
MARSHALL, Lovat
Duncan, William Murdoch
MARSHALL, Raymond
Raymond, Rene
MARSTEN, Richard
Hunter, Evan
MARTELL, James
Bingley, David Ernest
MARTENS, Paul
Southwold, Stephen
MARTIN, Abe
Hubbard, Frank McKinney
MARTIN, Ann
Best, Carol Ann

MARTIN, Bruce
  Paine, Lauran Bosworth
MARTIN, Christopher
  Hoyt, Edwin Palmer Jr
MARTIN, Chuck
  Martin, Charles Morris
MARTIN, Dorothea
  Hewitt, Kathleen Douglas
MARTIN, Frederick
  Stern, Frederick Martin
MARTIN, Gil
  Overy, Jillian P. J.
MARTIN, John
  Tatham, Laura
MARTIN, Nancy
  Salmon, Annie Elizabeth
MARTIN, Peter
  Chaundler, Christine
MARTIN, R. J.
  Mehta, Rustam
MARTIN, Rex
  Martin, Reginald Alec
MARTIN, Richard
  Creasey, John
MARTIN, Richard
  Harman, Richard
MARTIN, Robert
  Martin, Reginald Alec
MARTIN, Ruth
  Rayner, Claire
MARTIN, Scott
  Martin, Reginald Alec
MARTIN, Stella
  Heyer, Georgette
MARTIN, Tom
  Paine, Lauran Bosworth
MARTINDALE, Spencer
  Wolff, William

MARTINEZ, J. D.
  Parkhill, Forbes
MARTON, Francesca
  Bellasis, Margaret Rosa
MARTYN, Don
  Borbolla, Barbara
MARTYN, Henry
  Perry, Martin
MARTYN, Miles
  Elliott-Cannon, Arthur Elliott
MARTYN, Oliver
  White, Herbert Oliver
MARVEL, Holt
  Maschwitz, Eric
MARVEL, Ik
  Mitchell, Donald Grant
MARX, Magdeleine
  Paz, Magdeleine
MASON, Carl
  King, Albert
MASON, Chuck
  Rowland, Donald Sydney
MASON, Frank W.
  Mason, F. Van Wyck
MASON, Howard
  Ramage, Jennifer
MASON, Michael
  Smith, Edgar
MASON, Stuart
  Millard, Christopher S.
MASON, Tally
  Derleth, August William
MASS, William
  Gibson, William
MASSON, Georgina
  Johnson, Marion
MASTERS, Robert
  Boehm, David Alfred

MASTERS, Steve
  Mason, Sydney Charles
MASTERS, William
  Cousins, Margaret
MASTERSON, Whit
  Wade, Robert *and* Miller,
    William
MATELOT
  Uren, Malcolm
MATHER, Anne
  Grieveson, Mildred
MATHER, Berkely
  Davies, John Evan Weston
MATHER, Virginia
  Liebler, Jean Mayer
MATHESON, Hugh
  Mackay, Lewis
MATHESON, Sylvia A.
  Schofield, Sylvia Anne
MATT
  Sandford, Matthew
MATTHESON, Rodney
  Creasey, John
MATTHEWS, Brander
  Matthews, James Brander
MATUSOW, Marshall
  Matusow, Harvey Marshall
MAUGHAM, Robin
  Maugham, Robert Cecil Romer
    Viscount
MAURICE, Furnley
  Wilmot, Frank Leslie
    Thompson
MAURICE, Michael
  Skinner, Conrad Arthur
MAXTON, Anne
  Best, Allena

MAXWELL, Ann
  Pattinson, Lee
MAXWELL, C. Bede
  Maxwell, Violet S.
MAXWELL, Clifford
  Leon, Henry Cecil
MAXWELL, Vicky
  Worboys, Anne Ayre
MAY, Roberta E.
  Davidson, Edith May
MAYBURY, Anne
  Buxton, Anne
MAYHEW, Elizabeth
  Bear, Joan E.
MAYNE, Cora
  Walker, Emily Kathleen
MAYNE, Rutherford
  Waddell, Samuel
MAYO, Arnold
  Meredith, Kenneth Lincoln
MAYO, James
  Coulter, Stephen
MAYRANT, Drayton
  Simons, Katherine Drayton
    Mayrant
MAZ
  Mazure, Alfred Leonardus
MAZE, Edward
  Mazzocco, Edward
MEDHURST, Joan
  Liverton, Joan
MEDICA
  Malleson, Joan Graeme
MEDICUS
  MacLaren, James Paterson
MEDILL, Robert
  McBride, Robert Medill

MEE
  Schube, Purcell G.
MEE, Mary
  Dean, Mary
MEIKLE, Clive
  Brooks, Jeremy
MEINIKOFF, Pamela
  Harris, Pamela
MELBOURNE, Ida
  Ransome, L. E.
MELLOR, Michael
  Spooner, Peter Alan
MELMOTH
  Tullett, Denis John
MELVILLE, Alan
  Caverhill, William Melville
MELVILLE, Jean
  Cummins, Mary Warmington
MELVILLE, Jennie
  Butler, Gwendolyn
MELVILLE, Lewis
  Benjamin, Lewis S.
MENANDER
  Morgan, Charles
MENDEL, Jo
  Bond, Gladys Baker
MENDEL, Jo
  Gilbertson, Mildred
MENDL, Gladys
  Schütze, Gladys Henrietta
MENTOR
  Jones, Frank H.
MERCER, Frances
  Hills, Frances E.
MERCURY
  Eames, Helen Mary
MEREDITH, Anne
  Malleson, Lucy

MEREDITH, David William
  Miers, Earl Schenk
MEREDITH, Hal
  Blyth, Harry
MEREDITH, Peter
  Worthington-Stuart, Brian
  Arthur
MERIVALE, Margaret
  Frost, Kathleen Margaret
MERLIN, David
  Moreau, David
MERLINI, The Great
  Rawson, Clayton
MERRICK, Hugh
  Meyer, Harold Albert
MERRICK, Spencer
  Mason, Sydney Charles
MERRIL, Judith
  Grossman, Judith
MERRILL, Lynne
  Gibbs, Norah
MERRILL, P. J.
  Roth, Holly
MERRIMAN, Chad
  Cheshire, Gifford Paul
MERRIMAN, Henry Seton
  Scott, Hugh Stowell
MERRITT, E. B.
  Waddington, Miriam
METCALF, Suzanne
  Baum, Lyman Frank
METHUEN, John
  Bell, John Keble
MEURON, Skip
  Sands, Leo G.
MEWBURN, Martin
  Hitchin, Martin

MEYER, Henry J.
  Hird, Neville
MEYER, June
  Jordan, June
MIALL, Robert
  Burke, John Frederick
MICHAEL, Manfred
  Winterfield, Henry
MICHAEL X
  De Freitas, Michael
MICHAELHOUSE, John
  McCulloch, Joseph
MICHAELS, Barbara
  Mertz, Barbara G.
MICHAELS, Steve
  Avallone, Michael Angelo Jr
MICHELMORE, Susan
  Harvey, Margaret Susan Janet
MIDLING, Perspicacity
  Millward, Pamela
MILBURN, Cynthia
  Brooks, Ann
MILES
  Southwold, Stephen
MILES, David
  Cronin, Brendan Leo
MILES, John
  Bickham, Jack Miles
MILES, Miska
  Martin, Patricia Miles
MILES, Susan
  Roberts, Ursula
MILLBURN, Cynthia
  Brooks, Ann
MILLER, Ellen
  Pattinson, Lee
MILLER, Frank
  Loomis, Noel Miller
MILLER, Joaquin
  Miller, Cincinnatus H.

MILLER, John
  Samachson, Joseph
MILLER, Marc
  Baker, Marcell Genée
MILLER, Margaret J.
  Dale, Margaret
MILLER, Mary
  Northcott, Cecil
MILLER, Olive Thorne
  Miller, Harriet
MILLER, Patrick
  Macfarlane, George Gordon
MILLER, Wade
  Miller, William *and* Wade,
   Robert
MILLS, Alan
  Miller, Albert
MILLS, Martin
  Boyd, Martin à Beckett
MILLS, Osmington
  Brooks, Vivian Collin
MILNA, Bruno
  Painting, Norman
MILNE, Ewart
  Milne, Charles
MILNER, George
  Hardinge, George
MINGSTON, R. Gresham
  Stamp, Roger
MINICAM
  Russell, Henry George
MINIER, Nelson
  Baker, Laura
MIRYAM
  Yardumian, Miryam
MITCHAM, Gilroy
  Newton, William Simpson

203

MITCHELL, Ewan
  Janner, Greville
MITCHELL, K. L.
  Lamb, Elizabeth Searle
MITCHELL, Kerry
  Wilkes-Hunter, Richard
MITCHELL, Scott
  Godfrey, Lionel Robert
  Holcombe
MO, Manager
  Cassity, June
MODELL, Merriam
  Piper, Evelyn
MOKO
  Mead, Sidney
MOLE, Oscar
  Seaver, Richard
MOLE, William
  Younger, William Anthony
MONIG, Christopher
  Crossen, Kendell Foster
MONKLAND, George
  Whittet, George Sorley
MONMOUTH, Jack
  Pember, William Leonard
MONNOW, Peter
  Croudace, Glyn
MONRO, Gavin
  Monro-Higgs, Gertrude
MONTAGU, Robert
  Hampden, John
MONTGOMERY, Derek
  Simmons, J. S. A.
MONTROSE
  Adams, Charles William Dunlop
MONTROSE, David
  Graham, Charles

MONTROSE, Graham
  Mackinnon, Charles Roy
MONTROSE, James St David
  Appleman, John Alan
MONTROSS, David
  Backus, Jean L.
MOODIE, Edwin
  De Caire, Edwin
MOOLSON, Melusa
  Solomon, Samuel
MOORE, Arthur
  Matthews, Clayton
MOORE, Edward
  Muir, Edwin
MOORE, Frances Sarah
  Mack, Elsie Frances
MOORE, Rosalie
  Brown, Rosalie
MOORHOUSE, E. Hallam
  Meynell, Esther H.
MOORHOUSE, Hopkins
  Moorhouse, Herbert Joseph
MORDAUNT, Elinor
  Mordaunt, Evelyn May
MORE, Caroline
  Cone, Molly
MORE, Euston
  Bloomer, Arnold
MORE, J. J.
  Moffatt, James
MORENO, Nick
  Deming, Richard
MORESBY, Louis
  Beck, Lily Adams
MORETON, John
  Cohen, Morton N.
MORGAN, Angela
  Paine, Lauran Bosworth

MORGAN, Arlene
  Paine, Lauran Bosworth
MORGAN, Bryan
  Morgan, Brian Stanford
MORGAN, Carol McAfee
  Appleby, Carol McAfee
MORGAN, Claire
  Highsmith, Patricia
MORGAN, De Wolfe
  Williamson, Thames Ross
MORGAN, Frank
  Paine, Lauran Bosworth
MORGAN, John
  Paine, Lauran Bosworth
MORGAN, Michael
  Carle, C. E. *and* Dean, M. D.
MORGAN, Phyllis
  Thompson, Phyllis
MORGAN, Valerie
  Paine, Lauran Bosworth
MORISON, Elizabeth
  Moberly, Charlotte Anne
    Elizabeth
MORLAND, Peter Henry
  Faust, Frederick
MORPHY, *Countess*
  Forbes, Marcelle Azra
MORRIS, Ira J.
  Jefferies, Ira
MORRIS, John
  Hearne, John *and* Gargill,
    Morris
MORRIS, Julian
  West, Morris
MORRIS, Ruth
  Webb, Ruth Enid
MORRIS, Sara
  Burke, John Frederick

MORRISON, J. Strang
  Thom, William Albert Strang
MORRISON, Peggy
  Morrison, Margaret Mackie
MORRISON, William
  Samachson, Joseph
MORROW, Betty
  Bacon, Elizabeth
MORROW, Charlotte
  Kirwan, Molly
MORTIMER, June
  Ryder, Vera
MORTIMER, Peter
  Roberts, Dorothy James
MORTON, Anthony
  Creasey, John
MORTON, Leah
  Stern, Elisabeth Gertrude
MORTON, William
  Ferguson, William Blair
    Morton
MOSES, Ruben
  Wurmbrand, Richard
MOSS, Nancy
  Moss, Robert Alfred
MOSS, Roberta
  Moss, Robert Alfred
MOSSMAN, Burt
  Keevill, Henry John
MOSSOP, Irene
  Swatridge, Irene M. M.
MOSTYN-OWEN, Gaia
  Servadio, Gaia
MOTTE, Peter
  Harrison, Richard Motte
MOUTHPIECE
  Porter, Maurice

205

MOWBRAY, John
  Vahey, John George Haslette
MOWERY, Dorothy
  Dunsing, Dee
MOYES, Robin
  Bateman, Robert Moyes
MUIR, Alan
  Morrison, Thomas
MUIR, Dexter
  Gribble, Leonard Reginald
MUIR, Jane
  Petrone, Jane Gertrude
MUIR, John
  Morgan, Thomas Christopher
MUIR, Willa
  Muir, Wilhelmina Johnstone
MULDOON, Omar
  Matusow, Harvey Marshall
MULLER, Paul
  King, Albert
MULLINGS, Ann
  Dally, Ann
MUN
  Leaf, Munro
MUNDY, Max
  Schofield, Sylvia Anne
MUNDY, V. M.
  Cunningham, Virginia Myra
    Mundy
MUNRO, C. K.
  Macmullan, Charles W.
    Kirkpatrick
MUNRO, James
  Mitchell, James
MUNRO, Mary
  Howe, Doris
MUNRO, Ronald Eadie
  Glen, Duncan Munro

MUNROE, R.
  Cheyne, *Sir* Joseph
MUNTHE, Frances
  Minto, Frances
MURPHY, C. L.
  Murphy, Charlotte *and*
    Murphy, Lawrence
MURPHY, Louis J.
  Hicks, Tyler Gregory
MURRAY, Cromwell
  Morgan, Murray C.
MURRAY, Edna
  Rowland, Donald Sydney
MURRAY, Geraldine
  Murray, Blanche
MURRAY, Jill
  Walker, Emily Kathleen
MURRAY, Michael
  McLaren, Moray David Shaw
MURRAY, Sinclair
  Sullivan, Edward Alan
MURRAY, William
  Graydon, William Murray
MURRELL, Shirley
  Scott-Hansen, Olive
MURRY, Colin
  Murry, John Middleton Jr
MURRY, Colin Middleton
  Murry, John Middleton Jr
MYATT, Nellie
  Kirkham, Nellie
MYERS, Harriet Kathryn
  Whittington, Harry

N. D. H.
  Dick-Hunter, Noel
N. I.
  Camm, Frederick James

N. O. B.
  Bettany, F. G.
NA gCOPALEEN
  O'Nolan, Brian
NADA, John
  Langdon-Davies, John
NAMLEREP, Sidney
  Perelman, S. J.
NANKY POO
  O'Connor, Patrick
NAPIER, Geraldine
  Glemser, Bernard
NAPIER, Mark
  Laffin, John
NASH, Daniel
  Loader, William
NASH, Newlyn
  Howe, Doris
NASH, Simon
  Chapman, Raymond
NAST, Elsa Ruth
  Werner, Elsa Jane
NATHAN, Daniel
  Dannay, Frederic
NAUTICUS
  Seaman, *Sir* Owen
NAYLOR, Eliot
  Frankau, Pamela
NEAL, Hilary
  Norton, Olive Marion
NEIL, Frances
  Wilson, Christine
NELSON, Chris
  Huff, Darrell
NELSON, Gertrude
  Bobin, John W.
NELSON, Lois
  Northam, Lois Edgell

NELSON, Marguerite
  Floren, Lee
NEMO
  Douglas, Archibald C.
NEON
  Acworth, Marion W.
NESBIT, Troy
  Folsom, Franklin Brewster
NESS, K. T.
  Grant, Donald *and* Wilson,
    William
NETTLETON, Arthur
  Gaunt, Arthur N.
NEVILLE, C. J.
  Franklin, Cynthia
NEVILLE, Margot
  Joske, Neville *and* Goyder,
    Margot
NEVILLE, Mary
  Woodrich, Mary Neville
NEWCOMB, Norma
  Neubauer, William Arthur
NEWMAN, Margaret
  Betteridge, Anne
NEWTON, David C.
  Chance, John Newton
NEWTON, Francis
  Hobsbawn, E. J.
NEWTON, Macdonald
  Newton, William Simpson
NIALL, Ian
  McNeillie, John
NIALL, Michael
  Breslin, Howard
NICHOLAI, C. L. R.
  Clair, Colin
NICHOLLS, Anthony
  Parsons, Anthony

NICHOLS, Fan
  Hanna, Frances
NICHOLS, Peter
  Youd, Samuel
NICHOLSON, John
  Parcell, Norman Howe
NICHOLSON, Kate
  Fay, Judith
NICODEMUS
  Pearce, Melville Chaning
NICOLAS, F. R. E.
  Freeling, Nicolas
NIELSON, Vernon
  Clarke, Percy A.
NIELSON, Virginia
  McCall, Virginia
NIGHTINGALE, Charles
  Duddington, Charles Lionel
NILE, Dorothea
  Avallone, Michael Angelo Jr
NILSON, Bee
  Nilson, Annabel
NINA
  Nelson, Ethel
NITSUA, Benjamin
  Austin, Benjamin
NINESPOT
  Phillips, Hubert
NIXON, Kathleen
  Blundell, V. R.
NOBLE, Emily
  Gifford, James Noble
NOEL, John
  Bird, Dennis Leslie
NOEL, L.
  Barker, Leonard Noël
NONG
  Lobley, Robert

NOON, T. R.
  Norton, Olive Marion
NOONE, Edwina
  Avallone, Michael Angelo Jr
NORBURN, Martha
  Mead, Martha Norburn
NORDEN, Charles
  Durrell, Lawrence R.
NORDICUS
  Snyder, Louis Leo
NORHAM, Gerald
  James, J. W. G.
NORMAN, James
  Schmidt, James Norman
NORMYX
  Douglas, Norman *and*
  Fitzgibbon, Elsa
NORRIS, P. E.
  Cleary, C. V. H.
NORTH, Andrew
  Norton, Alice Mary
NORTH, Colin
  Bingley, David Ernest
NORTH, Eric
  Cronin, Bernard
NORTH, Gil
  Horne, Geoffrey
NORTH, Howard
  Dudley-Smith, Trevor
NORTH, Mark
  Miller, Wright
NORTHE, Maggie
  Lee, Maureen
NORTHERNER
  Hughes, William
NORTHROP, *Capt.* B. A.
  Hubbard, L. Ron

NORTHUMBRIAN GENTLEMAN
  Tegner, Henry
NORTON, André
  Norton, Alice Mary
NORTON, Bess
  Norton, Olive Marion
NORTON, Jed
  Lazenby, Norman
NORTON, S. H.
  Richardson, Mary Kathleen
NORTON, Victor
  Dalton, Gilbert
NORVELL, Anthony
  Trupo, Anthony
NORWAY, Kate
  Norton, Olive Marion
NORWOOD, Elliott
  Kensdale, W. E. N.
NORWOOD, John
  Stark, Raymond
NOSTALGIA
  Bentley, James W. B.
NOTT, Barry
  Hurren, Bernard
NOVAK, Joseph
  Kosinski, Jerzy
NUDNICK
  Nerney, Patrick W.
NUNQUAM
  Blatchford, Robert
NURAINI
  Sim, Katharine Phyllis

Cases of a man writing under a woman's name are rare.
—Cassell's Encyclopaedia of literature

O. P.
  Eccleshare, Colin
O. S.
  Seaman, *Sir* Owen
OATES, Titus
  Bell, Martin
OBOLENSKY, Ilka
  List, Ilka Katherine
O'BRIAN, Frank
  Garfield, Brian
O'BRIEN, Bernadette
  Higgins, Margaret
O'BRIEN, Deirdre
  McNally, Mary Elizabeth
O'BRIEN, Flann
  O'Nolan, Brian
O'BRIEN, John
  Hartigan, Patrick Joseph
O'BRIEN, Richard C.
  Conly, Robert Carroll
O'BYRNE, Dermot
  Bax, *Sir* Arnold
O'CONNELL, Robert Frank
  Gohm, Douglas Charles
O'CONNER, Clint
  Paine, Lauran Bosworth
O'CONNER, Elizabeth
  McNamara, Barbara Willard
O'CONNOR, Dermot
  Newman, Terence

O'CONNOR, Frank
  O'Donovan, Michael Francis
O'CONNOR, Patrick
  Wibberley, Leonard Patrick
    O'Connor
OCTAVIA
  Barltrop, Mabel
ODDIE, E. M.
  O'Donoghue, Elinor Mary
ODELL, Carol
  Foote, Carol
ODELL, Gil
  Foote, Carol *and* Gill, Travis
O'DONNELL, Donat
  O'Brien, Conor Cruise
OGDEN, Clint
  King, Albert
O'GRADA, Sean
  O'Grady, John
O'GRADY, Rohan
  Skinner, June O'Grady
O'GRADY, Tony
  Clemens, Brian
O'HARA, Kenneth
  Morris, Jean
O'HARA, Kevin
  Cumberland, Marten
O'HARA, Mary
  Sture-Vasa, Mary
OKADA, Hideki
  Glassco, John
OKE, Richard
  Millett, Nigel
OKE, Simon
  Vann, Gerald
OLD COYOTE, Sally
  Old Coyote, Elnora A.

OLDCASTLE, John
  Meynell, Wilfred
OLDFIELD, Peter
  Bartlett, Vernon
OLDHAM, Hugh R.
  Whitford, Joan
OLGA
  Phillips, Olga
OLIVER, Gail
  Scott, Marian Gallagher
OLIVER, Jane
  Rees, Helen
OLIVER, Laurence
  Brown, Laurence Oliver
OLIVER, Owen
  Flynn, *Sir* J. A.
OLIVER, Robert
  Carrier, Robert *and* Dick,
    Oliver Lawson
OLIVER, Roy
  Walker, Roy
OLIVIA
  Bussy, Dorothy
OLSEN, D. B.
  Hitchens, Dolores
OLSEN, Herb
  Olson, Herbert Vincent
OLYMPIC
  Hutton, Andrew Nielson
O'MALLEY, Frank
  O'Rourke, Frank
OMAN, Carola
  Lenanton, *Lady*
O'MARA, Jim
  Fluharty, Vernon
O'NAIR, Mairi
  Evans, Constance May

O'NEIL, Kerry
  MacIntyre, John Thomas
O'NEILL, Egan
  Linington, Elizabeth
ONIONS, Berta
  Oliver, Amy Roberta
ONIONS, Oliver
  Oliver, George
ONLOOKER
  Grant, William
OPHIEL
  Peach, Edward C.
ORAM, John
  Thomas, John Oram
ORBISON, Keck
  Orbison, Roy *and* Keck, Maud
ORCHARD, Evelyn
  Swan, Annie S.
ORDON, A. Lang
  Gordon, Alan Bacchus
O'RILEY, Warren
  Richardson, Gladwell
ORION
  Brooks, Ern
ORME, Alexandra
  Barcza, Alicja
ORME, Eve
  Williamson, Leila Isobel
ORMSBEE, David
  Longstreet, Stephen
ORR, Mary
  Caswell, Anne
ORVIS, Kenneth
  Lemieux, Kenneth
ORWELL
  Smith, Walter Chalmers
ORWELL, George
  Blair, Eric

OSBORN, Reuben
  Osbert, Reuben
OSBORNE, David
  Silverberg, Robert
O'SHEA, Sean
  Tralins, S. Robert
O'SULLIVAN, Seumas
  Starkey, James Sullivan
OUIDA
  Ramé, Maria Louise
OVERY, Claire May
  Bass, Clara May
OVERY, Martin
  Overy, Jillian P. J.
OWEN, Dean
  McGaughy, Dudley Dean
OWEN, Edmund
  Teller, Neville
OWEN, Hugh
  Faust, Frederick
OWEN, John Pickard
  Butler, Samuel
OWEN, Ray
  King, Albert
OWEN, Roderic
  Fenwick-Owen, Roderic
OWEN, Tom
  Watts, Peter Christopher
OXENHAM, Elsie Jeanette
  Dunkerley, Elsie Jeanette
OXENHAM, John
  Dunkerley, William Arthur
OYVED, Moysheh
  Good, Edward

P. B.
  Braybrooke, Patrick

211

P. C.
  Chalmers, Patrick
PACKER, Vin
  Meaker, Marijane
PADESON, Mary
  Magraw, Beatrice
PADGETT, Lewis
  Kuttner, Henry
PADMORE, George
  Nurse, Malcolm Ivan Meredith
PAGE, Eileen
  Heal, Edith
PAGE, Eleanor
  Coerr, Eleanor Beatrice
PAGE, Lorna
  Rowland, Donald Sydney
PAGE, Marco
  Kurnitz, Harry
PAGE, Stanton
  Fuller, Henry B.
PAGE, Vicki
  Avey, Ruby D.
PAGET, John
  Aiken, John
PAIN, Barry
  Guthrie, P. R.
PALINURUS
  Connolly, Cyril
PALMER, Edgar A.
  Posselt, Eric
PALMER, John
  Watts, Edgar John Palmer
PAN
  Beresford, Leslie
PANBOURNE, Oliver
  Rockey, Howard
PANDORA
  Moore, Mary McLeod

PANTOPUCK
  Philpott, Alexis Robert
PARADISE, Mary
  Eden, Dorothy
PARIOS
  Lee, Henry David Cook
PARK, Jordan
  Kornbluth, Cyril M.
PARKER, Seth
  Lord, Phillips H.
PARKES, Lucas
  Harris, John Wyndham Parkes
    Lucas Beynon
PARKS, Ron
  Guariento, Ronald
PARR, *Dr* John Anthony
  Anthony, E.
PARRISH, Jean J.
  Church, Elsie
PARRISH, Mary
  Cousins, Margaret
PARSONS, Bridget
  Cox, Euphrasia Emeline
PARTRIDGE, Anthony
  Oppenheim, E. Phillips
PASSMORE, Aileen E.
  Griffiths, Aileen Esther
PASTON, George
  Symonds, E. M.
PATIENT OBSERVER, The
  Strunsky, Simeon
PATRICK, Diana
  Wilson, Desemea
PATRICK, John
  Goggan, John Patrick
PATRICK, Keats
  Karig, Walter

PATRICK, Q
  Wheeler, Hugh Callingham *and*
  Webb, Richard Wilson
PATTEN, J.
  Cobb, Clayton W.
PATTERSON, Duke
  Leyland, Eric
PATTERSON, Harry
  Patterson, Henry
PATTERSON, Innis
  Patterson, Isabella Innis
PATTERSON, Olive
  Rowland, Donald Sydney
PATTERSON, Shott
  Renfrew, A.
PAUL, Adrian
  McGeogh, Andrew
PAUL, Barbara
  Øvstedal, Barbara
PAUL, James
  Warburg, James Paul
PAUL, John
  Webb, Charles Henry
PAULSON, Jack
  Jackson, Caary Paul
PAVITRA
  Saint-Hilaire, P. B.
PAWNEE BILL
  Lillie, Gordon W.
PAXTON, Lois
  Low, Lois
PAYE, Robert
  Campbell, Gabrielle Margaret
  Vere
PAYNE, Robert
  Payne, Pierre Stephen Robert
PEACE, Frank
  Cook, William Everett

PEACHUM, Thomas
  Oxman, Philip
PEARCE, A. H.
  Quibell, Agatha
PEARL, Irene
  Guyonvarch, Irene
PECKHAM, Richard
  Holden, Raymond
PEDRICK, Gale
  Pedrick-Harvey, Gale
PEEK, Bill
  Peed, William Bartlett
PEEL, Wallis
  Peel, Hazel
PEGDEN, Helen
  Macgregor, Miriam
PELHAM, Anthony
  Hope, Charles Evelyn Graham
PELHAM, Randolph
  Landells, Richard
PENDER, Marilyn
  Jacobs, Thomas Curtis Hicks
PENDLETON, Conrad
  Kidd, Walter E.
PENDLETON, Ford
  Cheshire, Gifford Paul
PENDOWER, Jacques
  Jacobs, Thomas Curtis Hicks
PENLAKE, Richard
  Salmon, P. R.
PENMARE, William
  Nisot, Mavis Elizabeth
PENN, Ann
  Jacobs, Thomas Curtis Hicks
PENN, Arthur
  Matthews, James Brander
PENN, Christopher
  Lawlor, Patrick

PENN, Richard
  Sproat, Iain Macdonald
PENN, Ruth Bonn
  Rosenberg, Ethel
PENNAGE, E. M.
  Finkel, George
PENNY, Rupert
  Thornett, Ernest Basil Charles
PENT, Katherine
  Shann, Renée
PENTECOST, Hugh
  Philips, Judson Pentecost
PEPPER, Joan
  Alexander, Joan
PEPPERWOOD, Pip
  Stoddard, Charles Warren
PERCY, Edward
  Smith, Edward Percy
PERCY, Florence
  Akers, Elizabeth
PEREZ, Faustino
  Hoffenberg, Mason
PERKINS, Eli
  Landon, Melville de Lancy
PERRY, Clay
  Perry, Clair Willard
PETERS, Alan
  Spooner, Peter Alan
PETERS, Bill
  McGivern, William Peter
PETERS, Bryan
  George, Peter
PETERS, Elizabeth
  Mertz, Barbara G.
PETERS, Ellis
  Pargeter, Edith Mary
PETERS, Fritz
  Peters, Arthur A.

PETERS, Geoffrey
  Palmer, Madelyn
PETERS, Geoffrey
  Trippe, Peter
PETERS, Jocelyn
  Oakeshott, Edna
PETERS, Lawrence
  Davies, Leslie Purnell
PETERS, Ludovic
  Brent, Peter Ludwig
PETERS, Maureen
  Black, Maureen
PETERS, Noel
  Harvey, Peter Noel
PETERS, Roy
  Nickson, Arthur
PETRIE, John
  Hewison, Robert John Petrie
PEYTON, K. M.
  Peyton, Kathleen Wendy *and*
  Peyton, Michael
PHELIX
  Burnett, Hugh
PHILATICUS
  Finlay, Ian
PHILIPPI, Mark
  Bender, Arnold
PHILIPS, Steve
  Whittington, Harry
PHILIPS, Thomas
  Davies, Leslie Purnell
PHILLIP, Alban M.
  Allan, Philip Bertram Murray
PHILLIPS, John
  Marquand, John Phillips
PHILLIPS, King
  Perkins, Kenneth

PHILLIPS, Leon
  Gerson, Noël Bertram
PHILMORE, R.
  Howard, Herbert Edmund
PHIPPS, Margaret
  Tatham, Laura
PHIPSON, Joan
  Fitzhardinge, Joan Margaret
PHOENICE, J.
  Hutchinson, Juliet Mary Fox
PICKARD, John Q.
  Borg, Philip Anthony John
PICTON, Bernard
  Knight, Bernard
PIERCE, Katherine
  St John, Wylly Folk
PIKE, Charles R.
  Harknett, Terry
PIKE, Robert
  Fish, Robert Lloyd
PIKE, Robert L
  Fish, Robert Lloyd
PILGRIM
  Wright, Marjory Beatrice
PILGRIM, Adam
  Webster, Owen
PILGRIM, Anne
  Allan, Mabel Esther
PILGRIM, David
  Palmer, John Leslie *and*
    Saunders, Hilary Aidan St
    George
PILGRIM, Derral
  Coleman, John
PILIO, Gerone
  Whitfield, John
PINDELL, Jon
  Paine, Lauran Bosworth

PINDER, Chuck
  Donson, Cyril
PINE, M. S.
  Finn, *Sister* Mary Paulina
PIPER, Evelyn
  Modell, Merriam
PIPER, Peter
  Langbehn, Theo
PIPER, Roger
  Fisher, John
PITCAIRN, Frank
  Cockburn, Claud
PITCHFORD, Harry Ronald
  Ebbs, Robert
PLAIDY, Jean
  Hibbert, Eleanor Alice Burford
PLAIN, Josephine
  Mitchell, Isabel
PLAUT, Martin
  Marttin, Paul
PLAYER, Robert
  Jordan, Robert Furneaux
PLEDGER, P. J.
  Tonkin, C. B.
PLOWMAN, Stephanie
  Dee, Stephanie
PLUMMER, Ben
  Bingley, David Ernest
POCRATES, *Dr* Hip
  Schoenfeld, Eugene L.
POE, Bernard
  Hausman, Leon Augustus
POLLOCK, Mary
  Blyton, Enid
POMFRET, Joan
  Townsend, Joan
PONT
  Laidler, Graham

215

POOK, Peter
  Miller, J. A.
POOLE, Michael
  Poole, Reginald Heber
POOLE, Richard
  Wells, Lee Edwin
POOLE, Vivian
  Jaffe, Gabriel
POOTER
  Hamilton, Alex
PORLOCK, Martin
  MacDonald, Philip
PORTER, Alvin
  Rowland, Donald Sydney
PORTOBELLO, Petronella
  Anderson, *Lady* Flavia
POTTER, Beatrix
  Heelis, Beatrix
POTTER, Margaret
  Betteridge, Anne
POWELL, Fern
  Samman, Fern
POWERS, Margaret
  Heal, Edith
POY
  Fearon, Percy
PREEDY, George
  Campbell, Gabrielle Margaret
  Vere
PREEDY, George R.
  Campbell, Gabrielle Margaret
  Vere
PRENDER, Bart
  King, Albert
PRENTIS, Richard
  Agate, James
PRENTISS, Karl
  Purdy, Ken
PRESCOT, Julian
  Budd, John

PRESCOTT, Caleb
  Bingley, David Ernest
PRESCOTT, John
  Lucchetti, Anthony
PRESLAND, John
  Bendit, Gladys
PRESTON, James
  Unett, John
PRESTON, Jane
  Thomas, Reg
PRESTON, Richard
  Lindsay, Jack
PREVOST, Francis
  Prevost-Battersby, H. F.
PRICE, Evadne
  Smith, Helen Zenna
PRIESTLEY, Robert
  Wiggins, David
PRIESTLY, Mark
  Albert, Harold A.
PRIVATE 19022
  Manning, Frederic
PROBERT, Lowri
  Jones, Robert Maynard
PROBYN, Elise
  McKibbon, John
PROCTER, Ida
  Harris, Ida Fraser
PROCTOR, Everitt
  Montgomery, Rutherford
  George
PROLE, Lozania
  Bloom, Urusla
PROUDFOOT, Walter
  Vahey, John George Haslette
PRUITT, Alan
  Rose, Alvin Emmanuel

PRUTKOV, Kozma
 Snodgrass, W. D.
PRYDE, Anthony
 Weekes, Agnes Russell
PULLING, Pierre
 Pulling, Albert Van Siclen
PULVERTAFT, Lalage
 Green, Lalage Isobel
PUNDIT, Ephraim
 Looker, Samuel Joseph
PURE, Simon
 Swinnerton, Frank
PUTRA, Kerala
 Panikkar, Lavalan

Q
 Quiller-Couch, *Sir* Arthur
QUAD, M.
 Lewis, Charles Bertrand
QUAESTOR
 Byford-Jones, Wilfred
QUARRY, Nick
 Albert, Marvin H.
QUEEN, Ellery
 Dannay, Frederic *and* Lee,
  Manfred B.
QUENTIN, Patrick
 Webb, Richard Wilson *and*
  Wheeler, Hugh Callingham
QUEX
 Nichols, *Captain* G. H. F.
QUILIBET
 Fowler, Henry Watson
QUILL
 Puddepha, Derek
QUILLET
 Fowler, Henry Watson
QUIN, Dan
 Lewis, Alfred Henry
QUIN, Shirland
 Guest, Enid

QUINCE, Peter
 Day, George Harold
QUINCE, Peter
 Thompson, J. W. M.
QUINLAN, Will
 Lash, William Quinlan
QUIRK
 Squibbs, H. W. Q.
QUIROULE, Pierre
 Sayer, Walter William
QUOD, John
 Irving, John Treat

No names, no pack-drill.
—British Army saying

R. H. F.
 Fairburn, R. H.
R. S.
 Zinsser, Hans
R. T. L.
 Vining, Charles A. M.
RACHEL
 Ferguson, Rachel
RACHEN, Kurt von
 Hubbard, L. Ron
RADIO PADRE
 Wright, Ronald Selby
RADYR, Tomos
 Stevenson, James Patrick
RAE, Scott
 Hamilton, Cecily
RAG MAN
 Burrows, Hermann
RAGGED STAFF
 Coley, Rex

RAIMOND, C. E.
 Robins, Elizabeth
RAINE, Richard
 Sawkins, Raymond Harold
RAKOSI, Carl
 Rawley, Callman
RALSTON, Jan
 Dunlop, Agnes M. R.
RAMAL, Walter
 De la Mare, Walter
RAME, David
 Divine, Arthur Durham
RAMEAUT, Maurice
 Marteau, F. A.
RAMPA, T. Lobsang
 Hoskin, Cyril Henry
RAMSAY, Fay
 Eastwood, Helen
RAMSEY, Michael
 Green, T.
RAN, Kip
 Randolph, Lowell King
RANA, J.
 Bhatia, June
RAND, Brett
 Norwood, Victor George
  Charles
RAND, James S.
 Attenborough, Bernard George
RAND, William
 Roos, William
RANDALL, Clay
 Adams, Clifton
RANDALL, Janet
 Young, Janet Randall
RANDALL, Rona
 Shambrook, Rona

RANDALL, William
 Gwinn, William R.
RANDELL, Beverly
 Price, Beverly Joan
RANDOLPH, Ellen
 Ross, William Edward Daniel
RANDOM, Alan
 Kay, Ernest
RANDOM, Alex
 Rowland, Donald Sydney
RANGELY, E. R.
 Coleman, John
RANGELY, Olivia
 Coleman, John
RANGER, Ken
 Creasey, John
RANKINE, John
 Mason, Douglas Rankine
RANSOME, Barbara
 Ransome, L. E.
RANSOME, Stephen
 Davis, Frederick Clyde
RAPHAEL, Ellen
 Hartley, Ellen R.
RASKIN, Ellen
 Flanagan, Ellen
RATH, E. J.
 Brainerd, Edith *and* Brainerd,
  J. Chauncey
RATTRAY, Simon
 Dudley-Smith, Trevor
RAVENSCROFT, Rosanne
 Ravenscroft, John R.
RAYMOND, Mary
 Keegan, Mary Constance
RAYNER, Richard
 McIlwain, David

RAYTER, Joe
  McChesney, Mary F.
READ, Miss
  Saint, Dora Jessie
READE, Hamish
  Gray, Simon
REDMAN, Joseph
  Pearce, Brian
REDMAYNE, Barbara
  Smithers, Muriel
REDWAY, Ralph
  Hamilton, Charles Harold St
    John
REDWOOD, Alec
  Milkomane, George Alexis
    Milkomanovich
REED, Cynthia
  Nolan, Cynthia
REED, Eliot
  Ambler, Eric *and* Rodda,
    Charles
REES, Dilwyn
  Daniel, Glyn Edmund
REES, J. Larcombe
  Larcombe, Jennifer Geraldine
REEVE, Joel
  Cox, William Robert
REEVES, James
  Reeves, John Morris
REEVES, Joyce
  Gard, Joyce
REFUGITTA
  Harrison, Constance Cary
REID, Desmond
  Baker, William Howard
REID, Marshall
  McBride, Robert Medill

REID, Wallace Q.
  Goodchild, George
REILLY, William K.
  Creasey, John
REINER, Max
  Caldwell, Janet Taylor *and*
    Reback, Marcus
REJJE, E.
  Hyde, Edmund Errol Claude
REMENHAM, John
  Vlasto, John Alexander
REMINGTON, Mark
  Bingley, David Ernest
RENAULT, Mary
  Challans, Mary
RENIER, Elizabeth
  Baker, Betty
RENNIE, Jack
  Spooner, Peter Alan
RENO, Mark
  Keevill, Henry John
RENTON, Cam
  Armstrong, Richard
RENTON, Julia
  Cole, Margaret A.
RENZELMAN, Marilyn
  Ferguson, Marilyn
REYNOLDS, Adrian
  Long, Amelia R.
REYNOLDS, Dickson
  Reynolds, Helen Mary
    Greenwood Dickson
REYNOLDS, Jack
  Jones, Jack
REYNOLDS, John
  Fear, William H.
REYNOLDS, Peter
  Long, Amelia R.

RHODE, John
Street, Cecil John Charles
RHOSCOMYL, Owen
Vaughan, Owen
RICH, Robert
Trumbo, Dalton
RICHARDS, Clay
Crossen, Kendell Foster
RICHARDS, Francis
Lockridge, Frances Louise *and*
Lockridge, Richard
RICHARDS, Frank
Hamilton, Charles Harold St
John
RICHARDS, Hilda
Hamilton, Charles Harold St
John
RICHARDS, Paul
Buddee, Paul
RICHARDS, Peter
Monger, Ifor
RICHARDS, Stella
Starr, Richard
RICHES, Phyllis
Sutton, Phyllis Mary
RICHMOND, Fiona
Harrison, Julia
RICHMOND, Grace
Marsh, John
RICHMOND, Mary
Lindsay, Kathleen
RICKARD, Cole
Barrett, Geoffrey John
RIDDELL, John
Ford, Corey
RIDING, Laura
Gottschalk, Laura Riding

RIFT, Valerie
Bartlett, Marie
RIGHT CROSS
Armstrong, Paul
RILEY, Tex
Creasey, John
RIMMER, W. J.
Rowland, Donald Sydney
RING, Adam
Reed, Blair
RING, Basil
Braun, Wilbur
RING, Douglas
Prather, Richard S.
RINGO, Johnny
Keevill, Henry John
RINGOLD, Clay
Hogan, Ray
RIORDAN, Dan
Cooke, William Everett
RIPLEY, Alvin
King, Albert
RIPOSTE, A
Mordaunt, Evelyn May
RITA
Humphreys, Eliza M. J.
RITCHIE, Claire
Gibbs, Norah
RITSON, John
Baber, Douglas
RIVERS, Ronda
Sveinsson, Solveig
RIVES, Amelia
Troubetzkoi, *Princess*
RIX, Donna
Rowland, Donald Sydney
RIXON, Annie
Studdert, Annie

RIZA, Ali
  Orga, Irfan
ROADSTER
  Bays, J. W.
ROBB, John
  Robson, Norman
ROBBINS, Harold
  Rubins, Harold
ROBBINS, Tod
  Robbins, Clarence Aaron
ROBERTS, David
  Cox, John
ROBERTS, Desmond
  Best, Rayleigh Breton Amis
ROBERTS, Ivor
  Roberts, Irene
ROBERTS, James Hall
  Duncan, Robert Lipscomb
ROBERTS, John
  Bingley, David Ernest
ROBERTS, Ken
  Lake, Kenneth Robert
ROBERTS, Lee
  Martin, Robert Lee
ROBERTS, McLean
  Machlin, Milton
ROBERTSON, E. Arnot
  Robertson, Eileen Arbuthnot
ROBERTSON, Elspeth
  Ellison, Joan
ROBERTSON, Helen
  Edmiston, Helen J. M.
ROBERTSON, Muirhead
  Johnson, H.
ROBIN
  Roberts, Eric
ROCK, Richard
  Mainprize, Don

ROCKWELL, Matt
  Rowland, Donald Sydney
RODD, Ralph
  North, William
ROE, M. S.
  Thomson, Daisy
ROE, Richard
  Cowper, Francis
ROE, Tig
  Roe, Eric
ROFFMAN, Jan
  Summerton, Margaret
ROGERS, Anne
  Seraillier, Anne
ROGERS, Floyd
  Spence, William
ROGERS, Kerk
  Knowlton, Edward Rogers
ROGERS, Phillips
  Idell, Albert Edward
ROGERS, Rachel
  Redmon, Lois
ROHMER, Sax
  Wade, Arthur Sarsfield
ROLAND, John
  Oliver, John Rathbone
ROLAND, Mary
  Lewis, Mary Christianna
ROLAND, Nicholas
  Walmsley, Arnold
ROLLS, Anthony
  Vulliamy, Colwyn Edward
ROLPH, C. H.
  Hewitt, Cecil Rolph
ROMANY
  Evens, George Bramwell
ROMNEY, Brent
  Larralde, Romulo

ROMNEY, Steve
  Bingley, David Ernest
ROME, Anthony
  Albert, Marvin H.
ROME, Tony
  Albert, Marvin H.
RONALD, E. B.
  Barker, Ronald Ernest
RONNS, Edward
  Aarons, Edward Sidney
ROOKE, Dennis
  Rotheray, Geoffrey Neville
ROOME, Holdar
  Moore, Harold William
ROOS, Kelley
  Roos, William *and* Kelley,
    Audrey
ROSCOE, Charles
  Rowland, Donald Sydney
ROSCOE, Janet
  Prior, Mollie
ROSCOE, Mike
  Roscoe, John *and* Ruso,
    Michael
ROSE, Hilary
  Mackinnon, Charles Roy
ROSE, Phyllis
  Thompson, Phyllis
ROSE, Robert
  Rose, Ian
ROSENTHAL, Richard A.
  Richards, Allen
ROSNA
  Rosman, Alice Grant
ROSS
  Martin, Violet Florence

ROSS, Barnaby
  Dannay, Frederic *and* Lee,
    Manfred B.
ROSS, Clarissa
  Ross, Dan
ROSS, Deborah
  Stoffer, Edith G.
ROSS, Diana
  Denney, Diana
ROSS, George
  Ross, Isaac
ROSS, Ivan T.
  Rossner, Robert
ROSS, J. H.
  Lawrence, T. E.
ROSS, Jean
  Hewson, Irene Dale
ROSS, John
  Winnington, Richard
ROSS, Jonathan
  Rossiter, John
ROSS, Katherine
  Walter, Dorothy Blake
ROSS, Leonard Q.
  Rosten, Leo C.
ROSS, Maggie
  Bermange, Maurine J. L.
ROSS, Marilyn
  Ross, Dan
ROSS, Martin
  Martin, Violet Florence
ROSS, Michael D. H.
  Rosenthal, Michael D. H. ·
ROSS, Patricia
  Wood, Patricia E. W.
ROSS, Sutherland
  Callard, Thomas H.

ROSSITER, Jane
  Ross, William Edward Daniel
ROSTAND, Robert
  Hopkins, Robert Sydney
ROSTREVOR, George
  Hamilton, *Sir* George Rostrevor
ROSTRON, Primrose
  Hulbert, Joan
ROTHMAN, Judith
  Black, Maureen
ROUSSEAU, Victor
  Emanuel, Victor Rousseau
ROWANS, Virginia
  Tanner, Edward Everett
ROWE, Alice E.
  Rowe, John Gabriel
ROWLAND, Iris
  Roberts, Irene
ROWLANDS, Effie Adelaide
  Albanesi, Effie Maria
ROWLANDS, Lesley
  Zuber, Mary E. I.
ROYAL, Dan
  Barrett, Geoffrey John
ROYCE, Kenneth
  Gandley, Kenneth Royce
RUBICON
  Lunn, *Sir* Arnold
RUCK, Berta
  Oliver, Amy Roberta
RUDD, Margaret
  Newlin, Margaret
RUDD, Steele
  Davis, Arthur Hoey
RUFFLE
  Tegner, Henry
RURIC, Peter
  Cain, Paul

RUSHTON, Charles
  Shortt, Charles Rushton
RUSSELL, Erle
  Wilding, Philip
RUSSELL, Raymond
  Balfour, William
RUSSELL, Sarah
  Laski, Marghanita
RUSSELL, Shane
  Norwood, Victor George
    Charles
RUTHERFORD, Douglas
  McConnell, James Douglas
    Rutherford
RUTHERFORD, Mark
  White, William Hale
RUTLEDGE, Brett
  Paul, Elliot Harold
RYAN, J. M.
  McDermott, John Richard
RYBOT, Doris
  Ponsonby, Doris Almon
RYDER, James
  Pattinson, James
RYE, Anthony
  Youd, Samuel
RYLAND, Clive
  Priestley, Clive Ryland

S. H. S.
  Spender, Stephen
S. S.
  Sassoon, Siegfried
SABBAH, Hassan i
  Butler, Bill
SABER, Robert O.
  Ozaki, Milton K.

SABIAD
  White, Stanhope
SABIN, Mark
  Fox, Norman Arnold
SABRE, Dirk
  Laffin, John
SABRETACHE
  Barrow, Albert Stewart
SACKERMAN, Henry
  Kahn, H. S.
SADBALLS, John
  Matusow, Harvey Marshall
SADDLER, K. Allen
  Richards, Ronald C. W.
SAGITTARIUS
  Katzin, Olga
ST CLAIR, Dester
  Winchell, Prentice
ST CLAIR, Philip
  Howard, Munroe
ST CLAIRE, Yvonne
  Hall, Emma L.
SAINT-EDEN, Dennis
  Foster, Donn
ST E. A. OF M. AND S.
  Crowley, Edward Alexander
ST GEORGE, Arthur
  Paine, Lauran Bosworth
ST GIRAUD
  Knott, William Cecil
ST JAMES, Andrew
  Stern, James
ST JOHN, Christopher
  Marshall, Christabel
ST JOHN, David
  Hunt, E. Howard
ST JOHN, Philip
  Del Rey, Lester

SAKI
  Munro, Hector Hugh
SALT, Jonathan
  Neville Derek
SALTEN, Felix
  Saltzmann, Sigmund
SALTER, Cedric
  Knight, Francis Edgar
SALTER, Mary D.
  Ainsworth, Mary Dinsmore
SALTER AINSWORTH, Mary D.
  Ainsworth, Mary Dinsmore
SAMPSON, Richard Henry
  Hull, Richard
SANBORN, B. X.
  Ballinger, William Sanborn
SANDERS, Brett
  Barrett, Geoffrey John
SANDERS, Bruce
  Gribble, Leonard Reginald
SANDERS, Daphne
  Rice, Craig
SANDERS, Dorothy Lucy
  Walker, Lucy
SANDERS, Jeanne
  Rundle, Anne
SANDERS, Winston P.
  Anderson, Poul
SANDHURST, B. G.
  Green, Charles Henry
SANDS, Martin
  Burke, John Frederick
SANDYS, Oliver
  Evans, Marguerite Florence
SANTA MARIA
  Powell-Smith, Vincent
SANTEE, Walt
  King, Albert

SAPPER
  Fairlie, Gerard
SAPPER
  McNeile, H. C.
SARA
  Blake, Sally Mirliss
SARAC, Roger
  Caras, Roger
SARASIN, J. G.
  Salmon, Geraldine Gordon
SARBAN
  Wall, John W.
SARGENT, Joan
  Jenkins, Sara Lucile
SARI
  Fleur, Anne Elizabeth
SARNE, Michael
  Plummer, Thomas Arthur
SARNIAN
  Falla, Frank
SASHUN, Sigma
  Sassoon, Siegfried
SAUER, Muriel S.
  Stafford, Muriel
SAUNDERS, Abel
  Pound, Ezra
SAUNDERS, Anne
  Aldred, Margaret
SAUNDERS, Carl McK.
  Ketchum, Philip
SAUNDERS, Ione
  Cole, Margaret A.
SAUNDERS, John
  Nickson, Arthur
SAUNDERS, Lawrence
  Davis, Burton *and* Davis, Clare
  Ogden

SAUNDERS, Marshall
  Saunders, Margaret Marshall
SAVA, George
  Milkomane, George Alexis
  Milkomanovich
SAVAGE, Leslie
  Duff, Douglas Valder
SAVAGE, Richard
  Roe, Ivan
SAVAGE, Steve
  Goodavage, Joseph F.
SAWLEY, Petra
  Marsh, John
SAXON
  Matthews, Edith J.
SAXON, John
  Gifford, James Noble
SAXON, John
  Rumbold-Gibbs, Henry St
  John C.
SAXON, Peter
  Baker, William Howard
SAYRE, Gordon
  Woolfolk, Josiah Pitts
SCARLETT, Roger
  Blair, Dorothy *and* Page,
  Evelyn
SCARLETT, Susan
  Streatfeild, Noel
SCHAW, Ruth
  Drummond, Alison
SCHWARTZ, Bruno
  Mann, George
SCIENCE INVESTIGATOR
  Speck, Gerald Eugene
SCOBEY, Marion
  Coombs, Joyce

SCOLOPAX
  Grant, Maurice Harold
SCOT, Neil
  Grant, *Lady* Sybil
SCOTT, Agnes Neill
  Muir, Wilhelmina Johnstone
SCOTT, Bradford
  Scott, Leslie
SCOTT, Bruce
  McCartney, R. J.
SCOTT, Casey
  Kubis, Patricia Lou
SCOTT, Dana
  Robertson, Constance Noyes
SCOTT, Denis
  Means, Mary *and* Saunders,
    Theodore
SCOTT, Douglas
  Thorpe, John
SCOTT, Elizabeth
  Capstick, Elizabeth
SCOTT, Grover
  King, Albert
SCOTT, Jane
  McElfresh, Adeline
SCOTT, Norford
  Rowland, Donald Sydney
SCOTT, O. R.
  Gottliebsen, Ralph Joseph
SCOTT, Thurston
  Leite, George Thurston *and*
    Scott, Jody
SCOTT, Valerie
  Rowland, Donald Sydney
SCOTT, Warwick
  Dudley-Smith, Trevor
SCOTT-MORLEY, A.
  Oakley, Eric Gilbert

SCROPE, Mason
  Mason, Arthur Charles
SEAFARER
  Barker, Clarence Hedley
SEAFORTH
  Foster, George Cecil
SEAFORTH
  Skues, George Edward
    Mackenzie
SEA-LION
  Bennett, Geoffrey Martin
SEAMARK
  Small, Austin J.
SEARCH-LIGHT
  Frank, Waldo David
SEARS, Deane
  Rywell, Martin
SEA-WRACK
  Crebbin, Edward Horace
SEBASTIAN, Lee
  Silverberg, Robert
SEC
  Manner, Marya
SECRIST, Kelliher
  Kelliher, Dan T. *and* Secrist,
    W. G.
SEDGWICK, Modwena
  Glover, Modwena
SEEKER, A
  Eagan, Frances W.
SEFTON, Catherine
  Waddell, Martin
SEGUNDO, Bart
  Rowland, Donald Sydney
SEIFERT, Elizabeth
  Gasparotti, Elizabeth
SELDEN, George
  Thompson, George Selden

SELKIRK, Jane
  Chapman, Mary I. *and*
  Chapman, John Stanton
SELL, Joseph
  Haley, W. J.
SELMARK, George
  Seldon Truss, Leslie
SENCOURT, Robert
  George, Robert Esmonde
  Gordon
SERAFIAN, Michael
  Martin, Malachi
SERANNE, Ann
  Smith, Margaret Ruth
SERJEANT, Richard
  Van Essen, W.
SERNICOLI, Davide
  Trent, Ann
SETH, Andrew
  Pattison, Andrew Seth P.
SETON, Graham
  Hutchison, Graham Seton
SETOUN, Gabriel
  Hepburn, Thomas Nicoll
SEUFFERT, Muir
  Seuffert, Muriel
SEVERN, David
  Unwin, David Storr
SEVERN, Forepoint
  Bethell, Leonard Arthur
SEVERN, Richard
  Ebbs, Robert
SEYMOUR, Henry
  Hartmann, Helmut Henry
SHALIMAR
  Hendry, Frank Coutts
SHALLOW, Robert
  Atkinson, Frank

SHAN
  McMordie, John Andrew
SHANE
  Richardson, Eileen
SHANE, John
  Durst, Paul
SHANE, Martin
  Johnston, George Henry
SHANE, Rhondo
  Norwood, Victor George
  Charles
SHANE, Susannah
  Ashbrook, Harriette Cora
SHANNON, Carl
  Hogue, Wilbur Owings
SHANNON, Dell
  Linington, Elizabeth
SHANNON, Monica
  Katchamakoff, Atanas
SHANWA
  Haarer, Alec Ernest
SHARMAN, Miriam
  Bolton, Miriam
SHARON, Rose
  Grossman, Judith
SHARP, Helen
  Paine, Lauran Bosworth
SHARP, Luke
  Barr, Robert
SHAUL, Frank
  Rowland, Donald Sydney
SHAW, Adelaide
  O'Shaughnessy, Marjorie
SHAW, Artie
  Arshavsky, Abraham Isaac
SHAW, Irene
  Roberts, Irene

SHAW, Jane
  Evans, Jean
SHAW, Jill A.
  Keeling, Jill Annette
SHAW, Josephine
  Clarke, Dorothy Josephine
SHAW, T. E.
  Lawrence, T. E.
SHAYNE, Gordon
  Winter, Bevis
SHAYNE, Nina
  Gibbs, Norah
SHEARING, Joseph
  Campbell, Gabrielle Margaret
  Vere
SHELBY, Cole
  King, Albert
SHELLEY, Frances
  Wees, Frances Shelley
SHELTON, Michael
  Stacy, P. M. de Cosqueville
SHEPARD, Fern
  Stonebraker, Florence
SHEPHERD, Joan
  Buchanan, B. J.
SHEPHERD, John
  Ballard, Willis Todhunter
SHEPHERD, Neal
  Morland, Nigel
SHERATON, Neil
  Smith, Norman Edward Mace
SHERMAN, George
  Moretti, Ugo
SHERRY, Gordon
  Sheridan, H. B.
SHIEL-MARTIN
  Old, Phyllis Muriel Elizabeth

SHIVAJI, Mahatma Guru Sri
  Paramahansa
  Crowley, Edward Alexander
SHONE, Patric
  Hanley, James
SHORE, Norman
  Smith, Norman Edward Mace
SHORE, Philippa
  Holbeche, Philippa
SHORT, Luke
  Glidden, Frederick Dilley
SHOTT, Abel
  Ford, T. W.
SHROPSHIRE LAD
  Barber-Starkey, Roger
SHUTE, Nevil
  Norway, Nevil Shute
SHY, Timothy
  Wyndham Lewis, D. B.
SIBLEY, Lee
  Landells, Anne
SIDNEY, Margaret
  Lothrop, Harriet Mulford
SIDNEY, Neilma
  Gantner, Neilma B.
SIGMA SASHUN
  Sassoon, Siegfried
SILLER, Van
  Van Siller, Hilda
SILURIENSIS, Leolinus
  Machen, Arthur
SILVER, Nicholas
  Faust, Frederick
SILVESTER, Frank
  Bingley, David Ernest
SIMMONDS, Mike
  Simmonds, Michael Charles

SIMMONS, Catherine
  Duncan, Kathleen
SIMMONS, Kim
  Duncan, Kathleen
SIMON
  Blakeston, Oswell *and* Burford,
  Roger d'Este
SIMON, Robert
  Musto, Barry
SIMON, S. J.
  Skidelsky, Simon Jasha
SIMONS, Peter
  Punnett, Margaret *and* Punnett,
  Ivor
SIMONS, Roger
  Punnett, Margaret *and* Punnett,
  Ivor
SIMPLE, Peter
  Herbert, John; Hogg, Michael;
  Welch, Colin *and* Wharton,
  Michael
SIMPLEX, Simon
  Middleton, Henry Clement
SIMPSON, Warwick
  Ridge, William Pett
SIMS, John
  Hopson, William L.
SIMS, *Lieut* A. K.
  Whitson, John Harvey
SINBAD
  Dingle, Aylward Edward
SINCLAIR, Jo
  Seid, Ruth
SINDERBY, Donald
  Stephens, Donald Ryder
SINGER, Bant
  Shaw, Charles

SINGER, Burns
  Singer, James Hyman
SINJOHN, John
  Galsworthy, John
SIOGVOLK, Paul
  Mathews, Albert
SION, Mari
  Jones, Robert Maynard
SIR TOPAZ
  Agate, James
SKEEVER, Jim
  Hill, John Alexander
SLADE, Gurney
  Bartlett, Stephen
SLATER, Patrick
  Mitchell, John
SLAUGHTER, Jim
  Paine, Lauran Bosworth
SLINGSBY, Rufus
  Siddle, Charles *and* Peel,
  Frederick
SLOANE, Sara
  Bloom, Urusula
SLOLUCK, J. Milton
  Bierce, Ambrose
SMALL, Ernest
  Lent, Blair
SMEE, Wentworth
  Burgin, G. B.
SMEED
  Taylor, Deems
SMEED, Frances
  Lasky, Jesse L.
SMITH, Adam
  Goodman, George Jerome W.
SMITH, Caesar
  Dudley-Smith, Trevor

SMITH, Dodie
  Smith, Dorothy Gladys
SMITH, Essex
  Hope, Essex
SMITH, Harriet
  Scott, Hilda R.
SMITH, Jean
  Smith, Frances C.
SMITH, Jessica
  Penwarden, Helen
SMITH, S. S.
  Williamson, Thames Ross
SMITH, Shelley
  Bodington, Nancy Hermione
SMITH, Stevie
  Smith, Florence Margaret
SMITH, Surrey
  Dinner, William
SMITH, Wade
  Snow, Charles Horace
SMITH, Z. Z.
  Westheimer, David
SNAFFLES
  Payne, Charles J.
SNOW, Lyndon
  Ansle, Dorothy Phoebe
SOMERS, J. L.
  Stickland, Louise Annie
  Beatrice
SOMERS, Paul
  Winterton, Paul
SOMERVILLE
  Somerville, Edith Oenone
SOPHIE, May
  Clarke, Rebecca Sophia
SOSTHENES
  Coad, Frederick R.

SOUTHCOTE, George
  Aston, *Sir* George
SOUTHWORTH, Louis
  Grealey, Tom
SOUTTER, Fred
  Lake, Kenneth Robert
SOUZA, Ernest
  Scott, Evelyn
SPADE, Mark
  Balchin, Nigel
SPAIN, John
  Adams, Cleve Franklin
SPALDING, Lucille
  Jay, Marion
SPARLIN, W.
  Spratling, Walter Norman
SPENCE, Betty E.
  Tettmar, Betty Eileen
SPENCE, Duncan
  Spence, William
SPENCER, Cornelia
  Yaukey, Grace
SPENCER, John
  Vickers, Roy
SPENSER, James
  Guest, Francis Harold
SPERLING, Maria Sandra
  Floren, Lee
SPIEL, Hilde
  De Mendelssohn, Hilde
SPILLANE, Frank Morrison
  Spillane, Mickey
SPINELLI, Marcos
  Spinelli, Grace
SPOONHILL
  Reaney, James
SPRINGFIELD, David
  Lewis, Roy

SPROSTON, John
  Scott, Peter Dale
SPROULE, Wesley
  Sproule, Howard
SPURR, Clinton
  Rowland, Donald Sydney
SQUARE, Charlotte
  Haldane, Robert Aylmer
SQUIRES, Phil
  Barker, S. Omar
STACY, O'Connor
  Rollins, William
STAFFORD, Ann
  Pedlar, Ann
STAFFORD, Peter
  Tabori, Paul
STAGGE, Jonathan
  Webb, Richard Wilson *and*
    Wheeler, Hugh Callingham
STAMPER, Alex
  Kent, Arthur
STAN, Roland
  Rowland, Donald Sydney
STAND, Marguerite
  Stickland, M. E.
STANDISH, Buck
  Paine, Lauran Bosworth
STANDISH, Burt L.
  Patten, Gilbert
STANDISH, J. O.
  Horler, Sydney
STANDISH, Robert
  Gerahty, Digby George
STANCE, Nora K.
  Stanley, Nora Kathleen Begbie
STANHOPE, Douglas
  Duff, Douglas Valder

STANHOPE, John
  Langdon-Davies, John
STANLEY, Arthur
  Megaw, Arthur Stanley
STANLEY, Bennett
  Hough, Stanley Bennett
STANLEY, Chuck
  Strong, Charles Stanley
STANLEY, Dave
  Dachs, David
STANLEY, F.
  Crocchiola, Stanley Francis
    Louis
STANLEY, Margaret
  Mason, Sydney Charles
STANLEY, Marge
  Weinbaum, Stanley Grauman
STANLEY, Michael
  Hosie, Stanley William
STANLEY, Warwick
  Hilton, John Buxton
STANSBURY, Alec
  Higgs, Alec S.
STANTON, Borden
  Wilding, Philip
STANTON, Coralie
  Hosken, Alice Cecil Seymour
STANTON, Marjorie
  Phillips, Horace
STANTON, Schuyler
  Baum, Lyman Frank
STANTON, Vance
  Avallone, Michael Angelo Jr
STAR, Elison
  Comber, Rose
STARK, Joshua
  Olsen, Theodore Victor

231

STARK, Michael
  Lariar, Lawrence
STARK, Richard
  Westlake, Donald Edwin
STARR, Henry
  Bingley, David Ernest
STARR, Leonora
  Mackesy, Leonora Dorothy
  Rivers
STARRET, William
  McClintock, Marshall
STAVELEY, Robert
  Campbell, R. O.
STEEL, Byron
  Steegmuller, Francis
STEEL, Kurt
  Kagey, Rudolf
STEELE, Erskine
  Henderson, Archibald
STEEN, Frank
  Felstein, Ivor
STEER, Charlotte
  Hunter, Christine
STEFFAN, Jack
  Steffan, Alice Jacqueline
STERLING, Helen
  Hoke, Helen L.
STERLING, Maria Sandra
  Floren, Lee
STERLING, Peter
  Stern, David
STERLING, Stewart
  Winchell, Prentice
STERN, Elizabeth
  Uhr, Elizabeth
STERN, John
  Stearn, John Theodore

STEVENS, Christopher
  Tabori, Paul
STEVENS, Dan J.
  Overholser, Wayne D.
STEVENS, J. D.
  Rowland, Donald Sydney
STEVENS, Jill
  Mogridge, Stephen
STEVENS, S. P.
  Palestrant, Simon
STEVENS, William Christopher
  Allen, Stephen Valentine
STEVENSON, Christine
  Kelly, Elizabeth
STEWART, C. R.
  Adam, C. G. M.
STEWART, Eleanor
  Porter, Eleanor
STEWART, Jay
  Palmer, Stuart
STEWART, Jean
  Newman, Mona A. J.
STEWART, Logan
  Savage, Lee
STEWART, Logan
  Wilding, Philip
STEWART, Marjorie
  Huxtable, Marjorie
STEWART, Scott
  Zaffo, George J.
STEWART, Will
  Williamson, Jack
STEWART-HARGREAVES,
E. H. I.
  White, Frank James
STEWER, Jan
  Coles, Albert John

STIRLING, Stella
    Ransome, L. E.
STITCH, Wilhelmina
    Collie, Ruth
STODDARD, Charles
    Strong, Charles Stanley
STOKES, Cedric
    Beardmore, George
STONE, Eugene
    Speck, Gerald Eugene
STONE, Hampton
    Stein, Aaron Marc
STONE, Simon
    Barrington, Howard
STORM, Lesley
    Clark, Mabel Margaret
STORM, Virginia
    Swatridge, Irene M. M.
STORME, Peter
    Stern, Philip Van Doren
STORY, Josephine
    Loring, Emilie
STORY, Sydney A. Jr
    Pike, Mary Hayden
STRAND, Paul E.
    Palestrant, Simon
STRANG, Herbert
    L'Estrange, C. James *and* Ely,
    George Herbert
STRANGE, John Stephen
    Tillett, Dorothy Stockbridge
STRANGEWAY, Mark
    Leyland, Eric
STRATEGICUS
    O'Neill, Herbert Charles
STRATTON, John
    Alldridge, John Stratten

STRATTON, Thomas
    Coulson, Robert Stratton *and*
    De Weese, T. Eugene
STRONG, Susan
    Rees, Joan
STRUTHER, Jan
    Maxtone-Graham, Joyce
STRYDOM, Len
    Rousseau, Leon
STRYFE, Paul
    Newman, James Roy
STUART, Alan
    Weightman, Archibald John
STUART, Alex
    Mann, Violet Vivian
STUART, Brian
    Worthington-Stuart, Brian
    Arthur
STUART, Charles
    Mackinnon, Charles Roy
STUART, Clay
    Whittington, Harry
STUART, Don A.
    Campbell, John Wood Jr
STUART, Florence
    Stonebraker, Florence
STUART, Frederick
    Tomlin, Eric
STUART, Gordon
    Wood, James
STUART, Ian
    Maclean, Alistair
STUART, John Roy
    McMillan, Donald
STUART, Logan
    Wilding, Philip
STUART, Margaret
    Paine, Lauran Bosworth

STUART, Matt
　Holmes, Llewellyn Perry
STUART, Sheila
　Baker, Mary Gladys Steel
STUART, Sidney
　Avallone, Michael Angelo Jr
STUART, Vivian
　Mann, Violet Vivian
STURGUS, J. B.
　Bastin, John
STUYVESANT, Polly
　Paul, Maury
STYLITES, Simeon
　Luccock, Halford Edward
SUBHADRA-NANDAN
　Prafulla, Das
SUBOND, Valerie
　Grayland, Valerie M.
SUDORF, Fingal von
　Rosenquist, Fingal
SULLIVAN, Eric Harrison
　Hickey, Madelyn E.
SUMMERS, D. B.
　Barrett, Geoffrey John
SUMMERS, Gordon
　Hornby, John W.
SUMMERSCALES, Rowland
　Gaines, Robert
SURREY, Kathryn
　Matthewman, Phyllis
SUTHERLAND, Joan
　Collings, Joan
SUTHERLAND, William
　Cooper, John Murray
SUTTLING, Mark
　Rowland, Donald Sydney
SUTTON, Henry
　Slavitt, David

SUTTON, John
　Tullett, Denis John
SUTTON, Rachel B.
　Sutton, Margaret
SVAREFF, *Count* Vladimir
　Crowley, Edward Alexander
SWAN, Annie S.
　Burnett-Smith, Annie S.
SWAYNE, Geoffrey
　Campion, Sidney
SWIFT, Anthony
　Farjeon, Joseph Jefferson
SWIFT, Benjamin
　Paterson, W. R.
SWIFT, Julian
　Applin, Arthur
SWIFT, Rachelle
　Lumsden, Jean
SWIFT, Stella
　Whish, Violet E.
SYLVESTER, Philip
　Worner, Philip A. I.
SYLVIA
　Ashton-Warner, Sylvia

T.
　Thorp, Joseph
T. J. V.
　Pound, Ezra
T. P.
　O'Connor, T. P.
TAAFFE, Robert
　Maguire, Robert A. J.
TABARD, Peter
　Blake, Leslie James
TAFFRAIL
　Dorling, Henry Taprell

TAGGART, Dean
  King, Albert
TAINE, John
  Bell, Eric Temple
TALBOT, Hake
  Nelms, Henning
TALBOT, Henry
  Rothwell, Henry Talbot
TALBOT, Hugh
  Alington, Argentine Francis
TALBOT, Kathrine
  Barker, Ilse Eva L.
TALBOT, Kay
  Rowland, Donald Sydney
TAPER
  Levin, Bernard
TARRANT, Elizabeth
  Leyland, Eric
TATE, Ellalice
  Hibbert, Eleanor Alice Burford
TATHAM, Campbell
  Elting, Mary
TAYLOR, Ann
  Brodey, Jim
TAYLOR, Daniel
  Schneider, Daniel Edward
TAYLOR, H. Baldwin
  Waugh, Hillary Baldwin
TAYLOR, John
  Magee, James
TAYLOR, Sam
  Goodyear, Stephen Frederick
TEARLE, Christian
  Jacques, Edward Tyrrell
TEG, Twm
  Vulliamy, Colwyn Edward
TELLAR, Mark
  Collins, Vere Henry

TELSTAR
  Goodwin, Geoffrey
TEMPEST, Jan
  Swatridge, Irene M. M.
TEMPLE, Ann
  Mortimer, Penelope
TEMPLE, Paul
  Durbridge, Francis *and*
    McConnell, James Douglas
    Rutherford
TEMPLE, Ralph
  Alexander, Robert William
TEMPLE, Robin
  Wood, Samuel Andrew
TEMPLE-ELLIS, N. A.
  Holdaway, Neville Aldridge
TEMPLETON, Jesse
  Goodchild, George
TENN, William
  Klass, Philip
TENNANT, Catherine
  Eyles, Kathleen Muriel
TENNENBAUM, Irving
  Stone, Irving
TERAHATA, Jun
  Kirkup, James
TERKEL, Studs
  Terkel, Louis
TERRY, C. V.
  Slaughter, Frank Gill
TEW, Mary
  Douglas, Mary
TEY, Josephine
  Mackintosh, Elizabeth
THANE, Elswyth
  Beebe, Elswyth Thane
THANET, Octave
  French, Alice

235

THAYER, Jane
  Wooley, Catherine
THAYER, Peter
  Wyler, Rose
THEOPHANY
  Tofani, Louise E.
THERION, The Master
  Crowley, Edward Alexander
THETA, Eric Mark
  Higginson, Henry Clive
THIRLMERE, Rowland
  Walker, John
THOMAS, Caroline
  Dorr, Julia Caroline
THOMAS, Carolyn
  Duncan, Actea
THOMAS, Dorothy
  Thomashower, Dorothy
THOMAS, G. K.
  Davies, Leslie Purnell
THOMAS, Gough
  Garwood, Godfrey Thomas
THOMAS, H. C.
  Keating, Lawrence Alfred
THOMAS, J. Bissell
  Stephen, Joyce Alice
THOMAS, Jim
  Reagan, Thomas B.
THOMAS, Joan Gale
  Robinson, Joan Gale
THOMAS, Lately
  Steele, Robert V. P.
THOMAS, Lee
  Floren, Lee
THOMAS, Michael
  Benson, Michael
THOMAS, Murray
  Ragg, Thomas Murray

THOMAS, Tay
  Thomas, Mary
THOMPSON, Buck
  Paine, Lauran Bosworth
THOMPSON, China
  Lewis, Mary Christianna
THOMPSON, Eileen
  Panowski, Eileen Janet
THOMPSON, Madeline
  Greig, Maysie
THOMPSON, Russ
  Paine, Lauran Bosworth
THOMSON, Audrey
  Gwynn, Audrey
THOMSON, Joan
  Charnock, Joan
THOMSON, Jon H.
  Thomson, Daisy
THOMSON, Neil
  Johnson, Henry T.
THORN, Barbara
  Paine, Lauran Bosworth
THORN, Whyte
  Whiteing, Richard
THORNTON, Maimee
  Jeffrey-Smith, May
THORNTON, W. B.
  Burgess, Thornton W.
THORP, Ellen
  Robertson, Margery Ellen
THORP, Morwenna
  Robertson, Margery Ellen
THORPE, Sylvia
  Thimblethorpe, June
THORSTEIN, Eric
  Grossman, Judith
THURLEY, Norgrove
  Stoneham, Charles Thurley

THURLOW, Robert
  Griffin, Jonathan
THURMAN, Steve
  Castle, Frank
TIBBER, Robert
  Friedman, Eve Rosemary
TIBBER, Rosemary
  Friedman, Eve Rosemary
TILBURY, Quenna
  Walker, Emily Kathleen
TILLEY, Gene
  Tilley, E. D.
TILTON, Alice
  Taylor, Phoebe Atwood
TIM
  Martin, Timothy
TIMON, John
  Mitchell, Donald Grant
TODHUNTER, Philippa
  Bond, Grace
TOKLAS, Alice B.
  Stein, Gertrude
TOLER, Buck
  Kelly, Harold Ernest
TOLLER
  Lyburn, Eric Frederic St John
TOMLINE, F. Latour
  Gilbert, William Schwenck
TONKONGY, Gertrude
  Friedberg, Gertrude
TOPICUS
  Goodwin, Geoffrey
TORQUEMADA
  Mathers, Edward Powys
TORR, Iain
  Mackinnon, Charles Roy
TORREY, Marjorie
  Hood, Torrey

TORRIE, Malcolm
  Mitchell, Gladys
TORROLL, G. D.
  Lawson, Alfred
TOWERS, Tricia
  Ivison, Elizabeth
TOWNE, Stuart
  Rawson, Clayton
TOWNSEND, Timothy
  Robey, Timothy Lester
  Townsend
TOWRY, Peter
  Piper, David Towry
TRACEY, Grant
  Nuttall, Anthony
TRACEY, Hugh
  Evans, Kay *and* Evans,
  Stuart
TRACY, Catherine
  Story, Rosamond Mary
TRAFFORD, Jean
  Walker, Edith
TRAILL, Peter
  Morton, Guy Mainwaring
TRAPROCK, Walter E.
  Chappell, George S.
TRASK, Merrill
  Braham, Hal
TRAVEN, B.
  Torsvan, Traven
TRAVER, Robert
  Voelker, John Donaldson
TRAVERS, Hugh
  Mills, Hugh Travers
TRAVERS, Stephen
  Radcliffe, Garnett
TRAVERS, Will
  Rowland, Donald Sydney

TRAVIS, Gerry
  Trimble, Louis
TRAVIS, Gretchen
  Mockler, Gretchen
TRAWLE, Mary Elizabeth
  Elwart, Joan Frances
TREADGOLD, Nye
  Tranter, Nigel
TREHEARNE, Elizabeth
  Maxwell, Patricia Anne
TRENT, Gregory
  Williamson, Thames Ross
TRENT, Lee
  Nuttall, Anthony
TRENT, Paul
  Platt, Edward
TRENT, Peter
  Nelson, Lawrence
TRESILIAN, Liz
  Green, Elizabeth Sara
TRESSALL, Robert
  Noonan, Robert
TRESSELL, Robert
  Noonan, Robert
TRESSIDY, Jim
  Norwood, Victor George
  Charles
TREVENA, John
  Henham, E. J.
TREVES, Kathleen
  Walker, Emily Kathleen
TREVOR, Elleston
  Dudley-Smith, Trevor
TREVOR, Glen
  Hilton, James
TREVOR, Ralph
  Wilmot, James Reginald

TREVOR, William
  Cox, William Trevor
TREW, Cecil G.
  Ehrenborg, *Mrs* C. G.
TRING, A. Stephen
  Meynell, Laurence Walter
TRIPP, Karen
  Gershon, Karen
TRITON, A. N.
  Barclay, Oliver Rainsford
TROTTER, Sallie
  Crawford, Sallie
TROTWOOD, John
  Moore, John
TROY, Alan
  Hoke, Helen L.
TROY, Katherine
  Buxton, Anne
TROY, Simon
  Warriner, Thurman
TRUAX, Rhoda
  Aldrich, Rhoda Truax
TRUSCOT, Bruce
  Peers, Edgar Allison
TSUYUKI SHIGERU
  Kirkup, James
TUCKER, Lael
  Wertenbaker, Lael Tucker
TUCKER, Link
  Bingley, David Ernest
TURNER, C. John
  Whiteman, William Meredith
TURNER, Josie
  Crawford, Phyllis
TURNER, Len
  Floren, Lee
TURNER, Mary
  Lambot, Isobel Mary

TURVEY, Winsome
  Rusterholtz, Winsome Lucy
TUSTIN, Elizabeth
  White, Celia
TWAIN, Mark
  Clemens, Samuel Langhorne
TWEEDALE, J.
  Bickle, Judith
TWIGGY
  Hornby, Lesley
TYLER, Clarke
  Brookes, Ewart Stanley
TYLER, Ellis
  King, Albert
TYSON, Teilo
  McFarlane, David

I am become a name.
—Alfred, Lord Tennyson. Ulysses

UBIQUE
  Guggisberg, *Sir* F. G.
UNCLE GUS
  Rey, Hans Augusto
UNCLE HENRY
  Wallace, Henry
UNCLE MAC
  McCulloch, Derek
UNCLE MONTY
  Hamilton-Wilkes, Edwin
UNCLE REG
  Woodcock, E. Page
UNCLE REMUS
  Harris, Joel Chandler
UNCUT CAVENDISH
  Meares, John Willoughby

UNDERWOOD, Keith
  Spooner, Peter Alan
UNDERWOOD, Michael
  Evelyn, John Michael
UNDERWOOD, Miles
  Glassco, John
UNDINE, P. F.
  Paine, Lauran Bosworth
UNOFFICIAL OBSERVER
  Carter, John Franklin
URIEL, Henry
  Faust, Frederick
URQUHART, Guy
  McAlmon, Robert
URQUHART, Paul
  Black, Ladbroke Lionel Day
USHER, Margo Scegge
  McHargue, Georgess

V. V. V.
  Lucas, E. V.
VAGABOND
  Blake, George
VAIL, Amanda
  Miller, Warren
VAIL, Philip
  Gerson, Noel Bertram
VALE, Keith
  Clegg, Paul
VALENTINE
  Pechey, Archibald Thomas
VALENTINE, Jo
  Armstrong, Charlotte
VAN BUREN, Abigail
  Phillips, Pauline
VAN DINE, S. S.
  Wright, Willard Huntington

VAN DYKE, J.
  Edwards, Frederick Anthony
VAN DYNE, Edith
  Baum, Lyman Frank
VAN HELLER, Marcus
  Coleman, John
VANCE, Ethel
  Stone, Grace Zaring
VANCE, Jack
  Kuttner, Henry
VANDEGRIFT, Margaret
  Janvier, Margaret Thomson
VANE, Brett
  Kent, Arthur
VANE, Michael
  Humphries, Sydney
VANE, Phillipa
  Hambledon, Phyllis MacVean
VANSITTART, Jane
  Moorhouse, Hilda
VARANGE, Ulick
  Yockey, Francis Parker
VARDRE, Leslie
  Davies, Leslie Purnell
VAUGHAN, Carter A.
  Gerson, Noel Bertram
VAUGHAN, Julian
  Almond, Brian
VAUGHAN, Richard
  Thomas, Ernest Lewys
VEDDER, John K.
  Gruber, Frank
VEDETTE
  Fitchett, W. H.
VEDEY, Julien
  Robinson, Julien Louis
VEHEYNE, Cherry
  Williamson, Ethel

VEITCH, Tom
  Padgett, Ron
VENISON, Alfred
  Pound, Ezra
VENNING, Hugh
  Van Zeller, Claud H.
VENNING, Michael
  Rice, Craig
VERNON, Claire
  Breton-Smith, Clare
VERNON, Kay
  Vernon, Kathleen Rose
VERNON, Marjorie
  Russell, Shirley
VERONIQUE
  Fisher, Veronica Suzanne
VERWER, Hans
  Verwer, Johanne
VESTAL, Stanley
  Campbell, Walter Stanley
VET, T. V.
  Straiton, Edward Cornock
VICARION, *Count* Palmiro
  Logue, Christopher
VICARY, Dorothy
  Rice, Dorothy
VICTOR, Charles B.
  Puechner, Ray
VIDENS
  Mumford, A. H.
VIGILANS
  Partridge, Eric
VIGILANS
  Rice, Brian Keith
VIGILANTES
  Zilliacus, Konni
VILLIERS, Elizabeth
  Thorne, Isabel Mary

VINCENT, Heather
  Walker, Emily Kathleen
VINCENT, Honor
  Walker, Emily Kathleen
VINCENT, Jim
  Foxall, P. A.
VINCENT, John
  Farrow, R.
VINCENT, Mary Keith
  St John, Wylly Folk
VINSON, Elaine
  Rowland, Donald Sydney
VINSON, Kathryn
  Williams, Kathryn
VIPONT, Charles
  Foulds, Elfrida Vipont
VIPONT, Elfrida
  Foulds, Elfrida Vipont
VIRAKAM, Soror
  Sturges, Mary d'Este
VISIAK, E. H.
  Physick, Edward Harold
VIVIAN, Francis
  Ashley, Arthur Ernest
VLOTO, Otto
  Parkhill, Forbes
VON MUELLER, Karl
  Miller, Charles Dean
VOX, Agnes Mary
  Duffy, Agnes Mary
VOYLE, Mary
  Manning, Rosemary
VUL' INDLELA
  Becker, Peter

*Bingo had told him that I was
the author of a lot of mushy
novels by Rosie M. Banks, you
know. Said that I had written
them, and that Rosie's name on
the title-page was my what d'you
call it.*
*—P. G. Wodehouse. Bingo and
the little woman*

WACE, W. E.
  Nicoll, *Sir* William Robertson
WADE, Bill
  Barrett, Geoffrey John
WADE, Henry
  Aubrey-Fletcher, *Sir* Henry
    Lancelot
WADE, Robert
  McIlwain, David
WADE, Thomas
  Looker, Samuel Joseph
WAGNER, Peggy
  Wagner, Margaret Dale
WAKE, G. B.
  Haynes, John Harold
WALDO, Dave
  Clarke, David
WALDRON, Simon
  King, Albert
WALES, Hubert
  Piggott, William
WALES, Nym
  Snow, Helen Foster
WALFORD, Christian
  Dilcock, Noreen

WALKER, Barbara
  Middleton, Maud Barbara
WALKER, Harry
  Waugh, Hillary Baldwin
WALKER, Holly Beth
  Bond, Gladys Baker
WALKER, Ira
  Walker, Irma Ruth
WALKER, Jean Brown
  Walker, Edith
WALLACE, Agnes
  King, Albert
WALLACE, Betty
  Wallace, Elizabeth Virginia
WALLACE, Doreen
  Rash, Dora
WALLACE, John
  Davis, Will R.
WALTER, Katherine
  Walter, Dorothy Blake
WALTER, Kay
  Walter, Dorothy Blake
WALTERS, Hugh
  Hughes, Walter Llewellyn
WALTERS, Rick
  Rowland, Donald Sydney
WALTERS, T. B.
  Rowe, John Gabriel
WAND, Elizabeth
  Tattersall, Muriel Joyce
WANDERER
  Smith, Lily
WARD, Artemus
  Browne, Charles Farrar
WARD, Brad
  Peeples, Samuel Anthony
WARD, Herbert B. S.
  Molloy, Edward

WARD, Kate
  Cust, Barbara Kate
WARD, Kirwan
  Kirwan-Ward, Bernard
WARDEN, Florence
  James, Florence Alice Price
WARE, Monica
  Marsh, John
WARNER, Frank
  Richardson, Gladwell
WARNER, Leigh
  Smith, Lillian M.
WARREN, Andrew
  Tute, Warren
WARREN, Mary D.
  Greig, Maysie
WARREN, Wayne
  Braun, Wilbur
WARRINGTON, George
  Agate, James
WARWICK, Pauline
  Davies, Betty Evelyn
WASH, R.
  Cowlishaw, Ranson
WATER, Silas
  Loomis, Noel Miller
WATSON, Andrew
  Watson, Albert Ernest
WATSON, C. P.
  Agelasto, Charlotte Priestley
WATSON, Frank
  Ames, Francis
WATSON, Will
  Floren, Lee
WAVERLEY, John
  Scobie, Stephen Arthur Cross
WAY, Wayne
  Humphries, Adelaide

WAYLAN, Mildred
  Harrell, Irene Burke
WAYLAND, Patrick
  O'Connor, Richard
WAYNE, Anderson
  Davis, Dresser
WAYNE, Heather
  Gibbs, Norah
WAYNE, Joseph
  Overholser, Wayne D.
WAYNE, Marcia
  Best, Carol Anne
WAYSIDER
  Camm, Frederick J.
WEALE, B. Putnam
  Simpson, Bertram L.
WEAVER, Ward
  Mason, F. Van Wyck
WEBB, Christopher
  Wibberley, Leonard Patrick
  O'Connor
WEBB, Neil
  Rowland, Donald Stanley
WEBSTER, Gary
  Garrison, Webb Black
WEBSTER, Jean
  Webster, Alice Jane Chandler
WEI WU WEI
  Gray, Terence J. S.
WEINER, Henri
  Longstreet, Stephen
WEIR, Jonnet
  Nicholson, Joan
WELBURN, Vivienne C.
  Furlong, Vivienne
WELCH, Ronald
  Felton, Ronald Oliver

WELCH, Rowland
  Davies, Leslie Purnell
WELCOME, John
  Brennan, John
WELLS, Hondo
  Whittington, Harry
WELLS, Jane Warren
  Picken, Mary
WELLS, John J.
  Coulson, Juanita *and* Bradley,
  Marion Z.
WELLS, Susan
  Siegel, Doris
WELLS, Tobias
  Forbes, Deloris Stanton
WELLS, Tracey
  Nuttall, Anthony
WENTWORTH, John
  Child, Philip A. G.
WENTWORTH, Patricia
  Turnbull, Dora Amy
WERNER, Jane
  Werner, Elsa Jane
WERNER, Peter
  Booth, Philip Arthur
WERRERSON, Talbot
  Robertson, Robert George
WESLEY, Elizabeth
  McElfresh, Adeline
WESLEY, James
  Rigoni, Orlando Joseph
WESSEX, Martyn
  Little, D. F.
WESSEX REDIVIVUS
  Dewar, Hubert Stephen Lowry
WEST, Anna
  Edward, Ann Elizabeth

WEST, Dorothy
  Wirt, Mildred
WEST, Keith
  Lane, Kenneth Westmacott
WEST, Laura M.
  Hymers, Laura M.
WEST, Mark
  Huff, Darrell
WEST, Nathanael
  Weinstein, Nathan Wallenstein
WEST, Rebecca
  Fairfield, Cecily Isabel
WEST, Token
  Humphries, Adelaide
WEST, Tom
  Reach, James
WEST, Trudy
  West, Gertrude
WEST, Ward
  Borland, Harold Glen
WESTALL, Lorna
  Houseman, Lorna
WESTERHAM, S. C.
  Alington, Cyril Argentine
WESTERN, Barry
  Evans, Gwynfil Arthur
WESTERN-HOLT, J. C.
  Heming, Jack C. W.
WESTGATE, John
  Bloomfield, Anthony John
    Westgate
WESTLAND, Lynn
  Joscelyn, Archie Lynn
WESTMACOTT, Mary
  Christie, *Dame* Agatha
WESTON, Allen
  Norton, Alice Mary *and*
    Hogarth, Grace Allen

WESTRIDGE, Harold
  Avery, Harold
WETZEL, Lewis
  King, Albert
WEYMOUTH, Anthony
  Cobb, Ivo Geikie
WHARTON, Anthony
  Macallister, Alister
WHEEZY
  Hounsfield, Joan
WHETTER, Laura
  Mannock, Laura
WHIM WHAM
  Curnow, Allen
WHITAKER, Ray
  Davies, John
WHITBY, Sharon
  Black, Maureen
WHITE, Dale
  Place, Marian Templeton
WHITE, Harry
  Whittington, Harry
WHITE, Heather
  Foster, Jess Mary Mardon
WHITE, James Dillon
  White, Stanley
WHITE, Jane
  Brady, Jane Frances
WHITEFRIAR
  Hiscock, Eric
WHITEHAND, Satherley
  Satherley, David *and*
    Whitehand, James
WHITEHOUSE, Arch
  Whitehouse, Arthur George
    Joseph
WHITEHOUSE, Peggy
  Castle, Frances Mundy

WHITINGER, R. D.
  Place, Marian Templeton
WHITLEY, George
  Chandler, Arthur
WHITNEY, Hallam
  Whittington, Harry
WHITTINGHAM, Sara
  Gibbs, Norah
WHITTLE, Tyler
  Tyler-Whittle, Michael Sidney
WHITTLEBOT, Hernia
  Coward, Noël
WHYE, Felix
  Dixon, Arthur
WICK, Stuart Mary
  Freeman, Kathleen
WICKLOE, Peter
  Duff, Douglas Valder
WIGAN, Christopher
  Bingley, David Ernest
WIGG, T. I. G.
  McCutchan, Philip D.
WIGGEN, Henry W.
  Harris, Mark
WILDE, Hilary
  Breton-Smith, Clare
WILDE, Leslie
  Best, Rayleigh Breton Amis
WILKINSON, Tim
  Wilkinson, Percy F. H.
WILL
  Lipkind, William
WILLEY, Robert
  Ley, Willy
WILLIAMS, Beryl
  Epstein, Beryl
WILLIAMS, F. Harald
  Orde-Ward, F. W.

WILLIAMS, J. R.
  Creasey, Jeanne
WILLIAMS, Jeanne
  Creasey, Jeanne
WILLIAMS, Joel
  Jennings, John Edward
WILLIAMS, Michael
  St John, Wylly Folk
WILLIAMS, Patry
  Williams, D. F. *and* Patry, M.
WILLIAMS, Rex
  Wei, Rex
WILLIAMS, Richard
  Francis, Stephen D.
WILLIAMS, Roth
  Zilliacus, Konni
WILLIAMS, Tennessee
  Williams, Thomas Lanier
WILLIAMS, Violet M.
  Boon, Violet Mary
WILLIAMS, Wetherby
  Williams, Margaret Wetherby
WILLIAMSON, Paul
  Butters, Paul
WILLOUGHBY, Hugh
  Harvey, Charles
WILLS, Chester
  Snow, Charles Horace
WILLS, Ronald
  Thomas, Ronald Wills
WILLS, Thomas
  Ard, William
WILMER, Dale
  Miller, William *and* Wade,
  Robert
WILSON, Ann
  Baily, Francis Evans

Pseudonyms

WILSON, Christine
  Geach, Christine
WILSON, D. M.
  Bentley, Frederick Horace
WILSON, Edwina H.
  Brookman, Laura L.
WILSON, Elizabeth
  Ivison, Elizabeth
WILSON, Holly
  Wilson, Helen
WILSON, John Burgess
  Wilson, John Anthony Burgess
WILSON, Lee
  Lemmon, Laura Lee
WILSON, Martha
  Morse, Martha
WILSON, Yates
  Wilson, Albert
WINCH, John
  Campbell, Gabrielle Margaret Vere
WINCHESTER, Kay
  Walker, Emily Kathleen
WINDER, Mavis
  Winder, Mavis Areta
WINDSOR, Rex
  Armstrong, Douglas
WING ADJUTANT
  Blake, Wilfred Theodore
WINFIELD, Allen
  Stratemeyer, Edward
WINFIELD, Arthur M.
  Stratemeyer, Edward
WINGFIELD, Susan
  Reece, Alys
WINN, Alison
  Wharmby, Margot

WINN, Patrick
  Padley, Arthur
WINSLOWE, John R.
  Richardson, Gladwell
WINSTAN, Matt
  Nickson, Arthur
WINTER, John Strange
  Stannard, Eliza Vaughan
WINTERS, Bernice
  Winters, Bayla
WINTERS, Mary K.
  Hart, Caroline Horowitz
WINTON, John
  Pratt, John
WITHERBY, Diana
  Cooke, Diana
WITHERS, E. L.
  Potter, George William
WODEN, George
  Slaney, George Wilson
WOLFENDEN, George
  Beardmore, George
WOOD, J. Claverdon
  Carter, Thomas
WOOD, Mary
  Bamfield, Veronica
WOOD, Quality
  Wood, Violet
WOODCOTT, Keith
  Brunner, John
WOODFORD, Cecile
  Woodford, Irene-Cecile
WOODFORD, Jack
  Woolfolk, Josiah Pitts
WOODROOK, R. A.
  Cowlishaw, Ranson
WOODRUFF, Philip
  Mason, Philip

246

WOODS, Jonah
  Woods, Olwen
WOODS, Ross
  Story, Rosamond Mary
WOODS, Sara
  Bowen-Judd, Sara Hutton
WOODWARD, Lillian
  Marsh, John
WOOLLAND, Henry
  Williams, Guy Richard Owen
WOOLRICH, Cornell
  Hopley-Woolrich, Cornell
  George
WORTH, Martin
  Wigglesworth, Martin
WORTH, Maurice
  Bosworth, Willan George
WRAITH, John
  Devaney, Pauline *and* Apps,
  Edwin
WRIGHT, Elnora A.
  Old Coyote, Elnora A.
WRIGHT, Josephine
  Weaver, Harriet Shaw
WRIGHT, Rowland
  Wells, Carolyn
WRIGHT, Sally
  Old Coyote, Elnora A.
WRIGHT, Ted
  Wright, George T.
WRIGHT, Wade
  Wright, John
WU WU MENG
  Beiles, Sinclair
WYANDOTTE, Steve
  Thomas, Stanley A. C.
WYATT, Escott
  Leyland, Eric

WYCLIFFE, John
  Bedford-Jones, Henry
WYLCOTES, John
  Ransford, Oliver
WYNDER, Mavis Areta
  Winder, Mavis Areta
WYNDHAM, Esther
  Lutyens, Mary
WYNDHAM, John
  Harris, John Wyndham Parkes
  Lucas Beynon
WYNDHAM, Lee
  Hyndman, Jane Andrews
WYNDHAM, Robert
  Hyndman, Robert Utley
WYNGARD, Rhoda
  Truax, Rhoda
WYNMAN, Margaret
  Dixon, Ella Hepworth
WYNNE, Anthony
  Wilson, Robert McNair
WYNNE, May
  Knowles, Mabel Winifred
WYNNE, Pamela
  Scott, Winifred Mary
WYNYARD, John
  Harrison, J. H.

X. Y. Z.
  Tilsley, Frank
XARIFFA
  Townsend, Mary Ashley

Y. Y.
  Lynd, Robert
YARBO, Steve
  King, Albert

YATES, Dornford
Mercer, Cecil William
YERUSHALMI, Chaim
Lipschitz, *Rabbi* Chaim
YES TOR
Roche, Thomas
YLLA
Koffler, Camilla
YORK, Andrew
Nicole, Christopher
YORK, Jeremy
Creasey, John
YORKE, Margaret
Nicholson, Margaret Beda
YORKE, Roger
Bingley, David Ernest
YORKE, Susan
Telenga, Suzette
YOUNG, Agatha
Young, Agnes
YOUNG, Edward
Reinfeld, Fred
YOUNG, Filson
Bell, Alexander
YOUNG, Jan
Young, Janet Randall

YOUNG, Kendal
Young, Phyllis Brett
YOUNG, Robert
Payne, Pierre Stephen Robert
YOUNG, Rose
Harris, Marion Rose
YOUNG, Thomas
Yoseloff, Thomas
YUILL, P. B.
Williams, Gordon Maclean *and*
Venables, Terry
YULYA
Whitney, Julie

ZED
Dienes, Zoltan
ZETA
Cope, *Sir* Zachary
ZINKEN
Hopp, Signe

*Wherefore is it that thou dost
ask after my name?*
—*Bible. Genesis 32, 29*

248